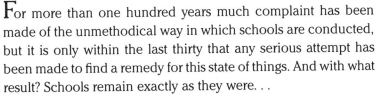
For more than one hundred years much complaint has been made of the unmethodical way in which schools are conducted, but it is only within the last thirty that any serious attempt has been made to find a remedy for this state of things. And with what result? Schools remain exactly as they were. . .

Let us isolate and examine the obstacles [to reforming the schools in the way we desire]:

(i.) There is a great lack of methodical teachers who could take charge of public schools and produce the results that we have in view (indeed, with regard to my Janua which is already used in schools, a man of great judgment has written to me complaining that in most places one thing is lacking, namely suitable men to use it).

(ii.) But even if teachers of this kind existed, or if they could all perform their task with ease by using time-tables and forms all ready prepared for them, how would it be possible to support them in each village and town, and in every place where men are born and brought up in Christ?

(iii.) Again, how can it be arranged that the children of the poor shall have time to go to school?

(iv.) The opposition of pedants, who cling to old ways and despise everything that is new, is greatly to be dreaded. . .

—John Amos Comenius, *The Great Didactic*,
published in 1630 A.D.

Redesigning Education

Redesigning Education

Kenneth G. Wilson
and
Bennett Daviss

Teachers College
Columbia University
New York and London

Published in paperback by Teachers College Press, 1234 Amsterdam Avenue, New York, NY 10027

This edition is reprinted by arrangement with Henry Holt & Company, Inc.

Library of Congress Cataloging-in-Publication Data

Wilson, Kenneth G. (Kenneth Geddes). 1936-
    Redesigning education / Kenneth G. Wilson and Bennett Daviss.
        p.   cm.
    Originally published: New York : H. Holt, 1994.
    Includes bibliographical references (p.   ) and index.
    ISBN 0-8077-3585-X (alk. paper)
    1. Educational change—United States.   2. Educational evaluation—United
States.   I. Daviss, Bennett.   II. Title.
[LA217.2.W55 1996]   96-24412
370'.973—dc20   CIP

ISBN 0-8077-3585-X (Paper)

Printed on acid-free paper
Manufactured in the United States of America

01   00   99   98   97   96   6   5   4   3   2   1

*To educators,
in schools and out*

Readers with access to the Internet can find additional information about the plan presented in this book and any initiatives arising from it. On the Internet, enter the World Wide Web and go to home page:

http://www-physics.mps.ohio-state.edu/~discover/RE.html

Contents

ACKNOWLEDGMENTS   xi

1. Reforming School Reform:
   Redefining the Mission, Means, and Meaning of U.S. Education   1

2. The Pursuit of Excellence:
   The Power of the Redesign Process   22

3. Reading Recovery:
   Precursor for a Process of Educational Redesign   48

4. Missing Links:
   How the Structure of the Teaching Profession
   Thwarts Innovation   78

5. The Culture of the School:
   Educational Politics and the Problem of Change   106

6. Measuring Up:
   Assessment and Evaluation in Educational Redesign   137

7. Enacting the New Paradigm:
   New Structures of the Redesigned School   156

8. The Key to Reform:
   The Systems Redesign School   197

   N O T E S   231

   B I B L I O G R A P H Y   237

   I N D E X   243

Acknowledgments

Any book is a collaboration involving many more people than those whose names appear on its cover. We thank the countless students, parents, teachers, administrators, and other educators who so generously have given us their ideas, listened to ours, and helped us learn. Among them, Arnold Arons, Michael Fullan, Dan Lortie, Lillian McDermott, Gay Su Pinnell, Seymour Sarason, and Robert Slavin—personally as well as through their writings—helped to chart and guide our explorations. Many of their ideas are present in this book. Although dozens of people have contributed to our effort, we bear ultimate responsibility for the arguments and conclusions that follow, and for any errors and omissions that have crept in.

Jonathan Dolger, our agent, first brought us together. Our editor, Jack Macrae, with his discerning eye, firm standards, and, above all, patience, has helped us find, after several drafts, the book we wanted to write. Dr. Constance Barsky, director of Project Discovery at Ohio State University, made invaluable suggestions about the book's approach and content. Sharon Kraft, Lorri Laudermilt, and Deborah McGee of the Discovery staff facilitated communication and handled endless details.

We owe debts to our wives that cannot be repaid. They endured the disruptions of family time that the consuming effort of writing a book inevitably demands. Alison Brown taught us much of what we came to know about technological change. Jackson Daviss contributed her considerable editorial skills, as well as her unfailing ability to detect inconsistent thinking, to crucial early drafts. Without their counsel and generosity of spirit, this book could not have been possible.

Kenneth Wilson wishes to express his profound gratitude to all who aided him while he experienced the forms of social change described in this book. During his four years as co-director of Ohio's Project Discovery initiative, the support of Nancy Eberhart, Jane Butler Kahle, E. Garrison Walters, the program's teacher-leaders, mathematician- and scientist-educators, regional directors, and many other participants has been vital, as has that of so many colleagues at the Ohio State University in physics, mathematics, biology, the college of education, and across the campus. He is grateful to Luther Williams and the National Science Foundation for establishing the Statewide Systemic Initiatives in Mathematics and Science Education, and to two Ohio governors, two Ohio State University presidents, and to Elaine Hairston and Ted Sanders for making his participation in Discovery possible. He is grateful to all members and staff of the National Academy of Sciences CoFRIER study committee, and for invaluable help in understanding the state of education research. For their help and support during the three years he spent immersed in technological change as director of the Cornell University Theory Center, he thanks the center's staff and management as well as marketing and administrative executives at IBM Corporation and Floating Point Systems, Inc. He is grateful also to Hans Bethe, Michael Fisher, Ben Widom, and the entire physics faculty for the warm and supportive atmosphere in which he worked during his twenty-five years in physics research at Cornell, where he experienced an evolving technical culture and many paradigm shifts. The National Science Foundation has graciously supported all his activities and initiatives. The support of the states of New York and Ohio is also gratefully acknowledged.

Finally, E. Bright Wilson, Jr., has demonstrated throughout his life an unflagging and unbiased search for fundamental causes, not only in science but in all things. We have done our best to honor his example.

Redesigning Education

1

Reforming
School Reform

*Redefining the Mission, Means, and
Meaning of U.S. Education*

The current crisis in education is costing us the American Dream. The democratic vision of Thomas Jefferson, Abraham Lincoln, and Martin Luther King, Jr.—a vision, finally, of equal opportunity and upward mobility for all—is today dimmed by structural unemployment, dwindling prospects for all but a highly educated elite, and the subsequent growth of what many observers fear is a permanent underclass. The base of well-paid factory jobs that built and sustained the American middle class after World War II is disappearing, lost in part to low-paid workers overseas and also to the relentless efficiencies of automation. At the same time, American workers haven't learned the sophisticated new skills they'll need to be as productive in the new service-based economy as yesterday's workers were in a manufacturing-based economy. Current estimates suggest that the inadequate skills of U.S. workers drain billions each year from the Gross Domestic Product. Americans, including those now graduating from school, simply are not educated to sustain middle-class incomes in an economy and society based in knowledge, driven by information, and defined by change.

Our inadequacies are rooted in this nation's outmoded schooling system. Indirectly, these same inadequacies lead Americans to complain of an increasing sense of powerlessness—the feeling that their lives are being taken over by huge, inhuman systems over which they have no control: from school-district bureaucracies to big government to Wall Street, organizational systems grow larger even as they show less and less ability to solve social and economic ills. This creeping and pervasive sense of powerlessness now threatens not only social cohesion but also the foundation of an American polity that was, until recently, the world's model. (Indeed, millions of Americans are forsaking the ballot box while millions elsewhere, especially in Eastern Europe and South Africa, are discovering its power for the first time.)

The crisis in our schools, from which so many other current difficulties stem, can be traced to America's failure to grasp the nature and power of education in a postindustrial world. We have yet to recognize that irreversible economic change has sapped the meaning from traditional concepts of education. Adequate schooling no longer means a set of basic skills acquired in childhood and perhaps polished by a few years at a local university; a conventional high-school diploma is no longer a ticket to the middle class. Education for the new century is a lifelong process of training the mind to manipulate information, to solve problems, to imagine, and to create, as well as to master specialized technical information. The past's piecemeal reforms will not—cannot—bridge the distance between the old definitions of education and the new. Instead, we must make a quantum change in our concept of education itself if our society and culture are to survive intact in the new century. The following pages detail a method by which our society can make real the opportunities implied in education's new meaning.

It won't be easy. The United States clings to a concept of education's nature and power that remains rooted in the last century. Learning holds the power to change a life from something small and weak to an ever-expanding, self-directed engine of development and opportunity; it alone offers the tools that will let us live together more smoothly, usefully, and harmoniously as citizens and workers. Yet American culture still venerates raw energy and initiative above scholarship; Americans pride themselves on "can do" and "getting the job done," not on their powers of analysis and reflection. They value education so little that they tell one another that "those who can, do; those who can't, teach." When school-district budgets across the country are cut, administrative bureaucracies and athletic programs consistently suffer fewer reductions than do academic courses.

During the last ten years, these traditional attitudes have begun to crack under the strain of prolonged failure. Technology and global competition have forced the United States to begin to understand that national prosperity no longer depends on raw materials and a vast pool of manual labor; it depends instead on every worker's ability to meet the diverging needs of increasingly sophisticated and demanding customers in services and in manufacturing. Meeting those needs is no longer a matter of pulling levers on a mass-production machine or ringing a cash register. It now demands the thinking skills and judgment to make the best creative use of a range of technological and information resources, often in competition with low-wage workers abroad. In service occupations and in manufacturing, workers without high levels of education cannot add enough value to work to earn a middle-class income. Americans are finally being forced to accept the idea that the future belongs to the trained mind.

This new understanding began in earnest in 1983 with the publication of *A Nation At Risk*. The booklet was the final report of the National Commission on Educational Excellence, an eighteen-member panel of educators and government officials who had been appointed two years earlier by the U.S. Secretary of Education. The panel's report warned that America's schools were sinking beneath "a rising tide of mediocrity that threatens our very future as a nation and a people."[1] The report set off the greatest concerted effort to reinvent education that this nation has seen in nearly a century. From that document, parents, politicians, and educators learned in graphic terms that our schools weren't educating children adequately for the future. However, the authors of *A Nation At Risk* also concluded that the reason our schools weren't working was largely that the schools had become lax in their adherence to the traditional icons of scholastic rigor. As a result, the report "rounded up the usual suspects" in education reform and, as reformers so often have, simply exhorted U.S. schools to apply them. "The topics are familiar," the group wrote. "There is little mystery about what . . . must be done."[2] Among its smorgasbord of well-worn proposals that promised "lasting reform" were proposals for longer school days and years, a rigid core curriculum of basic subjects, more homework, better textbooks, stiffer graduation requirements for high-school seniors, recruitment and training of better teachers, an increased role for classroom computers—thirty-eight directives in all, covering the spectrum of education's apparent ills.

Actually, the route to real reform pointed in a very different direction. America's national inadequacies, which we sense and which we attribute to our failing schools, have arisen not because our schools have changed, but precisely because *they continue to do what they always have, in the same ways they always have.* The authors of *A Nation At Risk*, like most of the reformers that their report has inspired, have failed to understand that genuine reform is not about repairing the dilapidated structure of traditional schooling. Instead, it is about discerning a new vision of what it means to educate and be educated in a world that is fundamentally different from the one our schools still believe themselves to inhabit.

Nevertheless, *A Nation At Risk*, embraced by then President Ronald Reagan and hailed by many opinion makers and educators across the country, became the guiding document in modern education reform. Unfortunately, by urging reformers to address these symptoms of educational failure instead of to search for its true causes, the report sent our national reform effort off in the wrong direction. As a result, our crusade to reform U.S. education has itself become mired in crisis. The evidence is overwhelming.

The State of Mathematics Education, a 1990 report prepared for the U.S. Department of Education's National Assessment of Educational Progress (the biennial federal measure of academic achievement among U.S. fourth-, eighth-, and twelfth-grade students), cites an Educational Testing Service report that 28 percent of the nation's fourth-graders ranked below their grade's traditional levels in mathematical understanding and skill. A third of all eighth-grade students weren't capable of routine fifth-grade work, while fewer than half of U.S. high-school seniors showed the consistent grasp of fractions, decimals, and percentages expected of competent seventh-graders. "Approximately half of the twelfth-graders graduating from today's schools appear to have an understanding of mathematics that does not extend much beyond simple problem-solving with whole numbers," the report stated. "These figures show that many students appear to be graduating from high school with little of the mathematics understanding required by the fastest-growing occupations or for college work."[3]

Numbers from the 1991 annual report of the National Education Goals Panel—a council of governors, members of Congress, and U.S. Department of Education officials—found the same broad weaknesses. While numbers of students graduating from high school had reached an all-time high in 1990, and more students than ever were showing at least minimal competencies, "these accomplishments . . . fall far short of what is needed to secure a free and prosperous future," the report warned. It noted that "scores on existing national tests have declined or stagnated during the past several years." According to the study, fewer than 20 percent of students tested in grades four, eight, and twelve were as competent in mathematics as the U.S. Department of Education expected them to be by that time. A third of the eighth-graders tested couldn't figure the price of a restaurant meal from a menu; a similar proportion of high-school juniors couldn't write a coherent paragraph about themselves. Scores on writing tests actually declined among eighth-grade students between 1984 and 1990, and remained virtually unchanged for children in the fourth and eleventh grades. In addition, while most adults are now at least functionally literate, "far fewer are able to perform more complex literacy tasks requiring them to process and synthesize many pieces of information"[4]—bad news for a country that has bet its future on an information-based economy. "Kids can go from page to page in workbooks getting nothing but one hundreds," a Connecticut English teacher says, "but if you talk to them about the ideas in a book, they just look at you."[5]

These reports and studies tell us nothing about U.S. educational achievement compared with that of children in the other nations with which we compete technologically and economically. If they did, our numbers would almost surely look far worse in comparison than they do already. The evidence we do have shows that in striving somehow to surpass our own past educational accomplishments, we're falling farther behind.

The findings are alarming not so much because they indicate a deterioration, but because they show no progress. It wasn't until the early 1950s that a majority of children graduated from high school instead of dropping out; there is no evidence that a greater proportion of our children then could solve these same exercises any more accurately than their counterparts can today. What alarms us is that now it matters so much. The National Education Goals Panel's 1992 survey echoed findings all too common among the endless stream of progress reports: "American first-graders may already be academically behind their counterparts in Japan and Taiwan. We now know that not only is the content studied by our students less challenging than what students in high-achieving countries are exposed to, but American parents expect less of their children academically." The panel's study also reported that those it calls our "lower-achieving eighth-grade students"—fully 55 percent— failed to master simple mathematical operations such as roots and decimals. Even worse, two thirds of them showed the same learning deficits even after two additional years of school. "Similar patterns are noted in science and reading," the report adds.[6]

The statistics are even more dismal for minority students. Demographers report that fully a third of the people needed to fill new jobs during the 1990s and beyond will be ethnic minorities, young people who are now quitting school in alarming numbers. Figures through October 1990 from the U.S. Department of Education indicate that, while 12.1 percent of all high-school students were dropping out, the rate was 13.2 percent among blacks and 32.4 percent among Hispanics. Experts now estimate that in several of the nation's largest urban centers, close to 50 percent of blacks and 60 percent of Hispanics leave school before graduating. According to the National Alliance of Business, during 1986 alone dropouts cost the U.S. economy $147 billion in lost wages and productivity.

These numbers add up to an inescapable conclusion: ten years of national effort intended to improve our schools have left them no more able—and, apparently, in some ways less able—to meet the needs of our children and our society. Meanwhile, the plight of many of our children is worsening, as David Hamburg has shown.[7]

The misleading course of reform that *A Nation At Risk* prescribed was not decisively redirected until the spring of 1990. In the report's aftermath, states burdened schools with huge numbers of new regulations designed to ensure compliance with various steps and procedures that the report urged. But in their "education summit" at Charlottesville, Virginia, in June 1989, newly inaugurated President George Bush and the nation's fifty state governors agreed to discard the emphasis on regulation and, implicitly, the prescriptive, superficial approach to reform that *A Nation At Risk* had advocated. Instead of dwelling on rules and procedures, the policy-makers set a new direction for our schools. The group worked together to develop a list of six educational goals that the nation is to achieve by the year 2000:

- ▸ *That all children enter school ready to learn*
- ▸ *That the U.S. high-school graduation rate rise to at least 90 percent*
- ▸ *That U.S. students lead the world in mathematics and science performance*
- ▸ *That each adult be competent as a worker and citizen*
- ▸ *That schools be disciplined environments free of drugs and violence*
- ▸ *That students demonstrate growing academic competencies in specific areas as they progress through school*

(The Educate America Act passed by Congress in March 1994 added two more goals: that parents become more deeply involved in their children's educational welfare, and that working teachers be helped to continue to expand and perfect their professional skills throughout their careers.) Implied throughout the goals is the assumption, revolutionary in education, that every child can learn—not just basic skills, but also the abilities of analysis, reflection, and invention. Schools were to be freed of much of the new regulation in exchange for their effort to reach these goals. For the first time, American schools were to be most strongly united not by common habits or textbooks, but by a new vision of learning.

By publicly removing the self-imposed limits from our national discussion about what education entails, the summit became the first step toward fundamental national reform. But it also stripped away our confidence in the traditional means of education that *A Nation At Risk* had insisted we cling to. States have begun to exchange their sheaves of old regulations and practices for what is called "standards-based systemic change." Under the new approach, traditional educational practices that are determined to be hindrances to the swift achievement of the national goals are to be swept away. Many states, following the examples set by California and Kentucky, have made bold beginnings. But redesigning a well-established bureaucracy that also embodies a social institution—school—is excruciatingly slow work. Although new structures are being fashioned, none are yet powerful enough to counteract the continuing decay in our current national educational achievement. Charged with the enormously difficult job of meeting new kinds of national goals but having no models to follow in identifying, developing, and implementing the innovations needed to do so, U.S. education reform has languished.

Paradoxically, while our national efforts at reform have stalled, effective innovations in teaching and learning are sprouting in individual classrooms around the country. When a Colorado geography teacher scrapped conventional classroom procedures and structures and made her students partners in planning and teaching lessons, students' interest soared and their test scores surged. By encouraging teachers to work together to redesign courses and to learn each other's most effective classroom techniques, a program called Success For All is building both self-esteem and a broad base of academic skills among once-forgotten children in Baltimore's urban core. South Pointe Elementary School in Miami, Florida, has replaced competition among students with cooperation; instead of grouping together students of similar abilities or ages, teachers negotiate with parents to formulate an individual learning plan for each child. In Wisconsin, a technique called Cognitively Guided Instruction enables teachers to help children learn not only how to "do math" but also how to think mathematically and grasp the concepts that underlie numerical relationships. Teachers in the program spend just half as much time teaching arithmetic facts and tables as do their colleagues leading traditional classes; yet tests show that their students surpass children outside the program in their knowledge of number facts and in their ability to solve practical problems. These kinds of success stories are being written in individual schools and classrooms all over the country.

We suggest that these reforms are showing consistent early success *precisely because* they violate, in one way or another, the structures of conventional schooling that *A Nation At Risk* and most subsequent reform efforts have implicitly or explicitly endorsed. As then President Bush said, they "break the mold" of traditional educational patterns. But the change they embody is actually greater than that. These reforms and reformers have realized what most of their colleagues have not: that the global and technological forces reshaping our economy and society are also rewriting our fundamental concepts of education's means, meaning, and purpose. To reform our schools we need not only new programs but a new vision of education itself.

TOMORROW'S SKILLS, YESTERDAY'S SCHOOLS

The pressures forcing the creation of a new educational vision are precisely the same ones forcing our economy to reinvent itself—pressures that value mind over muscle, process before product, and quality above quantity. Because our economy's strength grows directly out of the abilities of its workers, the same transforming pressures are reaching through to our schools and forcing us to redefine what it means to be educated.

In the industrial age—roughly from the 1870s through the 1950s—national wealth was rooted in an abundance of raw materials and a steady supply of factory labor, and the conventional structure of U.S. education was well matched to our society's needs. Most students learned, through rote exercises, to read and to do simple mathematics; all learned to memorize information and to follow instructions. The 10 to 15 percent who proved themselves most adept at this approach to learning were steered into high school—then a rigorous academic program for the elite—and finally into college and professional careers. The rest took up their places along the assembly line at the end of the eighth grade. The U.S. economy needed legions of minimally skilled workers to perform repetitive tasks, and the schools organized their patterns of teaching and learning accordingly. Blending a large manual workforce, mass production, research and development by a small cadre of trained professional engineers, and the natural wealth of a continent, our industrial economy turned out the huge quantities of goods that a developing country and world demanded. In commerce and thus in education, quality was subordinated to quantity.

Now, the engine of wealth is no longer physical resources but knowledge and the skills to use it creatively. Consumers take for granted the availability of an array of toasters, cars, or computers that perform adequately. The products that now command the high values needed to sustain middle-class living standards are those that perform more effectively and efficiently than their competitors; the people earning the highest wages will be those able to create customized technological products to suit the disparate individual needs of a sophisticated clientele. As a result, the companies and national economies that prosper are those whose products meet increasingly stringent tests of invention and quality. Those tests can be met only through the skillful manipulation of knowledge—creative, exacting, and sophisticated research, design, technical development, and market exploitation. These skills, in turn, pattern and integrate the processes that enable industry's endless search for improvement. Increasingly, societies that lack natural resources and huge pools of cheap factory labor define education to mean, among other things, the cultivation of these skills in their workers.

In contrast, the structure of U.S. schooling still bears the stamp of the antiquated, quantity-based economy that it was organized to serve. Students move through courses and grades at a fixed pace, like products moving along an assembly line that can't be slowed long enough to remedy the flawed processes that lead, inevitably, to flawed products. Schools still are organized to get a product—graduates—out the door, not to refine the processes by which students can meet increasingly stringent educational demands. Many educators have long sought to reorient schools' emphasis from quantity to quality, as the shift from a manufacturing to a service economy requires, but the structures within which they work push them back into the obsolete traditions of production-line schooling for a quantity-oriented economy.

Those educators know that it's no longer enough for workers to be able to comprehend the words in a simple sentence or do arithmetic correctly. According to the Hudson Institute's landmark 1987 study *Workforce 2000*, when the new century arrives even the least-skilled jobs will require a command of reading, computing, and thinking that was once necessary only for the professions. "Of the [job categories] that are growing faster than average, all but one—[the category of menial or low-wage] service occupations—require more than the median level of education for all jobs. . . . Only 4 percent of the new jobs can be filled by individuals with the lowest levels of skills, compared to 9 percent of jobs requiring such low skills today. At the other end of the scale, 41 percent of the new jobs will require skills ranked in one of the top [educational attainment] categories, compared with only 24 percent" in 1987."[8]

For more than a decade, leaders in American business have been grappling with the implications of these numbers. In 1992, a U.S. Department of Education study called *Measurement of Workforce Readiness Competencies* surveyed a battery of federal and private-sector reports and found that employers were already calling for workers who could do more than follow simple directions. "All . . . identified the need for higher-order [thinking] skills," the summary notes. "The most common . . . identified [were] skills in adapting to . . . changes." Among the abilities sought most: problem solving, creativity, decision making, knowing how to learn, and interpersonal and teaming skills. "Management now recognizes a need to have workers take on more responsibility . . . if we are to compete in rapidly changing world markets," the survey concludes. "This development means that much more is expected of even entry-level members of the American workforce."[9]

More may be expected, but it's not easily found. A November 1991 joint study of four hundred companies by the U.S. Department of Labor and the National Association of Manufacturers found that "manufacturers have plenty of job applicants. . . . The problem is [applicants'] skill deficiencies." The mismatch between employers' needs and workers' skills holds ominous significance, the report concludes: "As change accelerates and more training is needed, many workers will need advanced skills simply to give them access to useful job training. For example, assembly-line workers in many manufacturing plants are learning statistical process control, a system that is beyond the reach of those without a solid grounding in mathematics," says NAM president

Jerry Jasinowski: "The lack of basic workforce skills is jeopardizing workers' opportunities for employment mobility and success, and is seriously damaging manufacturing technological advancement and productivity." He notes that more than a third of U.S. manufacturers are having "serious problems" keeping up with technological advances or increasing productivity because workers aren't equal to the task. "For American manufacturers, remaining competitive in global markets will depend increasingly on workers' skills," he says. "This survey indicates that we have a tough road ahead."[10]

READY FOR REVOLUTION

That tough road leads back to our antiquated conception of traditional education's meaning and purpose. Specifically, U.S. education shows all the symptoms of having reached a historic divide similar to the one that astronomy had reached just before Copernicus proposed that the sun, not the earth, was the center of the solar system. Then, the system of fundamental assumptions and understandings that had defined the field of astronomy and held it together was breaking down. The discipline was bound by a framework of conceptual structures that its practitioners recognized to be more and more deeply at odds with the reality they sought to articulate. Moreover, that framework was unable to explain the growing body of contradictory experience without repudiating its own basic tenets. Attempts to label contrary evidence as mere exceptions, or to stretch the old conceptual framework to fit that evidence, strained that framework more. Astronomy was breaking down under the weight of the disparities between new experience and its own premises—as is conventional education today. As with astronomy, our national school-reform effort can move forward only if it stops trying to hold together a collapsing intellectual foundation and opens itself to a new paradigm—a systemwide conceptual revolution that allows people to understand the new meaning of education itself.

Progress in science and technology has always been driven by such conceptual upheavals. But schooling in the United States still conceives teaching and learning to be what they were ten decades ago, before computers, the global economy, or the information age added new dimensions to our concepts of knowledge and education. In most classrooms today, students' chairs still face the teacher, just as they have for more than a century. The teacher delivers information; children receive it passively. Teachers ask questions; children answer when called upon. For most of the rest of their class time, far too many students work silently and alone at their desks performing rote exercises. Their progress is measured in letter grades, which children must win at one another's expense. Most classrooms lack not only computers and electronic mail systems, but even a simple telephone that might connect teachers and students to experts and stores of knowledge beyond the closed classroom door. Today's typical school is one of the few places in the modern world where citizens of George Washington's America would feel right at home.

U.S. educators can't be blamed for clinging to their traditions. Deep conceptual change is personally tumultuous as well as enormously difficult to accomplish. But it's also periodically necessary to refresh an enterprise and to renew its relevance. When the Catholic Church in 1616 forbade the teaching of the Copernican idea that the earth moved around the sun, its intention was to affirm a paradigm of biblical truth. But the edict's practical effect was to place the church firmly outside of, and consequently make it far less relevant to, the evolving process of scientific inquiry. Because it continued to defend the Bible's supreme authority in matters of fact as well as faith, the church steadily lost its power over human scientific and technological imagination. If U.S. educators are to avoid a similar fate, they must be ready to exchange obsolescent structures of schooling for the new ones that a changing world requires. Only by understanding how paradigms change and why they must can we begin to grasp the forces behind the current crisis in education reform, and also glimpse the path to its resolution.

In every profession, paradigms satisfy the basic need for conceptual structure. In science, for example, "The activity in which most scientists inevitably spend almost all their time is predicated on the assumption that the scientific community knows what the world is like," explains Thomas Kuhn in *The Structure of Scientific Revolutions*, his landmark

1962 study of how scientific paradigms change. "Much of the [longevity] of the enterprise derives from the community's willingness to defend that assumption, if necessary at considerable cost."[11] Although largely unconsciously, the panel that authored *A Nation At Risk* was making precisely that kind of defense. The group didn't think to question its assumption that it knew what education means and, therefore, which educational standards and processes are to be used. If it had probed more deeply, it might have articulated a new vision of education. Instead, it directed an ultimately pointless attempt to salvage an antiquated one.

But, as Kuhn also points out, professionals virtually never set out to conceive new paradigms. Instead, they seek to articulate more fully and to apply more broadly the one within which they're working—just as *A Nation At Risk*'s authors did. "The . . . [worker] is a solver of puzzles, not a tester of paradigms," Kuhn writes. In solving a problem, "he may . . . try out a number of alternative approaches [but] he is not testing the *paradigm* when he does so. . . . These trial attempts are trials only of themselves, not of the rules of the game. They are possible only because the paradigm itself is taken for granted."[12] Again, the bromides that *A Nation At Risk* put forward as a basis for serious reform—all well couched within the traditional language and notions of schooling— offer proof of a dominant paradigm's power to pattern a professional's fundamental approach to his work. A scientist who assumes the atomic theory of matter to be basically accurate isn't going to spend her career trying to prove its basic tenets false; similarly, an educator who assumes that competitive grades or longer school days are essential to learning isn't likely to explore the usefulness of innovations that challenge them. "Paradigms provide . . . not only . . . a map, but also . . . some of the directions essential for map-making," Kuhn argues. "In learning a paradigm, [one] acquires theory, methods, and standards together, usually in an inextricable mixture."[13]

According to Kuhn, conceptual shifts begin when people working contentedly within the structure of a well-defined theoretical framework are startled by anomalies—events that can't be explained within, or that even contradict, the framework's premises. "The sense of malfunction that can lead to crisis," he writes, "is prerequisite to revolution." Copernicus himself felt that sense of malfunction. Perhaps the foremost astronomer of his day, the Polish aristocrat didn't set out to show that the earth revolved around the sun; he accepted the church's doctrine that the earth was the center of the universe. However, as mathematical techniques and observational equipment became more sophisticated, the model of an earth-centered universe became less and less reliable in predicting the motions and positions of stars and planets. In 1513, Copernicus declined to advise the church in revising its calendar, saying that the positions of the sun and moon couldn't be charted accurately enough to permit accurate recomputation. Such unreliability bothered him so much that he set out to solve the inaccuracies within the earth-centered model of the universe. As part of his effort, he studied the writings of several ancient Greek scientists who had held that the sun, not the earth, was the hub of the solar system. He considered the idea absurd, but when he applied the assumption in his calculations, he was able to devise more credible explanations for the motions of planets that other astronomers had observed. Over several years, he became increasingly convinced that the idea was right, but he still hesitated to publish because of the array of cultural forces—including the Catholic Church and Martin Luther—opposing the idea. As Kuhn notes, that sense of malfunction within the established conceptual order is so alien and so threatening in its implications that it can have the effect of reinforcing allegiance to the very concepts it challenges. "Though they may begin to lose faith and then to consider alternatives, they do not renounce the paradigm that has led them into crisis," Kuhn emphasizes. "They do not . . . treat anomalies as counterinstances. . . . They will devise numerous . . . *ad hoc* modifications of their theory in order to eliminate any apparent conflict." [14] Indeed, when Copernicus finally did publish *De Revolutionibus* (*On the Revolution of Celestial Spheres*) in 1542, his own publisher took it upon himself to insert a preface to the book declaring that the theory was only a convenience for making more accurate astronomical calculations and not to be taken literally.

Our current decade-long struggle to reform our schools fits Kuhn's larger model: we've been attempting to repair a building while its underlying foundation is shifting and crumbling. That's the source of the "sense of malfunction" that the United States is experiencing in education. We're still looking for ways to cling to old concepts instead of acknowledging that education has begun a revolution—that it's emerging from an outworn structure of assumptions in preparation for a new, more accurate, and more useful one.

A paradigm shift represents a new vision of a structure of ideas, in the same way that an architect's rendering represents a building to be built: both images imply a strategy—a process of detailed planning, design, and construction—that has to be carried out in order to transform the vision into useful reality. The key to reform is the understanding that such transformations are not only unavoidable and irreversible, but are put to effective and efficient use only through an *ordered process of strategic change*. In science and industry, for example, a well-established change process catalyzes, paces, and institutionalizes innovations in a ceaseless evolution of products and ideas that are more useful, more reliable, and that use resources more efficiently. It was this development process that sped the evolution of aircraft from the Wright brothers' wood-and-canvas contraption that flew at Kitty Hawk to the jumbo jet only sixty-five years later. Likewise, in less than half a century, it has changed computers from house-size glorified adding machines to laptop marvels that are able to draw electronic circuits one minute and prepare income taxes the next. The success of this process has been repeated in fields as diverse as medicine and telecommunications, and it can do the same for our schools. The reason: while this orderly and systematic process of guided change has been developed and applied largely in science and industry, its success does not depend on machines, equations, or products. It succeeds because it is, in essence, a human process that organizes and propels human energies in the service of a vision of appropriateness and excellence.

SEEDS OF CHANGE

Clearly, there are immense differences between educating children and building better tractors or devising a more enlightened theory of the origins of the universe. But the principles of an effective change process are no less applicable to one than the other. For example, if you were to conclude that the piston engine in your four-passenger car couldn't carry a four-passenger airplane into the sky, you'd be right. The car's engine is too small, too weak, and the wrong shape. But you'd be wrong to conclude that, therefore, piston engines can't power airplanes. By understanding the principles that make a piston engine work, one can conceive and design a piston engine to power a plane once it's understood that the engines are simply different expressions of the same concept. Similarly, by understanding the process of change that has powered the parallel triumphs of science and technology, educators can generalize its principles and modify them to work just as effectively in our schools.

To support that contention, we offer an example that illustrates how an orderly process of change has already succeeded in a field whose culture is not unlike that of education. The U.S. agricultural extension system used just such a process to transform a nation of individual farmers working in isolation into an integrated system that regularly produces extravagant surpluses.

A century ago, poverty and poor crops were endemic to America's farms. Eager for innovations that could better their lot, farmers were nevertheless suspicious of outside "experts" who tried to tell them their business. It took Seaman Knapp, an imaginative farmer and former president of Iowa's land-grant agricultural college, to transform American agriculture. His method: to expand agricultural research, integrate its various findings into a unified program of change, explain to farmers in simple language the practical meaning and benefits of those discoveries and programs, show farmers how to use them, and communicate back to researchers the problems farmers found most urgent or troublesome—thus beginning the cycle again.

Knapp's method began to take shape in 1885, when an English syndicate bought a million acres of southern Louisiana farmland—cheap because of its mediocre production history—and asked Knapp to find ways to make it more profitable. He suggested that the group subsidize one tenant farmer in each township to experiment with new strains and growing techniques for rice. It accepted his advice, and within a decade Louisiana was growing more rice than any other state in the nation. When the U.S. Department of Agriculture hired Knapp in 1898 to invigorate southern farming, he used government land in similar fashion. Although farmers agreed that the new seeds and techniques grew more and better crops, they were quick to assume that such innovations wouldn't work for private farmers who lacked the government's infinite resources of money and scientific expertise. To prove otherwise, Knapp offered a wager of sorts. In 1903, he convinced a group of Texas businessmen to put up $450 as a guarantee against losses to a local farmer willing to follow faithfully Knapp's instructions for one growing season. Knapp's office would provide only information and advice; the labor and other resources would be those of the farmer alone. When the experiment ended, not only were the businessmen able to keep their $450; the volunteer farmer figured that he made $700 more that year than he would have made by following his old practices. To achieve that result, Knapp had done only three things. First, he communicated information gleaned from agricultural laboratories directly to the farmer in practical terms. Second, he answered the farmer's questions with the best and most recent scientific information, couched in a language the farmer could understand. Third, he forbade the farmer to pick and choose among innovations. Instead, Knapp insisted that the farmer had to integrate the most effective individual methods of seed selection, cultivation, fertilization, crop rotation, marketing, and strategic use of capital into a single, unified approach to better farming.

The real power of Knapp's system proved itself in the early 1900s, as the Mexican boll weevil invaded Texas and threatened to wipe out the South's cotton crop. When U.S. Department of Agriculture researchers discovered that the weevils didn't begin to multiply until well into the growing season, Knapp urged farmers to switch to early-maturing strains of cotton and to use chemical stimulants to prod the stalks to early production. He "marketed" his advice by hiring agents to travel the countryside and explain the steps that, in combination, would boost farmers' chances of beating the weevil and saving their crops. His process of fostering change succeeded so well that it soon was boosting production of other crops in addition. In 1914 the Cooperative Extension Service became an official educational agency within the Agriculture Department.

Because it steadily compounds its own efficiencies, this process of change justifies the steadily growing investment needed to support it.

For example, the Extension Service's annual budget grew from $500,000 in 1915 to more than $250 million annually by 1980—a more than sixtyfold growth in real dollars. No one argues that the added investment has proved to be a poor one. Hybrid corn, developed at Connecticut's U.S. agricultural experiment station in the first years of this century, is credited with raising U.S. corn yields fivefold between 1930 and 1980 and adding several billion dollars to the national economy. American agricultural productivity in general tripled from 1945 to 1970, in no small measure because of the direct translation of research results into practice through the extension service. "Recent studies by economists have confirmed . . . that research has been a good investment of government money," write Richard Sauer and Carl Pray in their 1987 report, "Mobilizing Support for Agricultural Research at the Minnesota Agricultural Experiment Station."[15] Sauer, director of the University of Minnesota's agricultural experiment station, and Pray, an agricultural economist at Rutgers University, offered their own evidence as well. From 1880 to 1980, they found, agricultural research and extension raised the number of Minnesota's acres tended by a single worker from about fifty-five to almost 140. During the same period, the cash value of each acre's production went from $90 to almost $300 in constant dollars, and the value of each farm-worker's effort increased from about $5,000 to more than $35,000—indicating a greater productivity per worker as well as per acre. They also noted that a "study of soybean research indicates a rate of return to Minnesota soybean research above 50 percent. . . . The marginal product of every dollar spent on Minnesota research was $13.15 for cash grains and $75.55 for livestock."[16] Those rates of return, typical of an enterprise that depends on this ordered process of change, justify in purely practical terms the continuing pursuit of quality and the sizeable investment necessary to conduct it.

Today's education reformers face a task even more daunting than that of Knapp's early extension agents. The agents were backed by an elaborate research organization. They worked with individual farmers to implement an integrated program of change that researchers had tested and proved effective—new seeds, new techniques, new fertilizers, and so on, all working together to yield a better crop. Education reformers work alone, without the aid of a coordinated and supportive research and extension system. Instead, they attempt to insert their individual reforms into the $200 billion U.S. education conglomerate that, by its culture and structure, stymies change—even when those who work within it are themselves pleading for change. In the pages that follow, we will offer a means by which our schools can be transformed in much the same way that science and technology have been transformed throughout this century.

THE KEY TO REFORM

Our decade-long effort to reform U.S. education has failed. It has failed because it has not let go of an educational vision that is neither workable nor appropriate to today's needs. Until traditional assumptions about the nature and meaning of education are upset (and new paradigms replace outworn ones), good ideas will languish regardless of their appropriateness. Reforms that seek to correct symptoms without first addressing causes are doomed. Just as no amount of bailing could have kept the *Titanic* afloat, no amount of improved content can save our crumbling educational structure. To effect fundamental meaningful reforms, *all* educators must first be able to admit and agree that our traditional guiding vision of education is no longer relevant in a postindustrial, knowledge-based society. This admission and agreement are inevitable but, because of the discomforts of change, remain far from universal. Second, educators must accept, then build on, the model that the needs of a new society demand. Finally, when our schools do acknowledge education's new paradigm, they will need an ordered process of change that will enable them to exchange the patterns rooted in an antiquated structure of ideas for those needed to enact a new vision.

Luckily, industrial society has already perfected such a process of continuous, guided innovation. Though children are not products, schools are not factories, and educators are not assembly-line workers, human energies can be organized to produce the consistent improvement and excellence that have been achieved in agriculture and in industry. When our schools embrace the vision and adopt similar strategies of change that other enterprises have pioneered, we will have taken the first step not only toward improving our schools but toward addressing the social dilemmas that effective education alone can correct.

In the following pages we will propose a practical way in which an orderly process of progressive change can be incorporated into our educational infrastructure. Chapter 2 explores this process to understand how and why it is so consistently effective. Chapter 3 details one of today's most effective learning reforms, a program that has made education's most productive use of this process yet. Chapters 4 and 5 investigate the forces that have long rendered education impervious to structural change and also demonstrate how these traditional forces can be overcome. Chapter 6 takes special note of the role that educational measurement must play in effective reform. Finally, in chapters 7 and 8, we outline one method by which an ordered process of change can be made effective and affordable in our schools.

2
The Pursuit
of Excellence

*The Power of the Redesign
Process*

Ironically, U.S. education has remained in the grip of an outdated paradigm while for more than a century it has watched—and, to an extent, enabled—the triumph in science, technology, and industry of the process that could free it. For brevity's sake, we'll call it the redesign process. The redesign process is the integration of research, development, dissemination, and refinement by which innovations and the procedures that create them are originated, improved, and made affordable. But its usefulness reaches far beyond the laboratory or the marketplace. In essence, the redesign process is an institutionalized method of strategic, systemic change that works unceasingly to enact a vision of excellence as well as to redefine excellence itself when changing conditions make it necessary. The process's absence from school is the "missing link" in U.S. education reform, preventing reformers from integrating effective innovations and creating new ways to teach and learn that are rooted in a new, unifying vision of what it means to educate and be educated.

The redesign process is the theme that recurs throughout the evolution of the technologies that define our lives. That theme is played out through the steady succession of improved product models, in which each aspect of redesign contributes the fruits of its special expertise to each new product version and simultaneously supports the other phases of the process. Basic research works constantly to discover new materials and processes and find new relationships between existing ones. Development engineers refine those discoveries into practical ideas that improve products, render the company's wares more useful to consumers, boost quality, and reduce costs. No less important, the engineers pool separate smaller improvements to fashion a single new or enhanced component or product. Alone, a minor innovation's benefits may not be worth the cost of implementing it. In combination, however, small innovations can enhance one another's effectiveness and turn a good product into a markedly more effective and efficient one that justifies its purchase price even more clearly than before.

As development engineers build and test prototypes of their ideas, they bring manufacturing specialists into the creative process. Those specialists suggest changes that will render the product easier or cheaper to make. Then marketing specialists test prototypes with the new product's potential buyers, whose preferences compel the development engineers to reshape their prototypes more closely to the needs of customers. As a new model's design is finalized, marketing and sales staffs craft the most effective ways to persuade as many users as possible that the innovation's productivity gains and other benefits outweigh its purchase price. That step is no less crucial than the rest: marketing campaigns put innovations in the hands of as many users as possible, allowing a manufacturer not only to recover the costs of redesign, but also to continue the redesign process. Even repair technicians have a role in redesign: they note chronic problems in existing models and report them to development engineers, who then can "design out" those weaknesses in new versions.

Although the process comprises different aspects, its success depends on their close integration. Indeed, the successful process of improving successive product models is best likened to an ongoing conversation—a continuous circuit of information through which researchers, development engineers, marketing executives, salespeople, and consumers constantly communicate about their needs and goals. For example, when salespeople and market researchers discover the maximum price that consumers are willing to pay for a particular improvement, development engineers work to perfect a version of the improvement that meets that price in the finished product. Researchers and development engineers concentrate on creating the advances that consumers say they want most. This conversation guides the overall redesign effort in shaping successive product models that will be more useful and affordable than their predecessors. Modern air travel began in 1933 when Trans Continental and Western Air Line asked pioneering aircraft engineer Donald Douglas if he could produce a multiengine, single-wing plane to loft 2,300 pounds of payload for a thousand miles at a cruising speed of 150 miles an hour. Douglas huddled with his design team to determine if, and then how, the request could be met. The result was the DC-1, the predecessor of today's commercial airliner. Trans Continental worked with Douglas to improve the design, and subsequently ordered forty of the improved DC-2 version. By 1950, the DC-3 was the most common commercial plane in the world. It had come about because the product had been collaboratively redesigned through continuing communication among scientists, engineers, market researchers, and product users.

The conversation that the redesign process and its succession of innovations fosters in industry has no counterpart in our schools. The closest thing to a succession of new models that U.S. education sees is new editions of textbooks. But new editions of textbooks rarely result from new models of effective teaching and learning. Content and approach are swayed far more often by ideological lobbies and fads of intellectual style (religious conservatism or "political correctness," for example). Because new editions of textbooks so rarely grow from new understandings of the most effective ways to teach and learn, they foster no such conversation and thus accomplish little in the way of lasting progress.

There are other differences between industry's and education's approaches to change. First, each phase of industrial redesign is staffed by specialists trained and experienced in that phase. Scientists do research. Design engineers apply research results to practical problems and create products. Manufacturing engineers decide how to produce those products in the most efficient and effective ways. Marketing and sales people are experts in communication and persuasion. The efforts of each specialist complement the rest. Education makes few such distinctions, either conceptually or in practice. Second, the redesign process works most swiftly and effectively when it operates continually as an integrated whole. Each specialty constantly develops new projects and refines existing ones, but it also communicates incessantly with each of the others. Salespeople tell marketing executives which product features customers like, so future marketing campaigns can emphasize them. Manufacturing technicians tell development engineers about improved production technologies of which products can be designed to take advantage. Development engineers tell salespeople when to expect a particular product enhancement. (Indeed, specialists often work in interdisciplinary teams to accelerate the entire redesign cycle.) Such close integration focuses a variety of specialized expertise toward the common goal of success for the company, its processes, and its products. Educational researchers, innovators, and teachers work in isolation from each other. Third, in an endless pursuit of improvement, redesign builds on currently successful products and methods to create future paradigms of quality. Redesign is always tinkering with its own processes, relentlessly seeking to make itself and its results more useful and reliable and less expensive. In doing so, the redesign process becomes a guided, orderly pattern of strategic change—a pattern of behavior that points like a compass toward greater effectiveness and efficiency, both of products and of paradigms.

In education, we're glimpsing a few intriguing new approaches that signal the emergence of fundamentally new concepts. Results of Success For All, a school-restructuring program developed at Johns Hopkins University, hint strongly that when authority over the details of curriculum is taken away from regulatory bureaucracies and organized across a network of schools backed by a research and development organization, learning improves markedly and consistently. Studies prove that groups of students studying together learn more, better, and faster than individual students working silently and alone at their desks. The success of Reading Recovery, a unique method for teaching lagging first-graders to read, indicates that research, development, and ongoing teacher education can—contrary to conventional wisdom—play a crucial part in rapidly making teaching and learning more efficient and effective in the most difficult teaching situations. These small, isolated innovations are promising, but each in itself lacks the power to clear away old habits and paradigms and establish new ones. Reading Recovery can't refashion the high-school science curriculum, any more than computers in classrooms can by themselves revitalize learning in our nation's schools. Although they have certain things to teach us, these innovations aren't part of a deliberate, integrated effort of systemwide change. That doesn't diminish the crucial importance of these individual models; in effect, a handful of assorted seeds contains the plan for a thriving forest. But, as much as we need to keep inventing and testing new models, we also need to cultivate them to become something more. To construct a new paradigm, U.S. schools—as science, technology, and industry did long ago—must embrace their own version of the redesign process as an orderly pattern of strategic, systemic change. Presently, though, education lacks even the first of many prerequisites for doing so: an organizing and driving vision of its own future.

THE ROLE OF VISION

Institutional changes that are both sweeping and positive don't endure and succeed by chance. In education or any field, lasting fundamental change grows out of, and is sustained by, a compelling vision. That vision is gripping enough to inspire people to commit themselves to work for its realization—to begin and sustain the arduous processes of change in pursuit of the goals that the vision holds out. For the early few who perfected the airplane, the vision was powered human flight; for the industry they created, the enduring vision has been to carry more people and cargo farther, faster, safer, and more cheaply. The microprocessor industry from its inception has been driven by a vision of a computer that could be owned usefully by an individual; the continuing effort to make microcomputers ever smaller, more powerful, and more capable is the ongoing articulation of that vision through strategic redesign. Education's new paradigm—the raw material from which detailed and comprehensive reforms will be crafted—must express a vision of similar power. That vision will be neither rigid nor monolithic. Airline companies don't demand that every jetliner be made with the same brand of engine, nor must all computers be made with identical features; similarly, all children can't be taught effectively from one textbook or through a single pedagogical approach. In any search for excellence, the vision embodies goals more than means. Methods that bring one closer to those goals are valued and retained only until something even more effective is found. For that reason, it's not the place of this book to describe in full what education's new vision is; it and the new structural approach to education that such a vision will necessitate have yet to be properly articulated, and can be only by those who are enacting it. But parts of the vision and its attendant strategies already are coming into view. The National Education Goals formulated by President Bush and the nation's governors at their 1989 education summit (see page 7) embody a portion; so do many of the most effective individual reforms now making their way through our schools—programs like cooperative learning, Success For All, Reading Recovery, and certain uses of electronic technologies. The success of cooperative learning tells us that education's new strategic vision will give students far greater responsibilities in the classroom. The encouraging results of Success For All indicate that, under the new paradigm, educators and schools will share innovative programs instead of continually reinventing them independently. Reading Recovery's power makes it clear that a new educational strategy will call forth an infrastructure that helps professionals improve their skills and knowledge throughout their careers in pursuit of the vision's goals.

However, these aspects have yet to be combined into a single, overarching vision powerful enough to galvanize systemic reform. That vision can become clear and compelling only when disparate individual innovations are integrated into a working system that proves its power to overcome the problems that the old paradigm can't. Consequently, those now working for quantum change in our schools occupy the position in which aircraft builders found themselves before the Wrights flew at Kitty Hawk: they've seen enticing glimpses of the future, but no one has yet assembled those glimpses into a complete and compelling picture. The Wrights' flight at Kitty Hawk marks the beginning of powered human flight not because Orville and Wilbur invented the airplane; they didn't. Others had been aloft before them; others had developed the internal-combustion engine, the curved upper surface and flat bottom of the wing, elevator flaps to control climbs and dives, ailerons along a wing's trailing edge to aid steering, and the other parts needed to get a machine into the air. The Wrights' breakthrough was to integrate these different parts, test them in a wind tunnel under real-world conditions, and assemble them into a single, coordinated system that remained stable in the sky—and thus finally prove that controlled, sustained human flight was possible. The brothers' plane was the first to combine several different innovations into a single, workable system that demonstrated that the problems that had stymied the vision of powered human flight could be solved. In education, innovations such as Success For All or Reading Recovery are the equivalent of ailerons and wings: they're among the innovations that will be integrated to express a comprehensive new vision of education.

When clear, the vision will impel more and more people and organizations to embrace it. As a new structure of ideas proves its power to solve more and more problems, it builds a new context, or framework of meaning, that becomes irresistible. At first, a vision is expressed, or perhaps only suggested, by a rudimentary demonstration such as the Wrights' plane. Such early demonstrations of a new vision's workability usually win it a few influential converts, among whom may be clients with equally visionary goals, other inventors, institutional or governmental champions, the kinds of people who can begin to build a practical structure of support for the vision and for the steps required to begin to enact it. The first automobiles appealed to imaginative tinkerers who created a small but crucial market for the cars as well as an ad hoc feedback network to let carmakers tell their successes from their failures. Prototypical personal computers were embraced by hobbyists who played the same vital role. A technology's early enthusiasts also can be a deciding influence in luring adventurous capital to support visionary inventors. Those who embrace such visions do so largely on the faith that the vision can be achieved, even though the practical details of its implementation have yet to be addressed (or, in many cases, even imagined). They sustain the vision long enough for it to demonstrate its ability to address and resolve an increasing number of those details. As it does so, more and more people are drawn into the new paradigm as they recognize its power to advance their own goals.

Schools already are adopting some of the individual innovations that have attracted influential supporters. But educators haven't yet recognized their need for an organizing vision powerful enough to win a sizeable majority of their number to the cause of comprehensive reform the likes of which U.S. schools haven't seen in this century. That vision will continue to emerge as education reformers experiment. As the vision becomes clearer, an organization and structure will coalesce around it. The organization's purpose will be to study effective practices around the world, identify those that advance the vision, test them, refine them, integrate them into a comprehensive and coordinated structure of reform, teach educators to use them, and supervise their implementation—as well to continually improve teachers' general professional skills and knowledge. As part of its responsibility, the organization also will seed and cultivate new possibilities, a process that must include constant work to improve its own offerings and programs—to redesign its own products through successive "model changes" in pursuit of educational excellence.

A TEMPLATE FOR CHANGE

We suggest this approach not as a theoretical exercise, but because it has already proved its effectiveness. It is precisely the structure of basic research, development, marketing, and redesign that has brought technology the quantum increases in productivity and affordability that have come to define the way we live. The redesign process has transformed one complex technology after another—airplanes, automobiles, machine tools, computers, and others—from oddities and inefficient prototypes to giant industries that have changed the world in the span of a human lifetime. Obviously, children are not products and schools are not factories. But the redesign process works independently of commercial or technological contexts. It is the process by which human energies are harnessed to the steady pursuit of a vision of excellence. To understand how redesign channels and inspires those energies, we'll examine the version of the process that has come to define successful commercial industries.

In industry, the redesign process measures improvement against four specific criteria:

- *Capitalizing on success,*
- *Improving quality,*
- *Expanding usefulness, and*
- *Keeping the selling price of each unit as affordable as possible for as many consumers as possible.*

First, products that are candidates for redesign are those that already have shown the greatest success in the marketplace. (Ford did not invest millions to redesign the Edsel.) A company uses its resources efficiently when it seeks to improve a success, not to sustain mediocrity or to salvage a failed project. (Actually, the Edsel was an exception to this principle. Products that don't meet the four criteria rarely survive the prototype and test-marketing stages.) Second, each redesign tries to improve a product's quality so that it performs more effectively and efficiently. The third criterion is a corollary to the second: the redesign process seeks to expand and improve the product's features along with its quality. Improving a product's capabilities and reliability makes the redesigned version useful to more people than the old one was. The more people who find it worthwhile to buy a product, the lower the price at which the manufacturer can sell each copy—allowing, in turn, more people to buy it and earning even more money for the manufacturer. Finally, redesign works internally within a manufacturing organization to optimize the processes of design and fabrication. The goal is to produce each copy of a product at the lowest possible price without sacrificing any of the other three objectives.

In pursuing each of these goals, one of the most important techniques the redesign process employs is integration. Each time a product is redesigned, engineers try to combine as many improvements in the new version as are practical. By integrating improvements in a single product, both the manufacturer and user can more easily justify the cost of the new version instead of making do with the old one. Boeing's new 777 passenger jet is only one example. Thanks to years of testing, the new plane combines a wing contour and body shape that provide adequate strength and support while also improving aerodynamic efficiency. The plane's tail section is made from a synthetic composite instead of aluminum, which reduces the 777's weight by 15 percent. Similarly, in parts of the frame aluminum is being replaced by lighter-weight titanium. Although titanium is more expensive, engineers have calculated that each pound of eliminated body weight will save several hundred dollars' worth of fuel during the airplane's service life. Also, by combining a series of small, steady gains in engine design, engineers have given the two-engine 777 more power than many current three- and four-engine liners that will compete with it. By integrating so many improvements in one plane, Boeing has designed a craft that cuts wind resistance by 10 percent, boosts cruising speeds by up to 20 miles an hour while still using a thicker wing to add strength and store more fuel, and flies nonstop more than 9,000 miles fully loaded, farther than any other passenger jet previously could. The improvements mean that airlines can use the 777 to fly more passengers farther at less cost—a powerful incentive for them to buy Boeing's improved jet. Boeing's president, Phil Condit, says: "You retain your competitive position by continuously improving what you do."[1]

He might have added that continuous improvement is the result of continuous collaboration—the redesign conversation. The 777 was designed by committees of engineers representing not only Boeing, but also its suppliers and customers. When a customer or subcontractor urged a change in the 777's design, "we discussed it," says chief payload engineer, George Broady. "We may or may not have done it, but we listened. In the past, we didn't do that very well." In one case, United Airlines asked Boeing to redesign the luggage bins above the seats. "It could be done relatively easily," Broady says. "It opened up the passenger cabin more." In the past, the first chance a customer would have to comment on something like that would be when Boeing delivered the finished plane. In another instance, United's mechanics complained about Boeing's habit of enclosing wings' inner mechanisms under one long metal cover. "It was a nightmare," says a United representative on the Boeing team. "We had to remove scores of screws just to check out one problem." The design team simply replaced the one panel with several smaller ones.

Other conflicts required a more complex solution. For instance, some airlines pressured Boeing to equip the 777 with a new, top-performing two-hundred-foot-long wing, while others demanded that the plane take up no more groundspread than shorter-winged craft so it could still fit existing runways and loading areas. Boeing compromised; it gave the 777 a two-hundred-foot wing, but also offered buyers an optional twenty-one-foot hinged wingtip that can be raised vertically when the plane is on the ground. Using customers' ideas, Boeing also configured the passenger compartment to allow airlines to add or take out seats as traffic on different routes demands while still maximizing roominess and passenger comfort. By letting customers' needs and wants guide its research, development, and design process, Boeing did more than guarantee its 777 a ready market. It also saved itself and its customers money by slashing the amount of redesigning and customizing it would need to do after the plane was in production. "This is the ideal way to design a product," says one Boeing executive. "Everybody wins."

The conversationlike process of redesign also always uncovers the most useful product improvements, as Apple Computer learned. Apple saw sales of its new Macintosh machine weaken not long after the machine's 1984 introduction. The reason, customers told them, was that Apple wasn't "open." In other words, Apple wouldn't share its proprietary technology with others who could design new programs and specialized devices for the company's machines—programs and devices that would make the Mac more flexible and more useful in more ways to more people. In fact, Apple's Mac had no place in its circuitry to attach new devices. The Macintosh that Apple shipped from its factories was the only version of a Mac that the company permitted to exist. At the time, IBM not only was marketing its own personal computers but was taking more and more of the market. It shared its technologies with legions of programmers and hardware designers who were turning out arrays of compatible memory devices, programming aids, and other products—each of which made every IBM PC more useful than it was before. More and more buyers were choosing IBM's "open" system because it could be incrementally improved and customized to each user's tastes.

"It was quite controversial within Apple," recalls William Coldrick, who retired in 1989 as Apple's senior vice president in charge of U.S. sales. "Customers were telling us that unless we opened the machines to all the products that third parties could develop, it would be very difficult for our customers to stay with Macs. One faction in Apple pressed the company to be more responsive to what our market was telling us. Another faction thought that Apple was more intelligent than the user: that although the user wants something, we at Apple know what's best for him and therefore we won't do what he wants. The developers of the original Mac thought that way. But that mentality didn't work. As Mac sales began to slip and IBM sales gained, the people in product development decided that they'd better go along. Ultimately, customers influenced Apple *against its will* to develop an open-architecture Mac."

Redesign is equally powerful in leading a company to improve its processes as well as its products. Perhaps the greatest example is Henry Ford's creation of the moving assembly line. In 1909, Ford's automobile factory employed roughly one thousand workers. They turned out about eleven thousand cars that year, which Ford had to sell for $850 to cover his costs and earn a profit. In 1914, the year after the line began to move, his now eighteen thousand workers made three hundred fifty thousand Model Ts, each of which carried a retail price of $550. The motoring public hadn't demanded a moving assembly line; it wanted lower-priced cars. It was Ford's own relentless search for progressive efficiencies that led him to translate the public's desire into a new process that made automobiles affordable for average families.

As the redesign process pursues its four criteria, technology-driven products almost inevitably become increasingly complex: they add more features and capabilities in attempts to appeal to more consumers. Many of those products, such as airplanes and personal computers, are so complex that they're not so much products as they are systems composed of an array of specialized and integrated subsystems. As a result, each time a feature or subsystem is added, there are more subsystems to redesign in order to integrate the addition with them. Adding a more powerful amplifier to an existing stereo system also necessitates the addition of new speakers able to handle the increase, just as the advent of jet engines on airplanes required new methods of bracing and more streamlined surface contours. As such complexity increases, two consequences result. First, design becomes more and more centralized; a single, overarching intelligence is needed to ensure that subsystems will combine smoothly and that each complements the others to enhance the goals of the product as a whole and meet the four criteria. That central design intelligence is usually provided by companies, such as Boeing or Apple, that manufacture and market integrated products. Second, these design centers rely on networks of technically sophisticated and specialized suppliers, themselves constantly engaged in redesign. Each supplier works to perfect a few, or even just one, of the subsystems to ensure that they meet specifications set by the design center. Boeing's new 777 comprises 238 distinct subsystems, from the wings to the cockpit videoscreens. Each subsystem was designed by a team of engineers that included members representing the supplier who'll build the subsystem. The new plane's manufacture is carried out by more than one hundred suppliers on four continents.

In the same way, as a product, or system, becomes increasingly complex, so must the redesign process itself. First, it gives rise to new professions. When the Wright brothers flew at Kitty Hawk, there were no certified aeronautical engineers, aircraft mechanics, airport planners, or ticket agents. Those professions appeared over time as the demands of designing and operating airplanes became more complex—and, at the same time, busy and lucrative enough to support more workers. New businesses grew up around the air travel industry, such as publishers of in-flight magazines and catering companies that make meals to be served aloft. Similarly, new branches of science, such as aerodynamics, were born. New academic departments appeared on university campuses and new specialized departments grew up within aircraft manufacturing companies. As any redesign process matures, necessarily specialized professions, businesses, and even industries spring up in its wake. Second, as a result, the redesign process becomes increasingly expensive to support. Ford poured millions into streamlining his production system so he could make more cars faster and cheaper. More recently, Steven Wozniak engineered the first Apple personal computer in his parents' garage during his spare time in 1977. The first Apple was priced at $666, had too little memory space to have any truly practical uses, and was sold to a few hundred hobbyists—visionaries gripped by the implications of its design. As Apple invested more in improving its computers, the machines grew in strength and capabilities. More memory was added to the main circuitboard. Hard disks became standard equipment. The machines became able to manipulate pictures as well as text, first in black-and-white and later in color. Each time the company pursued an improvement, it had to expand its in-house staff of design and engineering specialists; as Apple expanded its engineering expertise, it was able to produce a more capable machine that more and more people could justify the expense of buying. The more people who bought its machines, the lower the price the company could charge for each individual computer and still cover its steadily growing costs of research, development, marketing, and redesign. Today, Apple employs 1,800 engineers and spends more than $1 billion annually to evolve better products. At the same time, the price of Apple's basic machine has been driven below $1,000—not much more than the price of the feeble prototype that spawned the company in 1977, and well within the price range of many middle-class families and college students. Apple's increasingly complex redesign process has developed products that have become steadily more affordable for more people, even while its infrastructure of redesign was demanding greater and greater investment.

Each successful large-scale manufacturer can tell a similar story. To bring its 777 out of the hangar, Boeing assigned more than four thousand of its staff engineers to the project. Each of them has invested between three and eight years of effort in the project. In rough terms, that's a commitment of at least forty million person-hours. Assuming each person involved in the 777's technical development has a four-year college degree, that alone represents more than sixteen thousand person-years of training brought to bear on the new plane's creation—a figure that doesn't include the practical know-how that those workers have gained on the job. Boeing's decision to commit its incalculably valuable infrastructure of design to the project wasn't a leap of faith, however, but a carefully calculated decision. The company had done enough engineering and market research to assure itself that the 777 would earn much more for Boeing over time than the company would invest in its development. It was right; by mid-1992, a full year before the first 777 would see a runway, Boeing had booked ninety-nine orders for the 777 and had sold options on eighty-six more—the largest number of advance orders in aircraft history for a new commercial plane.

The economies that the redesign process makes possible extend beyond the price of the product, however. Part of making a product more useful is making one that compounds the customer's own savings as the customer uses it. For example, airline companies have been eager to buy each new generation of passenger planes, even though each has been more expensive to purchase than its predecessor. The reason: each new model has carried more passengers farther without stopping, allowing the airlines to charge less per passenger-mile traveled and thus to attract more passengers. To illustrate, we can chart in constant dollars the declining fares that United Airlines charged passengers to fly from New York to San Francisco from 1927 to 1977.

In 1927, United ferried passengers between coasts in a $24,500, one-passenger Boeing 40A—what today would be a $250,000 airplane. The one-way trip took thirty-two hours, required fifteen stops, and a ticket cost $404, the current equivalent of $3,840. The in-flight cabin service consisted of a box lunch and a thermos of coffee on the way to Chicago. After Chicago, the amenities were limited to a single container of cold water. (After all those landings and takeoffs, that might have been all any traveler could stomach.) Ten years later, a twenty-one-passenger Douglas DC-3 cost an airline about $95,000 to buy, a sum that would be roughly $1 million in today's dollars. The DC-3 covered the distance in 15.5 hours with only three stops along the way. The $160 one-way fare—$1,370 today—included hot meals, stewardess service, and sleeper berths. In 1950, fifty-six passengers could board a $500,000 DC-6—a plane that would cost $3 million today—and cross the continent in 9.5 hours while sipping cocktails, making the same three stops, and paying a fare of $158, or about $960 in current terms. By 1967, United was paying $7 million or more apiece for Boeing 707 jets, a sum comparable to about $28.5 million now. A 707 could ferry one hundred thirty people from sea to sea in five hours without stopping or otherwise interrupting the buffet and in-flight movies. The fare was $145, which in today's dollars would be about $600.

In 1976, Boeing 747s took up the route—planes that cost $30 million each then and would sell for a little more than $70 million now. The fare had risen to $174, thanks to creeping inflation. But in constant terms, the ticket price had continued to fall, reaching today's equivalent of $350. "In constant dollars, the cost of air travel went down even though the cost of airplanes went up," says United spokesman Joe Hopkins, "in large part because the planes could carry more people at a lower individual cost."[2] Figures compiled by the Air Transport Association, the airlines' trade group, illustrate his point. Between 1970 and 1980, average passenger fares fell from 17.4 cents to 15.4 cents a mile, while the airlines' cost per passenger-mile fell from 6.9 cents to 6.3 cents. The companies' average rate of return on investment grew from 1.2 percent annually to 5.7, and operating profits went from an average of $43 million a year at the beginning of the decade to $199 million at the end—more than doubling from $155 million to $334 million in today's dollars. Airline profits boomed during the period that they were spending hundreds of millions of dollars to build new fleets of the costliest jetliners yet. They boomed because airlines made their product, air travel, affordable to more people through the regular replacement of older-model planes with new, more efficient ones.

The redesign process, however, doesn't develop without normal growing pains. In an industry's early years, the process is rife with failures, false starts, and wasted resources. Dozens of pilots lost their lives testing the second generation of airplanes during the early years of the twentieth century; tens of millions of dollars were spent during the 1950s, 1960s, and 1970s on computer designs that ultimately proved unworkable. Such risks are expected—perhaps even necessary— during an industry's infancy. A redesign process grows and strengthens by allowing people to work through those failures while an industry is still young. From one model change to the next, redesign allows engineers to identify failure's causes and "design out" the flaws that lead to disaster. During the first two decades of the twentieth century, there was a significant probability that a new design of airplane would fall out of the sky on its maiden voyage. The new models that flew often had other problems: they didn't always fit into existing storage or repair hangars; mechanics needed to devise exotic new tools and procedures to fix them; and those same mechanics sometimes had to learn to fix new models by hunch or trial and error—errors that sometimes weren't discovered until the plane was aloft. Today, those kinds of disasters are virtually impossible because of the techniques and processes that the airplane industry has learned and perfected through thousands of re-designs. Those who work with airplanes, from engineers and manufac-turing technicians to mechanics and baggage handlers, have learned to expect innovation. They know what it's like because they've been through it before and they understand what their respective roles are in making innovation succeed. They know that change demands adjust-ments on their part, but they also know that the process of change itself will help them make those adjustments. That collective expertise in creating and implementing innovation prevents the arrival of a new model from precipitating chaos and disaster.

But not in schools. Classroom innovations are still routinely falling out of the sky on their maiden voyages. The reason isn't hard to deter-mine: education has no redesign process that allows it to build on its past experience of change. Every experience in implementing an inno-vation is new, alien, approached as if it had never been done before. No broad vision infuses each task of educational change with a sense of context and continuity; no organizational culture or systematized pro-cess of change supports or guides educators as they cast about for better ways to do things. Education still confuses changing a program or procedure with the process of change itself.

THE HUMAN DIMENSIONS OF CHANGE

That by no means indicates that educators are less sophisticated or perceptive than engineers or executives. Tinkering with the shape or behavior of a tire, a computer, or an airplane is culturally, politically, and often technically far easier and more acceptable than revamping the patterns that shape people's ideas. No one questions the propriety of fuel injection in cars, but the artificial human heart remains a subject of debate on many levels. The appearance of a bigger memory chip in a new computer is a welcome event, while the idea of using drugs or genetic engineering to boost human intelligence sparks passionate argument. Because change (like redesign itself) is a human process that first asks for commitments of effort and resources before showing results, it typically confronts human resistance. Opposition to the new is endemic; to some degree, any change in a comfortable pattern forces those who have come to rely on that pattern to relearn or reorganize constellations of thought and behavior. The larger the change, the more disruption of the familiar it will cause and the more resistance it will meet.

It was that kind of resistance that chaos theory encountered as it emerged during the late 1970s and early 1980s. Chaos is a branch of mathematics that evolved to explain and to forecast events and patterns that had always remained beyond the reach of established patterns of human knowledge and thus unexplainable: the reasons for the rise and fall of gypsy moth populations, changes in weather patterns, the course of an arrhythmia in a human heart, the path that lightning takes through the sky. As James Gleick put it in his best-selling 1987 book *Chaos,* "Where chaos begins, classical science stops."[3] The handful of researchers who pioneered the mathematical descriptions of chaotic events felt they were learning to conceive the natural world in an entirely new way—that they were bringing forth a new paradigm in science.

As exciting as that was, virtually every early researcher who pursued the study of chaos ran into a wall of opposition. The reason was as clear as the reaction was predictable: chaos theory highlighted fundamental weaknesses in the assumptions, approaches, and theoretical structures of conventional physics. Traditionally, science had assumed that minute deviations in a pattern had no lasting or long-term effect on the pattern itself, that the pattern would absorb the anomaly. The mathematics of chaos demonstrates that such minute deviations have the very real power to obliterate the larger pattern and replace it with an entirely new one (or with utter randomness). In short, chaos theory suggests quite bluntly that the world does not work in the way that most physicists had long thought that it did.

For obvious reasons, researchers whose careers were vested in conventional science made chaos theorists feel something other than welcome. College professors worried that they risked their professional standing and hopes for promotion by following their curiosity into this uncharted intellectual territory. Graduate students faced the very real prospect of ending their careers before they began them if they chose to write their dissertations in a field that could muster neither experts nor mainstream acceptance. Many university departments were clearly hostile to chaos research and those who insisted on doing it; professional journals often showed the same bias. In particular, physicists specializing in conventional fluid dynamics openly resented the new science because it explicitly threatened the tenets of their discipline. Joseph Ford, a chaoticist at the Georgia Institute of Technology, might have been describing their feelings when he characterized reaction to his emerging specialty by quoting Tolstoy: "Most men . . . cannot accept even the simplest and most obvious truth if it would be such that would oblige them to admit the falsity of conclusions which they have delighted in explaining to colleagues . . . have proudly taught to others, and . . . have woven, thread by thread, into the fabric of their lives."[4] Yet the undeniable power and timeliness of the idea propelled the work forward. "Chaos now presages the future as none will gainsay," one advocate gushed in an early research paper on chaos. "But to accept the future, one must renounce much of the past."[5] In other words, to remain relevant and true to the goal, professionals had to forsake the comforts of an obsolete paradigm.

Like scientists, education reformers almost always face militant recalcitrance. Every classroom innovation challenges teachers' established habits and practices, and also often their basic beliefs about themselves and their work—something most of us, not just teachers, aren't willing to do without a struggle. Reforms can demand that administrators disrupt management structures or styles that they've become comfortable with and adept at controlling. New programs often require new budget outlays, and that can bring reformers into conflict with frugal school boards, pit school boards against taxpayers and taxpayers against teachers.

Because education lacks a shared vision as well as an orderly process of innovation, those conflicts can fester indefinitely and bring gridlock and stagnation to schools. In industry, by contrast, the redesign process and the vision it supports prod people to find solutions. For example, the early proponents of distributed computing—i.e., desktop machines scattered through an organization rather than centrally located mainframes run by a priesthood of technicians—first had to develop machines that could do the work of mainframes. But, just as crucial, they also had to overcome the opposition of the mainframe's advocates, as well as the skepticism of users and administrators, to establish their product and the vision it embodied.

In the early 1980s, everyone in a corporation depended for their data and information processing on huge, expensive centralized computers. Anyone wanting a financial forecast, a sales analysis, a payroll, or anything else done by the computer made a pilgrimage to the data-processing department and placed their request at the end of a line of tasks waiting their turn on the mainframe. It could take days to get a simple computing task back; developing and refining a customized computer program often took the data-processing department months. Although the delays were maddening (as well as inefficient), computing in a corporation remained in the hands of the specially trained bureaucracy that grew up around the mainframes. If knowledge is power, then the data-processing bureaucracy that controlled the flow of information was the regent of power within its corporation—and no bureaucracy surrenders power easily. When desktop computers threatened to break up that power and give a share of it to every office worker in a company, mainframe bureaucracies fought back. The microprocessor industry's marketing effort had to overcome that corporate resistance to change.

Coldrick recalls the campaign when Apple introduced its Macintosh in 1984.[6] "It was designed as a computer for people who didn't have access to computing yet," he says, "including those who weren't part of a corporation's central computing utility." Coldrick and his staff targeted one hundred major U.S. firms and called on the executives who headed each company's data-processing operation. "We were treated very cordially but not very seriously," he says. "So we began to work at the individual and departmental level." There, Coldrick and his sales force found legions of workers frustrated by the mainframe bureaucracy's stranglehold on the creation and management of information. "They realized that the mainframe organization wasn't serving their needs. We found that Macs were beginning to multiply in corporations out of sight of the data-processing department. People were buying their own Macs and a series of programs for them, taking them to work, using them, and then taking them home at night. And they became contagious." Workers had begun to experience the continuously expanding productivity that Apple's vision and ongoing strategic redesign process offered them. Apple won its corporate market the old-fashioned way: by gradually convincing enough users, even ultimately corporate data-processing executives, that its innovations were more useful than the products and systems that they replaced.

The Mac's progress is typical of the way in which industrial redesign overcomes the human resistance to change. First, marketing and sales campaigns show customers that the new product will deliver benefits greater than the trouble of the changes and inconveniences that must be made to accommodate it. Second, the product and the vision it embodies foster the expectation—and often the demand—for regular change. (Fashion designers, automakers, and computer manufacturers, among others, predicate their work on the assumption that regular change is not only necessary but inherently positive.) When a product's users come to understand that regular change ultimately means more effective and efficient use of their own resources, they still might not look forward to change but they also accept the ultimate futility of ignoring or resisting it. Until education as a profession can experience change as a continuous process of redesign that can be trusted to deliver the benefits it promises, every new reform will understandably remain alien—unfamiliar, unpredictable, and not to be trusted.

FLATTENING THE PYRAMID

To initiate a process that will keep schools evolving in the steady pursuit of quality as articulated by the new paradigm's vision, education will need to borrow one more innovation from industry: the flattening of organizations. To compete in the new global economy, companies have learned that they must be able to innovate more quickly than ever. There's no time anymore for questions to percolate up the management hierarchy and for decisions to find their way back down. The key to making the best product-related decisions in the shortest time—and to having those decisions accepted and acted upon—has turned out to be to give more and more responsibility for quality- and productivity-related innovations to teams of front-line workers.

In education, trends have taken the opposite direction. Between 1960 and 1990, the proportion of the education labor force working in administration instead of in classrooms grew by as much as 25 percent in some urban districts. Only recently have our schools begun to experiment with reducing administrative bureaucracies, most notably in Chicago, where in 1988 a new law mandated that school-district overhead costs be slashed and redirected to the city's schools. The law had the effect of reducing the number of managers and administrators in the district's downtown headquarters from almost twenty thousand to fewer than nine thousand. The power of decision once held by those managers was returned to "local school councils" made up of teachers, administrators, and parents. The councils hold real authority, from the right to hire and fire principals to set course content and allocate budget funds. Although it's still too soon to be certain that the changes have boosted students' learning, several studies have reported gains under the program: teachers now feel more energized and involved in their work, parents are taking a greater interest in their children's education, and more creativity and district dollars are flowing to the schools themselves. The path hasn't been smooth, but the new paradigm and the vision it embodies is giving the city's educational community new vitality, direction, and hope.

Such drastic reorganizations are almost unknown in education, although in industry decentralized power has come to be recognized as a necessity. The Union Pacific Railroad is one of the best examples. In 1985, the UP was in about the same shape as a conventional public school. It was rigidly controlled and sluggishly managed by a distant and centralized power elite and was wasting bushels of money through glaring inefficiencies. Even worse, although it assumed it was one of the best-run railroads in the country, it was regularly disappointing the people it was in business to serve. According to one UP report, United Parcel Service called Union Pacific "the 'least best' of the eleven railroads we deal with." A crisp note from an energy company pointed to "a major deterioration in service reliability" of UP's coal trains. "Some days," a client company executive told UP bluntly, "your service is a disaster." So was the company's organization. After subsuming two other railroads, UP was left with a rail system divided into thirty separate territories with 160 field offices staffed by four thousand people. Parallel bureaucracies spilled across the railroad's service territories, and nine layers of management separated boxcar from boardroom. With recession shrinking its revenues and profits, UP stopped buying new equipment and started laying off workers. Short-term profits perked up, but performance drooped. Twenty percent of the bills the railroad sent its customers were wrong and had to be done over, the typical locomotive was out of service 15 percent of the time, and shop workers and executives often had to struggle to maintain civil relations. The railroad estimated that its own sheer ineptitude was costing it $600 million a year. Then Mike Walsh took over as UP's new chairman.

Walsh knew nothing about railroads, didn't come to UP from another transportation company. He specialized in the management of change. His charge was simply to make UP the best-run, most efficient railroad in the country. As Walsh talked with groups of employees throughout the company as well as with the railroad's disgruntled customers, he pinpointed the major source of the company's troubles: the railroad's outmoded human systems.

He set to work to restructure them from top to bottom. At Union Pacific, work and authority had been organized according to the pyramid, based on a military-style chain of command, that has long defined corporations, schools, and most other organizations. The railroad's version was extreme: Problems percolated up to the central clutch of authority without middle managers' attempting to reach outside of their organizational niches to solve them. Decisions were made at the pyramid's pinnacle, then sent back down. Change was an alien concept. "At UP, 'good' employees were adept at following orders," a company executive recalls. "People rarely were chastised for following an order, regardless of the outcome." Walsh set out to wrest the company's preoccupation away from its internal processes and to redirect it squarely with the people the railroad exists to serve.

To do so, he turned the company's old power structure on its head, dispersing the authority to make decisions and changes while centralizing service and support. After the dust had cleared, nine layers of management had been cut to three. The number of territories was reduced from thirty to twenty-four. Field superintendents were empowered to make decisions and deal with customers' requests and problems on the spot. Many field-office staffs were halved, which alone saved the railroad an estimated $50 million annually. By 1989, trains were being dispatched and their travel managed over UP's twenty-two-thousand-mile line from a single control room in Omaha instead of from forty separate offices. According to UP, the new $50 million fiber-optic control center will trim $22 million a year from the company's previous operating budget. Customer-service work, once initiated at field offices and then bucked up the line of authority, has been centralized in one place; now, customers with questions or problems about the progress of their shipments call a single toll-free phone number. Duplication, delays, and inefficiencies are receding under the new organization, while a revitalized marketing effort has begun to win the railroad more business. At the same time, Walsh reconfigured the company's culture. As the new organization took form, he held eighteen meetings in nine of the railroad's regional offices and talked to an estimated ten thousand workers to bring them the message of a new Union Pacific. "The openness was not just encouraging," one worker recalls. "It was a foot in the door for change." The new structure forced blue- and white-collar workers to put their antagonisms aside, middle managers to come out of their organizational boxes, and executives and staff to move beyond their own isolation—not just to solve problems, boost quality, and please customers, but also to guarantee their own futures.

The new organization produced the results the railroad had hoped for. Revenues grew steadily from 1986 and profits grew even faster. Earnings of $322 million in 1985 swelled to $602 million in 1991. During 1990, UP toted 4 percent more freight than in 1989, while the industry's average fell by almost an equal amount. The railroad invested in new engines and equipment, began taking business away from truck lines, and also increased its share of the haulers' market among coal and food producers. Productivity jumped; the railroad shaved its work force by 22 percent and still handled 40 percent more traffic. At the same time, the number of workers' injuries dropped by almost a third. Billing accuracy rose from 80 percent in 1985 to 94 percent by 1989, and locomotives' downtime was halved. In 1990, UP won its second consecutive 3M Company Quality Award for all-around service, the only railroad that year to do so.

By leveling the traditional vertical organization and placing the power to change and to make decisions in the hands of front-line workers, hundreds of U.S. companies like Union Pacific are beginning to see similar gains in efficiency, productivity, and worker spirit. The reasons that make it a good idea in industry also make it a good idea in education: it guarantees the best innovations in the shortest time, and it guarantees that those innovations "stick." That facet is no less important than any other in constructing education's new paradigm and realizing the new vision's goals.

THE KEY TO REFORM

As a group, U.S. educators lack a clear, compelling, detailed, and unifying vision of the direction in which they want school reform to go. They also have yet to construct a process that will organize and energize their collective pursuit of the goals created by such a vision. Without a vision and a process of change, our current efforts at education reform are at best doomed to a fragmented and therefore limited success. By adapting the redesign process for use in education, U.S. schools can define that missing vision and begin to construct their own process of progressive innovation. By doing so, our schools could realize the same quantum gains that the process has brought again and again to science and industry: steadily improving quality, reliability, and usefulness while squeezing out waste and deploying resources more and more efficiently as defined by the goals that the process has been adapted to serve.

Because redesign is in essence a human process rather than a technical or industrial one, it can be adapted to do for schools what it has done for computers, aircraft, kitchen appliances, or any of the other industries that it has propelled to global success so quickly and forcefully. It can do so by fostering and maintaining a devotion to effectiveness and efficiency *as defined through the experience of students and teachers*, just as industrial redesign unwaveringly pursues effectiveness and efficiency as defined through the experience of its customers. That kind of adaptation can be structured in several ways, and it's not our purpose here to detail them all. However, it's clear that an effective redesign infrastructure in education would develop, test, refine, and integrate reforms. It would contract with a school or district to implement a comprehensive, integrated package of reforms—not just isolated, unrelated programs—aimed at restructuring school and district organizations. It would instruct teachers in new methods of teaching that the innovations required, help students adapt to change, and supervise the reforms' implementation to ensure that things don't go awry while educational communities are learning to incorporate innovations effectively. At the same time, an infrastructure of educational design would itself be constantly engaged in redesign to make its own programs better, more useful, and more cost-efficient. By helping schools accomplish their mission more efficiently, an infrastructure of educational redesign also would free some of the money already in school budgets to underwrite a portion of the cost of the redesign process.

Those assertions aren't speculation. We can see those approaches embodied in some of today's most effective reforms. Reading Recovery is consistently effective because it's based on careful research, teaches educators how to make practical use of the findings, and supervises them continuously. Cooperative learning and restructuring programs such as Success For All disperse power and responsibility among students and teachers. Because such programs make education more effective, they all trim the amount of money and effort schools must divert to remedial teaching—money, in effect, wasted because, for whatever reason, the job of educating wasn't done right the first time.

The process of educational redesign is not mere theory. In the next chapter, we'll glimpse the process's potential as evidenced by Reading Recovery, one of the most successful educational reforms to appear in U.S. schools—one thoroughly grounded in the process of redesign.

3
Reading Recovery

*Precursor for a Process
of Educational Redesign*

Jan Yanscik, a tutor coaching the poorest readers in Wickliffe Elementary School's first grade in suburban Columbus, Ohio, seems to be doing everything backward. She prods slow learners to read and write quickly. She praises children for their mistakes and cuts their writing to pieces with scissors. When they get stuck on a word, she doesn't tell them what it is but asks them what they're going to do about it. A twenty-year teaching veteran, she's never been happier in her work—or more effective in teaching lagging children to crack the code of printed English.

Billy, her first student this morning, is reading aloud from a book when he comes to the word *socks*. He pronounces it "soaks" and then stops.

"Does that sound right?" Yanscik asks. Billy stares at the word.

"Does it sound like good language?" she coaxes. "Does 'soaks' make sense in the story?" Finally, Billy shakes his head.

"What are you going to do?" Yanscik asks.

Billy looks at the picture on the page and sees a drawing of an old man in his socks. He reads the word correctly and goes on, but Yanscik interrupts.

"Now what did you do there?" she asks, and Billy explains. "You did what good readers do, didn't you?" Yanscik says. "You looked for other information that could help you. I like the way you did that."

To her visitor, Yanscik whispers, "That's a big change for Billy. A few weeks ago, he would have read 'soaks' and kept on going. But now he's learned to cross-check and he's reading for meaning."

Later in the story, Billy comes to the word *like* and stops dead. "What are you going to do?" Yanscik asks again.

He sounds the *l* and the *k*, but can't decide how to pronounce the *i* or explain the role of the *e*. She waits for Billy to initiate a strategy, then coaches him as he puzzles out the word.

"Do you know what good readers do?" she asks him after he's succeeded. "They take a really good look at that word and they say, 'That word gave me trouble so I'm going to have to remember that that's how 'like' looks. Now write 'like' for me." He does so. "Again." He complies. "Again, and faster," Yanscik commands. "Good readers are fast writers." Billy obediently picks up his pace.

After Billy has written *like* several times, Yanscik writes *bike* on the blackboard. "I bet now you know this word, too," she says. Billy reads it correctly and Yanscik follows with *hike* and *Mike*.

"Now you know 'like,' " Yanscik says. "We'll put a star by 'like' on the blackboard because you know it so well."

STRATEGIC READING

Until now, Billy, like most other U.S. first-graders who show abject confusion in learning to read, typically would have spent years in special classes. He would have filled out countless worksheets, drilled and drilled on phonics and other isolated bits of reading technique, and he still would never have caught up to his grade's average level of reading ability. Instead, after just twelve weeks Billy is reading with average first-grade skill. He's been rescued by an innovative program called Reading Recovery—probably the closest thing to a process of research, development, design, and marketing that U.S. education reform has yet seen.

Since its introduction in this country in 1984, the program has made its way into more than seven hundred schools in forty-eight states. From 1989 through 1992, the number of teachers trained and children served increased by 60 percent annually, a pace equaled in industry only by rare commercial successes such as skateboards in the 1970s or personal computers a decade later. There's a simple explanation for such phenomenal growth: Reading Recovery has proved to be more effective and efficient at correcting reading problems than its competitors. In poor urban and posh suburban schools alike, the program consistently rehabilitates more than four of every five failing first-grade readers in just twelve to twenty weeks of daily half-hour lessons.

Reading Recovery isn't an example of educational redesign—not quite, at least not yet. It lacks a comprehensive marketing effort and is only now beginning to evolve a mechanism to reconceive and elaborate its fundamental structure and approach periodically as new insights from research and experience dictate; it also hasn't integrated other innovations that might leverage its considerable power. Still, it gives U.S. education a more complete framework than any other single program on which to model a full-fledged redesign process. By examining the way in which Reading Recovery has been developed and disseminated, we can better understand both the nature of an effective design process in education and its power to replace outmoded paradigms with more relevant ones.

The program does incorporate several key features of a successful redesign process. It has shaped its methods according to the results of its own and others' research. It has tested and honed its techniques through years of trials and refinements, analogous to industry's processes of product prototyping and test marketing. It equips its specialists with a common body of proven knowledge and skills that allows instructors to tailor each lesson to each child's needs—in marketing terms, to shape the product to the customer—rather than expecting every child to adapt to an identical course of lessons that moves at an inflexible pace. Equally important, the program maintains rigorous systems of self-evaluation or quality control, and offers ongoing training and support to the teachers and schools—"dealers," in effect—that adopt it.

Reading Recovery also integrates its instructional frameworks and techniques so each can strengthen the others. A student and teacher meet privately for a daily half hour of intense and closely structured work. Teachers tailor each student's lessons to build on the child's individual strengths, no matter how meager, showing him or her how to broaden those skills and use them to master others. Reading Recovery teachers learn the program's techniques not in a quick workshop but through a year-long course of study. The course includes extensive practice teaching, which is critiqued by other Reading Recovery teachers-in-training. In schools, "teacher-leaders" supervise working Reading Recovery teachers to help them always to improve the effectiveness and efficiency of their work.

Not surprisingly, Reading Recovery's effectiveness and efficiencies are intimately linked. "The program isn't conventional remediation," Gay Su Pinnell, professor of reading at Ohio State University, explains. "It's intervention—catching a failing reader before he establishes counterproductive habits. It's also about acceleration in a very short period, moving these students along fast enough that they can keep up in class after a few weeks with us—and they do. Reading Recovery is more successful than any other program I've seen."[1]

A 1990 study sponsored by the Chicago-based John D. and Catherine T. MacArthur Foundation, a private philanthropy funding education reforms (among other things), reached a similar conclusion. The study compared results of five methods used to correct reading difficulties among first-graders, including the most common approach now used in U.S. public schools. "Some educators thought that any form of individual tutoring should be just as effective as Reading Recovery," Pinnell notes. "Others wondered if a long and expensive course of teacher training was really necessary, and there are those who believe that Reading Recovery's techniques might work as well in groups as they do in individual lessons. We designed a rigorous study that would address these questions directly."

From thirty-three schools in ten Ohio school districts, the investigation randomly assigned a total of 324 first-graders, all of whom had tested as the worst readers in their classes, to one of five intervention programs. The first was Reading Recovery with a fully trained teacher. The second method mimicked most aspects of Reading Recovery but used teachers trained in an abbreviated program. Children in the third group were tutored individually by experienced reading teachers not using Reading Recovery's techniques. In the fourth, trained Reading Recovery teachers led group sessions instead of private lessons. The fifth, a control group, relied on the skill drills and worksheets typical of federally funded group remediation classes common in U.S. public schools. At the end of their special classes, students took five tests to gauge their mastery of a wide range of literacy skills. To measure the lasting powers of the different forms of instruction, the students repeated the tests at the end of their first-grade year and again at the beginning of second grade.

The results not only endorse Reading Recovery's approach, but also indicate the power of integrated educational design. The study found that Reading Recovery's combination of individual tutoring, extensive reading and writing during lessons, and a carefully structured program of thorough, ongoing teacher training rescued failing first-grade readers far more effectively than either conventional techniques or Reading Recovery's individual aspects used separately from each other. "Reading Recovery was the only group for which the . . . effect was significant on all four measures at the conclusion of the experiment," the study's report concludes, "and was also the only treatment indicating lasting effects."[2]

The study corroborates classroom experience. Pinnell and others at Ohio State charted the program's results during the first three academic years that Columbus, Ohio, schools used Reading Recovery, beginning in 1985. Reading Recovery students, whether core-city black children or whites from wealthier suburbs, clearly outlearned those in other remedial programs, scoring three achievement levels above them on standard tests. Also, the number of Reading Recovery students able to reach their grade-level average climbed from 73 percent the first year to 82 percent and finally to 86 percent. The Marion, Ohio, school district tested Reading Recovery alumni one, two, and three years after they'd graduated from the program and found that 90 percent of the children maintained reading skills at or above their grade-level averages. In a similar test, Ohio State researchers followed the academic progress of Reading Recovery students statewide into the fourth grade. They found that 60 percent of those who had been part of the program were reading at or above their grade averages, 70 percent were spelling with at least average ability, and more than 80 percent were in the average or better reading groups in their classrooms. Reading Recovery students who hadn't completed the course showed some gains, and all of them were reading with skills consistent with their grades.

"Not only have we seen these results replicated in district after district in Ohio," Pinnell reports, "but we've seen them in other states over five or six years. Reading Recovery delivers very consistent performance."[3] To maintain that consistency, Pinnell's group at Ohio State University—serving as the program's de facto national leadership— collects statistics on every Reading Recovery student nationwide. "Every teacher sends back complete data and test scores every year on every child he or she has served," Pinnell says. "In 1993, for example, we collected numbers on more than sixty thousand students." With those figures, program leaders can identify problems and also districts where the program isn't performing as well as it should. "Once we spot a problem, we can work with teacher-leaders in that area to determine how we can better support those teachers or improve the program's implementation."

Techniques based in research and refined through practice, thorough teacher training, and the careful and continuing measurement of results all help to fashion what Pinnell calls "the growing foundation of evidence that Reading Recovery might well be the most efficient, cost-effective way we know of to save children who risk reading failure. For children in schools from inner cities to affluent suburbs, Reading Recovery works." Why? "For the first time," she explains, "we're teaching children to deliberately adopt and combine the actual strategies of reading."[4]

As sensible as that sounds, it's not the way reading is commonly taught in U.S. public schools. A typical first-grade class is segmented into ability groups, and the teacher offers a single reading program for each group. If a student can't keep pace, the child rather than the program is viewed as the problem. "In normal first-grade reading classes, teachers drill students on a list of words, then read a section of the reading text in which the words are used," Pinnell says. "Teachers are trained to teach by item, not for strategies." This traditional process works well enough for most, but about 20 percent of all first-graders have trouble catching on. Some can't relate spoken sounds to printed letters, for example, while others have trouble developing the habit of reading from left to right. In a class of thirty or more children, a lone teacher lacks not only the time to work individually with confused kids; she also lacks the technique. "Teachers mean well, but they have inadequate tools to teach kids who don't fit into the one system the teachers have been taught to use," Pinnell says. "The kids who don't fit into the conventional system of textbooks and vocabulary lists are automatically shoved out." Their destination: remedial classes where children may progress in some fashion, but almost never well enough to catch up to their classmates or to become genuinely good readers.

In contrast, Reading Recovery teachers tailor their tutorials to the needs of each child. "We determine what each individual student can do and we build on it," Pinnell says. "When kids learn, they're bringing their own cognitive strategies to reading. In coaching them minute by minute, a teacher supports their own thought constructions by showing them how to consciously use the strategies that good readers use by instinct." Robin Holland, a Reading Recovery instructor at Columbus's Second Avenue Elementary School, explains. "A skill is a tactic, a single pro- cedure. But using a strategy involves knowing that you don't know something and figuring out what to do about it. The goal is to make each child independent and able to continually learn on his own." One of Holland's students, for example, confuses the sounds represented by the letters *m* and *b*. "But now she knows that she does it and she's gotten to a point where she'll catch and correct herself," the teacher explains. "That's where we want these children to be."

The 1990 MacArthur study showed that Reading Recovery can get them there. As part of the study, first-graders in several Ohio schools were asked to name the best readers in their classes. When those best readers were asked what good readers do to read well, they mentioned such things as sounding out new words, looking for little words inside bigger ones to help figure out what the bigger word is, and trying to understand a word from an accompanying picture or from the rest of the sentence in which it appears. Asked the same question, less-skilled readers talked about paying attention to the teacher and being quiet in class. The only group to respond differently were the Reading Recovery graduates, whose answers matched those of the classes' top readers.

IMMERSED IN LANGUAGE

Candidates for Reading Recovery are first grade's worst reading students, winnowed first by classroom teachers. Students ranked among the lowest 30 percent are then evaluated through a battery of six tests. "In some schools, all kids might know the alphabet, so then we measure reading proficiency," Pinnell says. "In other schools, proficiency scores might all be zero and we'll have to go by the ability to identify letters or write a few words. It varies from context to context, but the process always gets us the children who need Reading Recovery the most"—in other words, the poorest performers.

Instead of using the rote drills and skill sheets that define conventional remedial efforts, in Reading Recovery those children are immersed in printed language. They read short storybooks instead of reading texts with their controlled vocabularies and sometimes stilted language. The teachers match the books read and the strategies emphasized to each student's expanding abilities, leading them upward through gradually sequenced levels of reading complexity. Ideally, the teacher will select a succession of books that the child can read the first time with 85 to 90 percent accuracy—good enough to bolster confidence, but still allowing room to learn and improve.

As each individual lesson begins, the student writes a series of small words—*an*, *there*, *him*, and the other little words that connect the larger parts of so many sentences. "We coach children to write these words quickly," Yanscik explains. "We want them to be able to whip them out without even having to think about them, the way any good writer or reader can."

Next, from the several dozen storybooks that make up Reading

Recovery's library, the child picks a favorite that he has read before. It's a confidence builder; he can "warm up" by reading aloud a book he likes and knows well. There's a larger point to it as well, though. Familiar books allow students to integrate more easily their growing arsenal of reading strategies and gain a sense of what it's like to read fluently. "If a child makes an error at this point in the lesson, I might not deal with it because that would interrupt the flow of reading," says Holland.

As the third part of each lesson, the child reads a book that he read for the first time the day before. This time, when the child stumbles or stops at a word the teacher is mute. Instead of coaching, she keeps a running record of the child's performance, noting each error he makes and what he does in attempting to correct or cope with the mistake. After the student finishes the story, the teacher leads him back over his successes as well as his most serious mistakes. She praises good-faith efforts, evaluates the child's strategies, and perhaps explains other ways in which the child can grasp the text's meanings. "If there has to be some skill instruction, it's done right there and put back immediately into the context of reading," explains Mary Fried, a clinical instructor in the Reading Recovery training program at Ohio State University. "It's not left as an abstraction in the child's mind."

Next, the student thinks of a sentence to write. The teacher coaches the child as he writes to attend to details—seeing that he leaves enough space between words, that the sentence ends with a period, that *d*s have stems and *p*s have tails, and that words are spelled correctly. As he writes, the child teaches himself to associate certain sounds with certain letters and combinations, expands his own store of words he can recognize quickly, and reinforces his own methods of self-checking. Billy, for example, decides to write, "I started reading a new book today." He leaves the *a* out of *reading*. Yanscik draws three boxes on the practice page of Billy's writing book. With him, she pronounces the word *read* slowly. Then Billy writes one of the word's three sounds—*r*, *ee*, and *d*—in each box. Yanscik then draws three more boxes and divides the middle one down the center with a dotted line. She explains the word's hidden *a* and writes the two vowels, *e* and *a*, in the divided box. From a nearby table, Yanscik pulls out a tray full of multicolored plastic letters. Billy pulls out the four letters that make up *read* and assembles them in order on the table in front of him. "Children often learn spelling more effectively when they can manipulate the letters as physical objects," she explains. The boy rehearses the new word twice on his practice page and then transfers it, properly spelled, to his sentence. While he finishes, Yanscik prints his sentence on a strip of paper and cuts up the strip into individual words. As Billy reassembles the sentence, he reminds himself that sentences begin with capital letters and end with periods and that words have spaces between them. She also lops *ing* off *reading* and separates *st* and *ed* from *started*, strengthening his ability to recognize chunks of words that can help him decipher new words later on. She dumps the snippets on the table and Billy reassembles the sentence with only a moment's hesitation over *started*.

At the end of each lesson, the teacher chooses a new book for the student. As the child reads, the teacher coaches—asking what techniques might work to help decode a troublesome word, or posing leading questions to prompt certain strategies. Finally, each child takes home a book or two to read that night and also his cut-up sentence to reassemble and read for his parents.

Clearly, Reading Recovery teachers are marketing strategists as much as they are technically skilled instructors. Their task is not just to communicate the integrated skills of reading, but to motivate children to make the effort to embrace them. Toward that end, simple praise is one of the program's key elements.

Josh, another of Yanscik's students, begins his lesson by writing all the *th* words he knows. For *they*, however, he writes *thea*. Yanscik stops him. "I like the way you used what you know to try to figure that out," she says. "You made a really good guess. It sounds just like an 'a,' doesn't it? But it's tricky." She spells it for him. "It's just one of those tricky words we have to remember. Now write it again." Later that morning, as his lesson is ending, Josh looks up at Yanscik. "It's okay to make mistakes," he says, "as long as you're trying not to make mistakes."

"We start teaching wherever the child is," Ohio State's Fried explains. "Every child knows something, even if it's just a few letters or his own name. If a child only knows eight letters of the alphabet, we praise her for how well she knows those eight letters. Then we start from there." When a child does something well, the teacher tells her so. When a child makes a mistake, in most cases the teacher suggests strategies that allow the child to discover the right answer for herself—cause for yet more approbation. Billy, for instance, tends to be chatty in his lessons as he puzzles out rules and strategies. "That's why we don't always finish in thirty minutes," Yanscik sighs. "But I honor that in him because I think he's helping himself with it and building his own confidence."

This can be as important as the actual strategies learned: a lack of confidence hampers many poor readers as much as their personal confusions do. Most of the program's children have been humiliated again and again by their mistakes in class reading groups. They've come to expect their answers to be wrong, so they no longer offer any. "You always have children who come to a word they don't know and just sit there," Yanscik says. "Many of the children coming into the program will think it's better to do nothing than to be wrong again." Her remedy: "Reading Recovery teaches kids to take risks again. I tell my students, 'Try it. It doesn't matter if you're not right the first time. Everyone learns by making mistakes, and if it's wrong we'll fix it.'" Experiencing no penalty for mistakes, students in the program usually are willing to take chances again—a critical step toward reading success.

Yanscik has seen the power of such simple reassurances. Ellen, her very first Reading Recovery student, "wouldn't risk anything," the teacher recalls. "She was very retiring. But once she was willing to risk, to try, her confidence and self-esteem started to grow." She learned quickly and left the program after just twelve weeks. A few weeks later, Ellen's classroom teacher encountered Yanscik and asked, "Do you know the best thing you've done for this child?" Yanscik replied, "I taught her how to read." The teacher shook her head. "Ellen's now the class leader," the teacher told her. "She's organizing things. She's in charge. Before, she'd do nothing. The confidence, the reading, the thinking, the praise she received in the program all carried over into her other work." At the end of first grade, Ellen was reading sixth-grade material. "Reading Recovery changed that child's personality, her future—her entire life," Yanscik says. As essential as the technical elements of any design are, the human aspects are no less crucial in determining its success.

ROOTS IN RESEARCH

Ellen's transformation is a result of more than two decades' work by Dr. Marie Clay, a professor of child psychology at the University of Auckland in New Zealand. In the 1960s she began working with children who had trouble learning to read. Frustrated by inconsistent improvements from one child to the next, she set out to craft a systematic approach that would remove the barriers standing between lagging children and literacy.

Clay began as all effective designers do: by isolating and articulating a problem. In evaluating common methods of reading instruction, she discovered that while most children are flexible enough to respond adequately to a variety of instruction programs, one child in every four or five is not. The reasons vary. Some are uniquely personal to each child, such as emotional turmoil or a home in which parents don't or can't read. Many more stem from the outmoded view of children as passive learners that has become part of the paradigm of reading instruction. Among them, Clay says, are entrenched assumptions about "reading readiness" and the simple faith that a child's natural intelligence will overcome any initial difficulties the child has with print. Both attitudes are formidable barriers to change in the design of reading instruction.

The notion of reading readiness, which dominates most teachers' approach, assumes that children are ready for formal reading instruction when they reach a certain stage of personal development. At that point, an internal mental switch is tripped and the child is suddenly ready to absorb the techniques of literacy. Clay's research led her to see that view as wrongheaded. Teachers and programs adhering to the readiness theory "expect all children to get to where the [reading] program starts before they're ready for formal instruction," she writes in her 1991 book, *Becoming Literate*.[5] Children who don't meet readiness criteria are simply (or simplistically, as Clay would argue) assumed to be abnormally slow in their personal development. Typically, such children are barred from entering the context of literacy that reading programs offer. Instead, they're relegated to special classes that try to accelerate their readiness through drills and worksheets about letters, phonics, and other isolated scraps of the reading process. As a result, these children fall behind their classmates and, years of experience show, rarely if ever catch up. These are the children who most often repeat grades, are identified as learning-disabled, and make up the majority of those who drop out of school later on.

In contrast, Clay's and other research in cognition is supplanting the concept of reading readiness with that of "emerging literacy." Rather than crossing an invisible threshold between being not ready and then ready, a child "emerges" into literacy gradually, the research suggests. Early in her evolution as a reader, for example, a child may be able to grasp some of the basic concepts in reading—that print carries the message or that one reads from left to right, for instance. As she grows further into literacy, she can succeed in tackling more subtle and sophisticated ideas—that a group of letters isolated together on a page corresponds to a single spoken word, or that sounds are represented by letters.

The view of literacy as a personal evolution fits neatly with a broader principle that has been widely established by research: that children actively construct their own unique methods of understanding. After all, Clay points out, children arrive in school already having learned how to learn. They spend their earliest years offering responses to what they experience, watching what happens as a result, and then modifying those initial responses to produce outcomes more to their liking. In learning to speak and understand her native language, for example, a child formulates a complex web of rules that allows her to construct and understand sentences that in turn enable her to transact business with people in predictable ways. She learns that if she says "I have to go potty" in the presence of her mother, her mother will take her to the bathroom; she also knows that the same words in a different order—"I have potty to go"—are likely to produce only confusion in her parent. No one is quite sure how she formulates those rules, but it is clear that every preverbal child structures for herself the rules by which she learns to use spoken language effectively. "Because of what we now know about oral language acquisition, we have to accept that children can be active constructors of their own language competencies," Clay writes. "Only the child can develop strategic control over the experiences and information coded somehow in his brain. No teacher can manipulate those strategic activities in any tightly controlled way."[6]

Unfortunately, instruction based on the idea of reading readiness usually attempts to do just that. "This concept of the early reading period as a time of transition when various preschool behaviors change into new forms suggests that there will be wide variations in the patterns of progress one might find among children during their first year at school," Clay contends. "It then becomes the responsibility of the school to arrange the early reading program in ways that do not require all [children] to fit a single shoe size." Such flexibility, though, is inimical to the prevailing paradigm in U.S. reading education. "For some children," Clay adds, "the first steps of the curriculum's predetermined sequences may be an insurmountable barrier which turns them off into a side-road of failure." If a teacher believes a child should be able to write her name before trying to read her first book, for example, a student with poor hand-eye coordination easily could be stopped dead as an emerging reader. But the same child, allowed to read before writing, could vault that same barrier and keep progressing. For whatever reasons, Clay says, "Some children begin to build inefficient literacy systems. They get confused because they do not add for themselves what the teacher has left unsaid. As they try to meet the instructional demands, they become more and more confused about where to direct their attention, they remain unsure about how to apply what they know to new tasks, and the doors to problem-solving on novel texts begin to close for them."[7]

Clay sees a larger irony reflected in that smaller one. "The more formalized the teaching sequence, and the more committed the teachers are to it, the larger could be the group of children who cannot keep in step with that particular program," she argues. "When a teacher says of a child, 'He's not ready for reading and writing,' too often that's only true if he has to learn by that teacher's program. There's probably another route by which he could learn—and, in that case, the instruction would start not where the teacher is, but where the child is" along his personal journey toward literacy.[8]

Learning to read, then, isn't only about mastering reading's rules. It also demands the active personal construction of a new system of understanding. "The initiative for this act of learning comes from the child engaging with his new environment and bears little relation [to the passivity assumed for a child by the idea of readiness]," Clay says.[9]

"The need to transform preschool competencies into new ways of responding . . . makes early reading success a product of learning" rather than of simple maturation. In other words, if educators wait for slow readers to mature to the point where they fit into established reading programs, the wait may never end. Instead, schools must reach out to each confused child at whatever point he or she has reached as an emerging reader and guide learning from that point. Clay writes: "The teacher [needs to] provide temporary scaffolds and support systems which help the child to function effectively and can lead to the child taking over independent action before long."[10]

The second barrier Clay's research challenges is the assumption that children of normal mental abilities, given enough time and opportunity, face no serious or long-lasting obstacles in learning to read. Wrong again, says Clay. Intensive, detailed research in recent years shows that a child's lagging grasp of the mechanics of literacy has little to do with native intelligence. For example, she regularly finds that some children have trouble following a line of print from left to right or a block of text from top to bottom on a page because their motor abilities aren't as well developed as most children's at the same age. Others who have had little exposure to books prior to school may take longer to understand that sequences of printed letters are precisely related to a series of spoken words. Both problems are unrelated to sheer mental ability.

Nevertheless, Clay notes that "there is an unbounded optimism among teachers and parents that children who are late starters will catch up. In particular, there is a belief that the intelligent child who fails to learn to read will catch up to his intelligent classmates once he's made a start."[11] Clinical studies prove that belief groundless, she contends: "Wrong responses are learned and practiced." In her own studies of lagging learners, Clay has shown that "inappropriate responses become habituated and automatic when they're practiced day after day and become quite resistant to change as early as twelve to eighteen months after entry into school."[12] As a result, "It's now possible to argue that some styles of teaching may facilitate the development of independent, constructive learners" while others "may either confuse the learners or impede progress towards independence."[13]

It was those insights, among others, that shaped Reading Recovery's design. In years of clinical observation, Clay charted the ways in which both effective and ineffective young readers go about deciphering print—everything from the ways they moved their eyes to whether they listened for and corrected their own mistakes. Eventually, she was able to articulate common strategies good young readers use instinctively as well as the kinds of problems that typically trip up poor ones. From those understandings she built an instructional framework that shows poor readers how to use consciously the strategies good readers use unconsciously. By teaching children those techniques and then guiding their practice, Reading Recovery guides poor readers as they construct effective personal understandings of how reading is done well.

Clay also learned that there was only one sure way to provide the "temporary scaffolds and support systems" that prevent a child from habituating inappropriate responses to print: teachers must work individually with each poor reader to spot opportunities for the child to practice "on the spot" the effective strategies to substitute. By supporting and praising a student moment by moment as the child learns to identify and correct habitual mistakes, the teacher helps the child construct a new and more effective way of reading. "Through the things a teacher attends to, she reveals to children what she values about their activities," Clay writes. "Every time she talks with a child about his activity, she places a value on it. . . . Such valuing of [children's] efforts and involvements are [*sic*] continuous, individual, personal, and powerful. Careful management of teacher attention can encourage children to change and take more control of their own activities and learning."[14]

As she integrated her ideas about instruction into a system of teaching, Clay recruited veteran reading teachers to help her test her method. She coached them in the use of the techniques she'd devised, explained their origins in research, then watched how well those techniques worked in practice. Through years of her own experiences and those of Reading Recovery's early tutors, Clay refined her design. Today, Reading Recovery reverses reading failure in more than ninety out of every one hundred New Zealand first-graders headed for illiteracy.

In 1982, New Zealand's government made Reading Recovery a national program. Two years later, a group of educators at Ohio State University's College of Education launched a Reading Recovery pilot project in a few Columbus public schools. Clay and an associate came to Columbus to train sixteen of the city's elementary-school teachers in Reading Recovery's techniques. Three of them also learned how to coach and supervise their fellow instructors. During and after training, twelve instructors worked in pairs in Columbus classrooms. One taught the regular class group for half the day while the other worked individually in Reading Recovery with the class's worst readers. After twelve weeks' instruction, two thirds of the program's first-graders were reading at or above their average grade levels. On every standardized test, the Reading Recovery students strongly outscored students who, like them, had begun as poor readers but who had not been through the program. Similar outcomes in subsequent trials moved the Ohio legislature in 1985 to fund Reading Recovery training statewide for every school district that wants to adopt the program. Since then, the U.S. Department of Education's $6 billion "Chapter One" funding program for remedial education has designated Reading Recovery as "exemplary" and now encourages schools nationwide to use it.

No Good Alternatives

Without the program, Reading Recovery's students would almost certainly be sidetracked into conventional remediation—programs that have been shaped not by research, design, and refinement, but by assumption and convention. Predictably, their results are quite different from Reading Recovery's effective and efficient outcomes.

"Children like Billy often are forced to repeat first grade," says Fried. "That's been one way that people have traditionally thought poor readers could be strengthened. In fact, it's better to pass kids even though they're having trouble. Research has proved over and over again that retention is detrimental." Retention, the polite word for flunking, often communicates a powerful message to a child: that by the end of first grade he's already a failure. "The highest statistical correlation you find among children who've been retained is that these are the children who'll eventually drop out of school," she points out. "Retaining a child is trying to make the child fit the program. It means dragging the child back through the same material again that he didn't understand the first time, and it's been shown that doing that does no good. Educators agree on that in theory, but in practice a lot of kids are still being retained."

Whether a poor reader repeats a grade or not, he's usually assigned to a remedial reading class. Most, designed to meet Chapter One's strict and detailed qualifications for funding, are organized identically: lagging students meet daily in small groups where teachers use rote drills and worksheets to strengthen them in the isolated skills of reading—differentiating vowel sounds, remembering *i*-before-*e* rules, and so on. For example, a remedial reading teacher might decide to drill the group on the spelling difference between an *ah* sound and an *oo* sound. Typically, she might enunciate the sounds, explain their spelling differences, and then pass out worksheets on which the children would fill in blanks or circle correct responses. After that, the group might play a version of "vowel bingo," a popular teaching tool in remedial programs. "There might be thirty-five or forty minutes of instruction and then the kids return to their classrooms," Fried says. "Now what kind of transfer would there be from hearing vowel sounds, doing a worksheet, and playing bingo? Zero to none, as it turns out. There's some logic to it," she admits. "The teacher gives a student the parts, the student puts them together, and they add up to the whole. It's assumed that kids make this transfer of isolated skills to a whole text, but most of them don't."[15]

The reason, again, is to be found in the research that so many program officials haven't discovered: as Clay and other researchers have pointed out, the only way a person becomes an effective reader is by practicing his or her unique integration and orchestration of a complex suite of skills and strategies. Children learn to read and write most effectively by reading and writing, not by focusing separately on individual steps of the process.

Students in conventional remedial programs, however, barely practice real reading at all. In fact, a study by researchers at the State University of New York at Albany found that students spend less time reading in conventional remedial sessions than they would if they remained in their own classrooms. Richard Allington, a professor of reading in the university's school of education, led a team that measured the

time efficiency of typical Chapter One–funded classes and other corrective reading methods. His group found that an average of 76 percent
of any Chapter One group's time was wasted on things other than reading and writing—settling the class down, the teacher's lecture, filling
out worksheets, and so on. In the dozens of 45-minute classes the research team observed, children spent on average just 26.5 minutes on
meaningful work. Of that, 21 percent, or 5.5 minutes, were allotted to
actual reading, usually in round-robin style, giving each child the chance
to read no more than a few sentences. A scant 3 percent of the time,
barely a minute, was given to writing. Over the course of twelve lessons,
children in the conventional remedial classes Allington's group watched
read an average of sixteen stories. "If, in a typical week of reading
instruction, students only encounter one hundred fifty to five hundred
words in context, one has to ask: How they ever gonna get good?"
Allington wonders.[16] In contrast, Reading Recovery students usually
read more than sixty storybooks in the same number of sessions. The
Reading Recovery students Allington observed spent 60 percent of each
half-hour lesson actually reading, and another 25 percent writing. Although each lesson is supposed to be a half hour long, Allington's team
found the average lesson actually gave thirty-three minutes to real
studies.

"Chapter One children are missing up to forty-five minutes a day of
what's going on in their own classrooms and they're not learning," Ohio
State's Pinnell worries. "We're spending millions—billions—on remedial reading approaches that simply are not working well enough."
Conventional remedial methods persist in part because of sheer mo-
mentum, as any bureaucracy does, even though their inefficiencies are
manifest; the typical child in need of help, for example, spends three to
five years in other remedial programs funded by Chapter One. "In those
programs, I worked and worked and even if I made a year and a half's
progress with a child he might still be as much as a year behind his grade
level," elementary teacher Holland says. "Group work is valuable, but
you look at a student having trouble and you know how much faster he
could progress if you could work with him individually for just a few
weeks." Yanscik points out that "even with a small group, a teacher can't

pay constant attention to each child. While she's working with one, another is off perpetuating the mistakes and bad habits that make him a poor 'reader in the first place. Typical Chapter One–funded approaches almost can't help but allow those wrong practices to become even more deeply ingrained. Reading Recovery is specifically designed so that, the minute a bad habit shows up, we stop it. We don't allow a child to habituate anything that's not productive." In an attempt to thwart some of that inherent waste, a number of schools assign Reading Recovery teachers to spend the second half of each day teaching conventional remedial classes. The effect of their training quickly makes itself felt. "They're moving away from isolated skill drills and worksheets and are offering more books, more whole-text reading, and more writing," Fried says. "Reading Recovery has actually benefited a number of other Chapter One programs."

TEACHING TEACHERS

Those benefits grow from the design process's ability to enact new paradigms by repatterning behavior. In an educational context, that's done by teaching teachers to teach in different ways. Again, Reading Recovery sets a standard. Douglas Kammerer, director of compensatory services for the Marion, Ohio, city schools, calls Reading Recovery "the single most powerful teacher training program I've ever seen—and I've been involved in educational innovation since the late nineteen-sixties."

Teachers selected by their districts to be Reading Recovery instructors devote one night a week for a year to learning the method. Teachers in training forge a solid theoretical understanding of how children learn to read and of the techniques through which Reading Recovery pinpoints and resolves children's problems. While they're learning, they're also teaching. In tandem with their classroom work, the teachers use what they're learning to begin to tutor lagging first-grade readers. Theory and practice become extensions of each other, prodding Reading Recovery's teachers-to-be to stretch both their skills and their understanding through graduated experiences that demand increasingly sophisticated judgments and technique. As they take those measured steps, they weave their own integrated fabrics of knowledge and experience that they've tested and made their own.

It's not easy. "For most of them, it's hard to shift from teaching at the item level—teaching a child to give you the right answer—to the strategy level, where you're teaching a child a pattern of behavior," Fried says. She and other teacher-trainers coax the program's fledgling instructors past the notion that every word read must be correct before the child proceeds to the next. "They need to teach kids how to identify and solve problems for themselves instead of worrying about right and wrong, one by one," she says. "A lot of the teachers in training want the instructors to give them rules and standards, and we're constantly telling them that it depends entirely on the child in front of them at the moment." A few teachers can't make the shift. According to Fried, those who can adjust do so during their year in training. Those unable to change usually withdraw from the program before their year of training ends.

To help other teachers maintain and broaden their new understandings, Reading Recovery teaches some of its experienced instructors to train and supervise other teachers under the program. If no training center is close by, many school districts elect to pay the teacher's salary for the full year she spends studying on a distant university campus. "That districts are willing to do that is a testament to the power of the Reading Recovery method," Pinnell says.

One of the most effective training tools in preparing teacher-leaders is the sessions in which they observe one another teaching "behind the glass." At least three times during training, each teacher conducts a Reading Recovery lesson with a child in front of a one-way, soundproof window. On the other side, the other teacher-leaders-in-training note the child's stratagems, the teacher's responses and strategic decisions, and compare them with what their own decisions and reactions might have been. "They're like scientists," says Pinnell. "They watch a child's eye movements to see if he's rereading text or looking for clues in the book's pictures. They watch the teacher's gestures and listen to the inflections in her voice. They're constantly asking questions, trying to figure out what a child is doing and how a teacher could most powerfully call his or her attention to the most appropriate aspect of story or language or print or whatever's needed. It's constant, moment-by-moment problem solving." After a session is over, the group reassembles to dissect and critique the lesson they watched. The teacher-leader who conducted the lesson explains, defends, and often modifies the decisions and observations made during the course of the lesson. "Teachers are learning not only through their own teaching, but also by watching and discussing all the other teachers," Fried emphasizes. "No two lessons, and no two children, are the same. The more case examples we can put before teachers, the more they'll have to talk about and analyze. That makes them stronger in dealing with each individual child who comes to them in the program."

Once trained, teacher-leaders become circuit riders who regularly visit and observe Reading Recovery teachers in a given area. A teacher-leader sits in on individual lessons, emphasizes the teacher's strengths, suggests improvements, and coaches the teacher through weak areas. The teacher-leader might bring along a teacher who's strong in a particular area where another is weak, or bring together two or three teachers having the same problem to work with them in a miniclass focused on the particular shortcoming.

In addition, during the school year Reading Recovery teachers in a district or area will meet to exchange ideas and improve their technique. Teacher-leaders also regroup regionally each June for an intense four-day conclave. "At these sessions, the teachers expect to be taken to new levels in their thinking and understanding," notes Fried. "This ongoing monitoring, training, education, and support is permanent—an integral part of the program itself."

THE PRICE OF SUCCESS

Reading Recovery's rate of success with students isn't its only impressive statistic. The program also passes a critical test for any design program: its benefits must justify its costs. As costly as it first seems to adopt Reading Recovery, in several ways it more than earns back a district's initial investment.

Like any tutoring effort, Reading Recovery is costly compared with other programs. There's a library of storybooks and other materials to buy. A Reading Recovery teacher works with only one child at a time, and usually no more than four children in half a day because of the intensely demanding nature of the work. Districts with teachers training as teacher-leaders may need to keep them on the payroll during the year they're away studying. Pinnell puts the program's costs at $1,100 to $3,000 for every child that enters it, depending on how administrators apportion costs in different categories. It sounds expensive, but it's proved to be economical for two reasons. First, children move through the program quickly. Second, after they've left it they're usually able to keep pace with their classmates with no more need of special reading help for the rest of their school careers.

No formal studies have calculated the program's actual cost benefits. However, Philip Dyer, an elementary school principal in Wareham, Massachusetts, has made a detailed estimate of what Reading Recovery has meant in dollars to his district's budget just in its first year. The average salary of a Massachusetts elementary-school teacher at the time Dyer parsed the costs, in 1990, was $34,500. Typically, a Chapter One teacher works with about forty students each year. That means $862.50 will buy a year's worth of a Chapter One teacher's time for one Massachusetts child. But that child usually stays in Chapter One four years. That runs the state's average per-child Chapter One bill back up to about $3,450 in teachers' salaries alone. "That's conservative," he notes. "Chapter One teachers actually earn higher-than-average salaries because of their special training." A Reading Recovery teacher works only half of each school day in the program. That's a salary equivalent of $17,250 spread over eight children—four at a time for sixteen to twenty weeks each over the course of a thirty-two-week school season. At the end of those sixteen to twenty weeks, the typical child needs no more special reading instruction. Thus the salary bill for each Reading Recovery student is $2,156—more than a one-third savings over the same kind of expense for the most common remedial reading program now used.[17] The office of California's statewide Reading Recovery program, housed in the school of education at California State University at San Bernardino, used a similar approach in its 1993 annual report to calculate programs' comparative costs. It reported that the average cost of tutoring a student in Reading Recovery was $2,276—exactly half the outlay to achieve the same result through more conventional Chapter One–funded initiatives.[18]

In practice, the program can often save even more money and time: the average child graduates from the program in only twelve weeks instead of the full sixteen to twenty allotted. As more Reading Recovery teachers hone their expertise through experience, the program could eventually further reduce the average time from twelve weeks to perhaps ten—allowing three full groups of Reading Recovery students instead of two in each thirty-two-week academic year.

School officials in Wakeman, Ohio, report that Reading Recovery yielded savings of another kind. During 1987, 1988, and 1989, Wakeman's schools failed forty-two fewer first-graders than they did during the preceding three years, a change the officials attribute entirely to the district's adoption of Reading Recovery in 1986. The average cost at that time to keep a U.S. elementary-school student in class for a year was $5,638. By holding back forty-two fewer students Wakeman saved roughly $236,700, while paying out $148,000 in salaries to Reading Recovery teachers during the same period. In those three years, the program saved the district more than $88,000. That's enough to recoup much of the cost of implementing Reading Recovery in the first place.

Other systems log similar gains. In January 1987, halfway through its first year of Reading Recovery, one rural Ohio school system forecast that among the children chosen for Reading Recovery, 95 percent would fail first grade that year. But only 10 percent actually flunked when the school year ended. "Even if more of the children are retained in later grades," Pinnell says, "the savings can be substantial enough to pay for the program." In Upper Arlington, a Columbus suburb, the superintendent of schools reported that by February of Reading Recovery's second year, the district already had saved the program's cost in reduced demand for remedial services and in the lower numbers of kids repeating first grade. Such secondary savings are common. In Dyer's district of Wareham, for example, Reading Recovery is credited with slashing first-grade referrals to special-education programs by 57 percent and those to learning-disabled classes by 87 percent.

Those kinds of gains can make a critical difference to cash-strapped school districts trying to balance budget cuts and taxpayers' revolts with demands for better-educated kids. In Massachusetts and other states, Dyer notes, "School funding is being held at current levels or being reduced. Also, in most of our school districts the special-education costs are accelerating." Typically, 15 to 30 percent of students nationwide are being referred to such classes. "The general funds for schools are shrinking, while that portion of our costs are [*sic*] growing. That takes away from the overall money we can use to educate all children. We have to look at ways to decelerate that growth in special-education funding, and I think Reading Recovery is a major way of doing that." More and more districts seem to think so, too. In school budgets, money for in-service teacher training usually trails most other claims on funds. Reading Recovery, which graphically links educational design, rigorous teacher training, and consistently effective and efficient results, is convincing once-skeptical administrators to allot scarce funds to it, even over other priorities. "If administrators would weigh the costs of the program against its benefits to the children we serve—and that's why we're all here in the first place—there would be no choice but to adopt or expand it," Holland says. Besides, Fried asks, "Would you rather spend an extra $2,200 on a child in first grade or more than $20,000 a year to keep that same person in prison as an adult?" Her point is firmly rooted in statistics: according to the U.S. Department of Education, almost 70 percent of the people now in U.S. penitentiaries are functionally illiterate.

"The question isn't whether a school district can afford Reading Recovery," Dyer says, "but, rather, how long a school district can afford to keep operating without it."

DEATH OF A PARADIGM

Despite the program's successes, though, Reading Recovery has to fight for a place in U.S. schools. The first problem, of course, is money. In some urban school districts, it's estimated that as many as 40 percent of all first-graders read poorly enough to qualify for the program. In principle, Reading Recovery targets the poorest 20 percent, but fiscal reality now limits participation to an average of less than 5 percent across the districts now hosting the program. Short budgets can dwarf Reading Recovery's apparent impact by holding its results against the vast numbers of children it didn't help. "That proportion will grow," Pinnell says, "but not fast enough to rescue tens of thousands of kids who need it now." Some school districts, reluctant to commit a lot of money to an idea they haven't yet tried, will budget only enough money to field perhaps one or two teachers to reach a handful of students. Then, says Fried, "At the end of the school year, these administrators will say, 'Reading Recovery isn't working; we still have first-graders who can't read.' It's a lack of money, but also of understanding."

Career mobility also works against the program. Whether in a corporation or a school district, any innovation needs a high-level champion—someone in upper management who promotes and defends the new idea. Without a champion, the innovation can get lost in a gaggle of competing initiatives. "Superintendents want to bring in their own programs," Pinnell points out. "The fact that Ohio's associate superintendent of education and the assistant superintendent of schools in Columbus—the program's chief advocates in those agencies—were here to support the program during its first three years is the only reason we got established enough to survive." Says Fried: "In Columbus, we're now on our fourth superintendent of schools in seven years. Each time a new person takes office, those of us with our hearts in this program go talk to him to explain and try to win his support. We're listened to, but there isn't always the kind of follow-through we'd like to see. Without a champion, we're just another program."

Adding to the delays, a few administrators professionally wedded to other programs have been fighting rearguard actions against Reading Recovery's adoption—in effect protecting their deeded acreage within remedial reading's prevailing paradigm. In most states, Reading Recovery is paid for largely from Chapter One funds. But the idea to begin Reading Recovery doesn't always originate in Chapter One offices. In Ohio, for example, it was proposed by curriculum specialists and urged by the state to become part of Chapter One's portfolio. "That's left us sort of in the position of Cinderella," Fried explains. "We think we're the prettiest and that we'll be recognized in the end, but meanwhile the stepmother already has these other programs that she likes better."

Because Reading Recovery can shrink the number of children needing conventional Chapter One–funded services, the budgets for other state or local remedial programs could shrink in response. That may threaten program administrators who see the subsequent loss of funds and staff— coin of the realm in any bureaucracy—as a concomitant loss of power and influence within their school districts.

Ohio's Reading Recovery program has suffered the consequences of just such a battle. The director of remedial programs in one of the state's smaller cities had been a key figure in launching traditional remedial programs in Ohio and had amassed a degree of statewide professional clout and renown as a result. In 1986, he published a report purporting to prove that Reading Recovery wasn't delivering its promised results in his district. "He based his conclusions on results from nine half-time teachers and a handful of children who were not randomly selected or assigned," Fried says, "and he compared the performances of children who weren't of the same ability to begin with. It wasn't a valid research study, but if you include enough numbers and expound on things like standard deviations some people will decide you must know what you're talking about." The director mailed copies of his study to Chapter One directors around the United States. Incensed, Ohio State University's team of Reading Recovery specialists and the state's department of education each wrote a rebuttal to the paper. The director refuted their rebuttals in yet another paper, to which the OSU squad made a final reply. "Then we washed our hands of it," Fried says. "If we'd let it, it would have become tremendously wearing and time-consuming." It has been anyway: as a result of the director's fervor, she sighs, "We've had to fight this battle in so many places."

Once in a while, a school district administrator intrigued by Reading Recovery's apparent power will call the OSU staff and ask questions about the clouded study. Then, Fried says, "We can help them sort out the claims and they can understand that there's nothing much to it." Her favorite example is Ron Binckney, then in charge of special services for the schools of Wareham, Massachusetts. "He was on the phone to us constantly," she says. "He compared every number in the report with every number in our publications and he worked out every little discrepancy. He finally discounted the adverse report and brought Reading

Recovery into his district. But the report almost caused him not to." But Fried and her colleagues have no way to know how many administrators lacked Binckney's perseverance and dropped their interest in Reading Recovery after the report crossed their desks. "It seems to be a personal issue with that administrator," Fried says. "It would seem to be a turf question: his program has been there for twenty years, and here's this new program coming along and telling everyone it's better." There are ways to skirt the problem. The Dallas suburb of Richardson, Texas, for example, hadn't used much Chapter One money in its elementary schools until Reading Recovery came along. Then Richardson's Chapter One office lobbied for Reading Recovery's adoption. When it was approved, it was made part of Chapter One and brought new funds into the district's overall Chapter One initiative, expanding its importance and influence. "In that case, it worked very well," Fried says. "But when Reading Recovery isn't the funding agency's own innovative idea, it can cause some definite political problems."

Despite such "market resistance," Reading Recovery's use continues to spread. More than forty-eight states from Oregon to South Carolina are training teachers, while two Canadian provinces and eighteen U.S. regional centers are training teacher-leaders. California had opened three teacher-leader training sites by 1994. Legislatures in Connecticut, Illinois, and Massachusetts are moving to join Ohio's in funding the program statewide. Still, says Pinnell, "You won't see Reading Recovery spreading like wildfire, because fully trained people are an absolute necessity. If a school district decides to start, it can't just go hire fifty people to do it. You really need a two-year lead time." Says Fried: "When we say the program is now in forty-eight states, it might only be in one or two schools of a single district within many of those states. It's still a battle. This program still has to vie with every other for a piece of the shrinking budget pie." The proof, though, is in how that pie can be sliced. A school district's investment in Reading Recovery is proving repeatedly to be one of the most cost-effective it can make. According to Marion's Kammerer, "We now know that we can successfully teach ninety to ninety-five percent of the kids who have difficulty learning to read. It's simply a matter of will"—and of good design.

THE KEY TO REFORM

Reading Recovery offers U.S. education its first real demonstration of the power of a process combining research, development (including ongoing teacher education), marketing, and technical support in an orchestrated system of change. The research underlying the program shatters cornerstones of the old paradigm of reading education—readiness and the triumph of native intelligence—and supplants them with a new foundation. Its process of design and development then creates a structure that embodies a new, more accurate, and more useful paradigm. The new structure monitors its own results, detects and addresses problems among practitioners as they occur, and makes teachers leaders of change, instead of its victims, through extensive and ongoing education.

In three ways, Reading Recovery can encourage the process of educational redesign. First, it proves that a well-designed educational program can be replicated among teachers and schools across a wide array of locations and cultures and still yield uniformly superior results. Second, it indicates that an investment of money and effort in educational design can earn dramatic rewards—if it's made in a properly researched and designed program that offers thorough teacher training and support. Third, it shows that when educators find a program that meets these two criteria and proves that it can earn a good return, schools are willing to make its adoption a budget priority. Reading Recovery is the best evidence yet of the direct link between good design and educational excellence.

Like any prototype, though, the program is an indication of what is possible, but not all that's possible. Reading Recovery hasn't been integrated with other reforms to amplify its own strengths through those of the others; for example, it has not yet become part of a complete, systematic literacy program for early grades based on insights from cognitive research and teachers' growing experience. Reading Recovery has been completely adopted in its native New Zealand but in North America still faces the obstacles that beset any new school initiative. The program hasn't been fully evaluated by independent U.S. analysts or compared in effectiveness to a wide range of other American innovations pursuing broadly similar objectives. Instead, Reading Recovery is educational design's equivalent of the transistor—a breakthrough, a conceptual masterpiece capable of amazing feats. But a transistor is most effective only when it becomes an integral component in a larger device. In the same way, as the process of educational redesign matures it will incorporate the innovations that make Reading Recovery so successful and gradually build and elaborate upon them. Meanwhile, the program stands as a first model of a thorough and effective design process able to liberate students, teachers, and budgets. It does so by focusing a broad and powerful array of resources on a single goal: to enable hard-to-teach first-graders to read. As England's Office of Her Majesty's Chief Inspector of Schools pointed out in reporting on its investigation of the program, "The individual Reading Recovery lesson with a single pupil is the cutting edge of a coherent national system, the whole of which is geared to the effective delivery of that lesson." In that ability to focus resources on a single goal lies the power of redesign.

As we'll see in the next two chapters, it also stands as a clear challenge to two of the most deeply rooted, influential, and inflexible paradigms hindering genuine school reform: the structure of the teaching profession and many of the patterns that shape U.S. schooling itself.

4
Missing Links

How the Structure of the Teaching
Profession Thwarts Innovation

Nowhere is education's lack of a comprehensive and coordinated process of change more evident than in the structure of the U.S. teaching profession. While some promising new approaches to teaching facilitate innovation (as we'll see later), the American model's inherent structure thwarts it. To begin to understand how, we can contrast the support for change and improvement that U.S. education offers teachers with the support that a farmer receives in seeking new ways to boost his harvest.

First, a farmer is free to experiment with new crops and methods according to his own lights; his techniques are dictated far more by his calculation of possible results than by tools and procedures mandated by others. In addition, a farmer constantly talks to other farmers, trading insights and experiences about how to prepare soil, which seeds to use, what to plant when and where, how to irrigate, and when to harvest. He talks to knowledgeable salespeople at feed and grain stores to learn about new or improved products. He visits equipment showrooms to see what improvements are being made in specialized tools and machinery.

He meets with his county extension agent to find out what scientists have learned lately about growing and managing crops more effectively and efficiently.

To accomplish all that, a farmer doesn't have to leave town or even make a long-distance phone call. Through those salespeople and extension agents, the farmer has access to a network of experts—mechanical designers, genetic engineers, soil scientists, fertilizer chemists, livestock breeders, farm management specialists, university research laboratories, and demonstration farms—that exists expressly to find better ways for him to farm. A farmer, like a family doctor or auto mechanic, is only the most visible part of an integrated infrastructure of expertise that binds the individuals in a profession to an orderly process of continuous improvement.

The developed world has become so accustomed to these institutionalized structures of innovation that we take them for granted. If a farmer's annual average yield per acre falls from one harvest to the next, we don't assume that he'll simply quit farming; we expect that he'll call upon agriculture's accumulated body of knowledge and experience to try to find what caused the drop and try to correct it. If an airplane engine breaks down, the airline company that owns it doesn't throw it away and buy a new one; it doesn't commission a panel of experts to propose various ways to repair it. It doesn't occur to anyone at the airline company to do anything but deploy its mechanics to use the aircraft industry's cumulative store of expertise to diagnose the problem and fix it.

In contrast, when an educational program or technique doesn't yield the expected results it typically meets one of three fates: it's abandoned, it's analyzed again and again by successions of more- or less-qualified people who typically have little ability to enact real solutions, or it's patched with the easiest, quickest, and least expensive repair to be found. The reason is that unlike virtually all other professions, U.S. education a lacks technical culture, a common body of proven knowledge and technique that lets all members of a profession adapt and perform to the same standards of excellence, and to redefine those standards as technology progresses.

Farmers improve their yields and airplane mechanics can fix jet engines because their industries, like most professional enterprises, are rooted in bodies of collective knowledge that permeate their professions and are constantly expanding. A doctor in Seattle resections a colon in the same proven, effective way as a doctor in Boston; particle physicists in Dallas and Moscow pursue related experiments based on shared assumptions, knowledge, and techniques. The uniformity of knowledge and effective performance across a profession grows from research that creates new knowledge and an accompanying process to test new solutions, which then are disseminated throughout the profession in conferences, journals, training courses, and sales and marketing campaigns.

That process—the essence of a technical culture—allows a profession to articulate, expand, and, when necessary, to change its governing paradigm. First, a technical culture is rooted in, depends on, and actively cultivates the process of research and experimentation. Second, it embodies a process to transform the fruits of research into solutions for practical problems. Third, it includes ways to gather, preserve, codify, and disseminate the practical knowledge gleaned by its members in the course of their work to all other members of the profession. Fourth, it capitalizes on the exponential power of specialization to speed progress. Finally, a technical culture is held together by formal, enduring avenues of communication among a profession's practitioners, particularly those avenues linking distinct specialties to the common enterprise. In essence, a technical culture becomes the means by which a profession defines itself.

U.S. education has no such infrastructure of progress. The lingering debate about whether teaching can legitimately be termed a profession rises, in part, from education's lack of a technical culture and the resulting absence of an established process of growth. Teachers learn no repertoire of research-based classroom performance and management techniques that have proved to be consistently effective. Their profession has no structures through which to broadcast new understandings when knowledge of pedagogical methods or the psychology of learning advances. There are no acknowledged specialties or formal training programs in the profession to differentiate between, say, an educational designer and an educational troubleshooter. Although senior teachers may move into quasi-management roles such as department head or curriculum supervisor, the profession's training requirements and structure still declare that a teacher is a teacher.

This approach contrasts sharply with that of other professions. American society prides itself on its technical skills in medicine; how far would those skills have advanced if the medical profession had decided that there should be no obstetricians, cardiologists, or cancer specialists—that "a doctor is a doctor"? How quickly would the aircraft industry have advanced if design engineers weren't distinguished from repair mechanics—if the industry had decided that a technician is a technician, all equally capable of doing every job, each worker interchangeable with all others? Few of us would put our children on a jumbo jet flying cross-country if we knew that the airplane's lone pilot was also its only design engineer, mechanic, navigator, chef, and cabin attendant. Yet we regularly entrust our children's future to teachers expected to discharge flawlessly a similar array of burdens in their classrooms, with far less rehearsal, preparation, and support than even the smallest airlines give pilots.

THE MISSING ART OF INQUIRY: THREE FLAWS IN TEACHER EDUCATION

The profession's structural weaknesses are highlighted in the collision of emerging and waning paradigms. Prospective teachers study teaching as the old model of education defines it. Increasingly, they're expected to practice teaching as the new model defines it. The two approaches bear little resemblance.

As we've seen, education's old paradigm conceives learning to be a rote activity, a transfer of information. The new paradigm views learning as the development of increasingly sophisticated judgment and skills across a spectrum of integrated disciplines. By their nature, such skills are complex processes more effectively learned by practice than by rote, in which mastery is demonstrated far better by performance than by recitation. As the influential educational psychologist Jerome Bruner once put it, "I have never seen anybody improve in the art and technique of inquiry by any means other than engaging in inquiry." But teachers aren't trained to present reasoning, writing, mathematics, or any other discipline as the reflective, dynamic, skill-building processes that they are. In fact, industry's new demand that schools teach higher-order skills spotlights three fundamental flaws in teachers' professional education as educators struggle to cope with the new paradigm.

Flaw No. 1: Old Teaching Techniques Don't Adequately Impart the New Skills

Higher-order thinking skills demand a different kind of learning and, thus, a different approach to teaching. One masters a complex skill not by studying about it nor by rehearsing its parts in isolation from each other. Instead, a person masters it by slowly internalizing a complex, integrated suite of subtle and sophisticated abilities and judgments that strengthen and deepen by steady practice and reflection through a series of successively more demanding challenges. A person learns to play the piano not by reading about technique but by practicing and integrating those techniques and then playing progressively more demanding pieces. One learns to think skillfully by solving real problems that become more complex as one's thinking and imaginative skills grow. We develop strength and agility not by reading the sports page but through exercise.

A new kind of learning also demands a different kind of teaching. While data may be transferred by rote from one mind to another, higher-order skills must be evoked or coached. The difference is crucial in improving the results of what happens in our classrooms.

In education's traditional paradigm, teachers teach by lecturing; a student is expected to learn by listening to the teacher and then completing sets of exercises—often rote drills—about the information communicated. A coach, in contrast, doesn't simply tell an athlete to shoot a hundred baskets or hit fifty line drives. She monitors the athlete's performance, offering praise for things done well and showing the athlete exactly how to improve different aspects of the performance. By the time the athlete has shot a hundred baskets or hit fifty line drives, he's doing so more effectively and efficiently than he had before. As a student, however, this athlete may do a hundred mathematics problems before an overworked teacher correcting his homework discovers that he's been making the same mistake in each one and developing it into a habit. If a skill is to be mastered, basic techniques are practiced until they're executed expertly, as habits. A coach then introduces more complex techniques at a pace dictated by the strengths, skills, and development of the student rather than by the demands of a set lesson plan or school calendar. Instead of being linear, like beads on a string, higher-order skills are learned in a circular way, looping back again and again to use basic techniques in increasingly complex, subtle, and more integrated patterns.

Clearly, a coach must be a master of the discipline being learned and of the art of teaching it. An aspiring woodworker doesn't apprentice himself to someone because that person has read books about wood-working; he seeks out a master cabinetmaker with a knack for nurturing talent in others. Yet schooling's old paradigm asks us to entrust our children's education to people whose training requires them to know more about theories of teaching than about the subjects they teach, and whose training imparts those theories without giving them the chance to learn how to practice them effectively. The strictures of education's traditional model leave teachers prepared to perform duties comparable to those not of a coach but of a mailman: once a packet of information has been delivered, the person who brought it is permitted no means to observe over time whether the information has been put to use, kept on file, or simply thrown away.

Flaw No. 2: Teachers Too Often Lack Proper Subject Skills

Many teachers, especially those teaching elementary grades, don't know their subjects well enough to coach them as skills. An elementary-school teacher typically can earn a bachelor's degree in education and a state teaching certificate without studying in any depth at college the disciplines he'll teach. University-level education programs instruct students in the traditional theories and methods of teaching rather than in academic disciplines; higher-level college academic courses usually are built around advanced or specialized subjects that aren't relevant to elementary education. The education of elementary-school teachers

falls through the sizeable crack that lies between. The problem is exacer-
bated by budget shortages and seniority rules governing teachers' employment, which often lead schools to assign teachers to courses that
they're not certified to teach. An elementary-school art teacher we spoke
with recalls being told, "The science teacher just quit. You start tomorrow." Similarly, an industrial arts teacher told of suddenly being assigned
to take over a physics class and struggling to learn the material one
textbook chapter ahead of his students. Instructors who find themselves
in such a spot are conceptually unprepared to teach a new subject
competently, let alone to coach students in practicing the increasingly
subtle skills that lead to mastery.

Flaw No. 3: Educators Misunderstand the Nature of Teaching

Few teachers have been shown that effective teaching is itself a higher-
order skill. Most have never seen it practiced as such, and virtually none
have been taught to coach students toward mastery instead of to teach
by information transfer. Intentionally or not, the U.S. system of schooling
has decided that teacher education is something that takes place in
college and then is largely over. That notion kills innovation. Roland
Barth, Harvard University senior lecturer in education and a former
public-school teacher, writes in his 1990 book, *Improving Schools from
Within*: "When teachers . . . develop new practices . . . students are alive.
Just as potters cannot teach others to craft in clay without setting their
own hands to . . . the wheel, so teachers cannot fully teach others the
excitement, the difficulty, the patience, and the satisfaction that accom-
pany learning without themselves engaging in the messy, frustrating, and
rewarding [practice] of learning."[1]

TEACHER EDUCATION AS A CAREER-LONG PROCESS

Education's old paradigm fails in part because it assumes that teachers
learn to teach in teacher's colleges. Teachers themselves say that they
don't. Several studies—chief among them University of Chicago education professor Dan Lortie's 1975 book *Schoolteacher*,[2] still considered to

be the definitive look at the profession—have found that teachers acquire their professional behaviors not in college but through experience on the job and, ironically, during the sixteen or more years they spend as students.

Teachers can't learn to teach effectively simply by listening to lectures about teaching. Yet schools of education still train teachers largely through series of lectures and seminars, sprinkled with only brief chances to test in laboratory classrooms what they've studied. That training typically ends with one- to three-month internships, during which teachers-to-be correct papers, gain experience in maintaining classroom order and discipline, and try to pick up the techniques by which a seasoned teacher delivers information effectively to students. These newly minted teachers graduate from "teacher school" in June; the following September, they assume command of their own classrooms where they have little contact with, and virtually no supervision by, other educators. Teachers-in-training learn *about* teaching, they *watch* others teach, but they do little actual teaching on the way to becoming teachers themselves. Consequently, teachers commonly feel that they learn little during their formal schooling. "Teachers are inclined to talk about their training as easy ('mickey mouse')," Lortie reports. "I have yet to hear a teacher complain that education courses were too difficult or demanded too much effort. Teachers do not perceive their preparation as conveying something special. It may be true, as some suggest, that pedagogical instruction makes more sense *after* one has taught awhile."[3] Michael Fullan, dean of the University of Toronto's education faculty, says flatly in his 1991 book, *The New Meaning of Educational Change*, "Teacher training does not equip teachers for the realities of the classroom."[4]

Such superficial training can't reach deeply enough to uproot young teachers' assumptions about how teaching and schooling are properly conducted, assumptions rooted during a student's own twelve to sixteen years in school. "There are ways in which being a student is like serving an apprenticeship in teaching," Lortie writes. "Social psychologists have noted that some kinds of learning occur through a slow, unwitting process involving imitation; the individual takes on the ways of others without realizing he is doing so. . . . When we recall that students have protracted and consequential face-to-face interaction with many teachers, and that some young people identify strongly with their teachers, it is likely that many are influenced in ways they do not even perceive." Indeed, a number of the teachers that Lortie interviewed admitted as much. "One wonders," he says, "how effectively . . . [education] professors communicate with the many students who, it appears, see teaching as the 'living out' of prior conceptions of good teaching."[5] Obviously, those conceptions were formed largely in the kinds of education settings from which our schools now are struggling to free themselves.

John Goodlad, a professor of education at the University of Washington and a leading analyst of school reform, reached the same conclusion in his 1990 book, *Teachers for Our Nation's Schools.* "What future teachers experience in schools and classrooms during their years as students profoundly shapes their later beliefs and practices," he writes. "As teachers, they follow closely the models they have observed. Mental stereotypes developed over years of observing their own teachers are not challenged or fundamentally changed . . . by their experiences in formal teacher preparation programs." Those programs are "not powerful enough or long enough to dissuade them from what has already been absorbed from role models. In fact, these programs *do not necessarily try to dissuade them*" (emphasis added).[6]

Because teachers' training doesn't lead them to confront their assumptions about how teaching "should" be done, it casts up an additional barrier to reform. Prepared only superficially, a new teacher has no arsenal of effective techniques to fall back on when he or she confronts the anxieties and uncertainties all new teachers face— feelings that "push teachers back into their pasts," Lortie says. "Uncertainty . . . may evoke the need for conformity. Anxious people . . . may rely on orthodox doctrines to buttress their self-confidence."[7] Acutely conscious of their own inexperience, new teachers can easily fall back on the assumptions and habits of teaching they learned during their sixteen-year "apprenticeship"—the same habits of mind and practice that attempts at reform are trying to root out and replace. Seymour Sarason, a former professor of psychology at Yale University who spent four decades as a consultant to schools involved in change, notes the result: "Being a teacher for a number of years may be in most instances antithetical to being an educational leader or vehicle of change."[8]

Dan Lortie offers two reasons to help explain that seeming paradox. First, after interviewing ninety-four public-school teachers in Massachusetts and Florida, he found most of them to be professionally conservative. Teachers become teachers because they liked school and did well in it just as it is. As a result, he notes, they're "favorably disposed toward the existing system of schools" and unlikely to feel a great need to change that system. Second, Lortie found that each teacher is left alone to reinvent "good teaching" for himself. Because the profession lacks a technical culture, teachers see their work as intensely individualistic, subjective, and expressive. The techniques that become part of an individual teacher's repertoire evolve almost entirely through personal experiences on the job—techniques that he's conceived, tested, and adapted to suit his personality and approaches. Teachers consistently report that they find their greatest satisfactions in perfecting their own approaches to students and learning, not in mastering proven professional techniques learned from others. "Teachers do not acquire new standards to correct and reverse earlier impressions, ideas, and orientations," Lortie reports. "The result is that . . . the beginner in teaching must start afresh, largely uninformed about prior solutions and alternative approaches to recurring practical problems."[9] In contrast, in Japan teaching has begun to evolve a technical culture. There, most schools are equipped with reference works such as the twenty-volume *Arithmetic and Mathematics Educational Practice Lectures*. The collection's three thousand articles were written by six hundred outstanding teachers nominated by university professors and boards of education throughout the country. Entire volumes are given over to discussions of the best ways to teach computation, set theory, problem solving, and creativity and thinking skills. The articles often include actual lesson plans, setting out the goals teachers had intended the lessons to accomplish, and critical reviews of the lesson's strengths and weaknesses. Other books in the set help teachers devise effective ways to use equipment in their lessons, evaluate student performance, and understand current trends in mathematics education.

"There are tons of similar resources," says Makoto Yoshida, a Japanese graduate student in psychology at the University of Chicago. "Every school has something like this."

Not so in American schools where, according to Lortie, the "ethos of the occupation is tilted against engagement in pedagogical inquiry. Conservatism implicitly denies the significance of technical knowledge, assuming that energies should be centered on realizing conventional goals in known ways. Individualism leads to distrust of the concept of shared knowledge; it portrays teaching as the expression of individual personality . . . [whereas] inquiry rests on the opposite value." Teachers like to talk about "tricks of the trade" that they've picked up, he adds— "not broader conceptions which underlie classroom practice."[10]

It's not the usual approach among professions. A lawyer who learns to draw up wills or prepare court cases by trial and error would have more malpractice suits coming his way than clients. A doctor who relies on hunches in deciding how to perform surgery or diagnose an illness would be judged a quack or worse. But the intuitive path is the only one that teachers find open to them. Left alone in front of thirty children to teach and "control" them, a new teacher combines a unique group of random examples of teaching she's experienced as a student with an equally unique subjective idea of what good teaching is. Her inadequate professional training hasn't prepared her to do anything else.

The obvious places to introduce proven new methods of effective teaching and learning that working teachers so often lack are in the in-service workshops, seminars, and training sessions that dot their calendars. But these one-day or half-day gatherings rarely address substantive issues about the practice of teaching. As one school principal told us, "It's AIDS awareness this week and computer literacy the next." *Rarely, if ever, do most practicing U.S. teachers come together to study each other's work and help each other to become better teachers.* Schools as institutions and education as a profession effectively allow teachers no continuing opportunities systematically to improve their own effectiveness in the classroom.

Instead, innovation in school typically means importing new curricular programs. Unfortunately, the considerable workaday pressures on teachers' time and schools' budgets often limit teachers' training in the innovation's concepts and methods to a day or two. Because teachers and those who design classroom innovations share a lack of funds, time, and, frequently, evaluation expertise, teachers using a new program typically receive little or no supervision, feedback, or ongoing instruction after they've begun it. As a result, programs commonly fail—or, at least, don't show clear-cut success. An innovation in education, even something as seemingly simple as a new textbook or new kind of test, is a plan for a new way to do something—a small-scale change of paradigm that often demands changes in deeply rooted assumptions and long-practiced habits. People rarely can make such changes permanently without lengthy periods of supervision and coaching. To innovate, teachers must have not just good ideas but also the time and available psychic resources to study them, comprehend them, reflect on them, and practice them to a high level of skill.

Compounding the problem, administrators and taxpayers too often regard teachers' in-service training sessions as frills rather than as integral, ongoing elements of continuously improving what happens in classrooms. For example, the small Fall Mountain school district in southwestern New Hampshire budgeted $31,477 in its 1991–92 school year directly for the education of working teachers—three-tenths of one percent of its annual budget of $10.5 million. Although the sum increased to $41,020 for the 1993–94 school year, the proportion of the budget remained the same: three-tenths of one percent, or about $279 for each of the district's 147 classroom teachers. One teacher said, "That doesn't even cover one course's tuition at the local college." (During the state's same hard economic times, the proportion of the district's budget taken by extracurricular activities—chiefly sports—actually rose, from 1.5 percent of the budget to 1.6 percent.) Those amounts are typical, according to the Syracuse-based National Council of States for In-Service Education: across all fifty states, an average of just one half of 1 percent of school funds is budgeted to help working teachers improve their professional skills and knowledge.

Such disregard for teachers' continuing professional growth runs deep in education's conventional paradigm. The teaching profession's norms were fixed at a time when most teachers were women needing to support themselves during the brief interval between leaving school and marrying. School boards made up of taxpayers who usually were not educators themselves saw little point in investing public money to build the expertise of what were, in practical terms, temporary employees. In addition, many taxpayers hold a deeply rooted and often unconscious belief that teachers are doing real work only when they're leading a class. As a result, school boards and administrators give as little thought to budgeting for in-service teacher education as they do for any other programs considered marginal. Education officials stoutly agree that teachers should improve themselves throughout their careers, but their actions say that teachers have little legitimate claim to public support when they try to do so.

Even where some money is available for ongoing professional improvement, there is another barrier: the structural conventions of teaching allow teachers neither the time nor psychic resources to engage in it. Custom and regulation keep U.S. teachers in front of classes five to seven hours every school day. Michael Fullan writes: "This 'classroom press' . . . draws [teachers'] focus to day-to-day effects or a short-term perspective; it isolates them from other adults, especially meaningful interactions with colleagues; it exhausts their energy . . . at the end of the week they are tired; at the end of the year, they are exhausted."[11] Teachers whose hours, energy, and imagination are drained away by the relentless demands of moment-to-moment and day-to-day obligations can't be expected to engage in serious reflection or study at the same time.

For all these reasons, Dan Lortie says, typical efforts at in-service teacher education are "superficial . . . school systems generally have not assumed responsibility for systematically improving staff performance through serious training programs."[12] Fullan's findings support Lortie's view: "Nothing has promised so much and has been so frustratingly wasteful as the thousands of workshops and conferences that led to no significant change in practice when the teachers returned to their classrooms." For those and other reasons, he says flatly, "Most professional development programs fail. If the individual attempts to put the ideas into practice, there is no convenient source of help or sharing when problems are encountered. All of this sounds rather depressing, but it is true. It is hard to be a lone innovator."[13]

But most teachers don't want to be lone innovators. Fullan goes on to point out that "there is a strong body of evidence that indicates that other teachers are often the preferred source of [innovative] ideas. On the other hand, the evidence is equally strong that opportunities to interact with other teachers [are] limited. . . . Individual teachers are less likely to come into contact with new ideas, for they are restricted to the classroom and have a limited network of ongoing professionally based interaction within their schools or with their professional peers outside."[14]

Teachers normally meet regularly at only three places: the faculty lounge, faculty meetings, and union meetings. Teachers see each other in the faculty lounge during whatever sporadic short breaks they can manage away from their students—not an atmosphere conducive to reflective and insightful discussions of tradecraft. At faculty meetings, the gatherings are short—often less than a half hour at the end of a hectic day—and are usually dominated by the principal, who makes announcements, fields questions, and raises and settles tactical questions of school management. Union meetings are usually poorly attended, and agendas are dominated by discussions about workplace conditions. Only recently have teachers' groups begun considerable efforts to foster experiments with reforms.

Other traditions and taboos of the teaching profession inhibit teachers from sharing innovations. For example, educators have a deep respect for the profession's ethic of individualism—and, therefore, for each teacher's autonomy in her own classroom. "A taboo prevents one teacher from watching another . . . engaged in the act of teaching," Barth notes. "Teachers develop subtle strategies for trying to influence the domain of others, but seldom venture there or relate substantively when they do." One teacher told him that "the unwritten rule is 'no talking about teaching in the teachers' [lounge]'." He recalls the field note from a graduate student's report: "The teachers' lunchroom contains fifteen large tables. When I visited during one lunch period, each table was occupied by a single, silent teacher." (The same is true of administrators. At a meeting of school principals in a suburban Boston district, a show of hands indicated that more administrators had visited schools in Great Britain than in their own districts.) Barth holds substantive professional interaction of teachers to be "the [essential condition] that allows, energizes, and sustains all other attempts at school improvements"; to him, such self-enforced isolation is nothing short of willful surrender to instructional mediocrity. "Professional isolation stifles professional growth. Unless adults talk with one another, observe one another, and help one another, very little will change. There can be no community of learners when there is no community and when there are no learners."[15]

MISSING LINKS

Technical cultures are shaped and driven by such communities of learners. In essence, they are webs that link research, development, evaluation, and dissemination into a single, synergistic, supportive system that increases the effectiveness and efficiency of creator, user, and process alike. In contrast, the teaching profession is marked by a series of missing links—separations between areas within the profession that, if joined, could create the technical culture necessary to sustain progressive innovation in education.

The Gap Between Basic and Applied Education Research

The contrast first becomes evident where industry's system of change begins: in basic and applied research. Industrial and university-based research looks for basic ways in which materials and processes can be improved; education research, such as it is, looks for new ideas and methods by which learning can be improved. In 1992, the U.S. National Science Foundation dispensed $2 billion in research grants, and the National Institutes of Health $6 billion. In contrast, the National Academy of Science estimates that during that same year the United States invested around $350 million in education research *and development*—less than one twentieth of the combined research budgets of just two of several government entities that fund the search for innovation in the sciences.

The federal government supports education research through direct grants as well as through twenty-five of its own specialized research and development centers. Despite some successes, the fruits of that work have been meager and inconsistent in their usefulness, thanks in part to budget deficits, spending cuts, poor management, and ideological conflicts that have conspired to gut the federal outlay for such work over the last twenty years. In fact, the federal government now spends three times more on research in agriculture and twenty-one times more for space research than it does to discover ways to improve our schools. In constant dollars, between 1973 and 1989, research funding by the federal National Institute of Education shrank by 88 percent, while the budget of its parent agency, the U.S. Department of Education, rose 7 percent and the national government's total investment in research and development rose by nearly 25 percent. In 1990, when the average federal agency was spending 4.7 percent of its budget on research and development, the education department was spending .8 percent.

Private sources of money contribute only a small amount to the cause of education research. A 1991 National Academy of Education report surveyed twenty-eight private funders, from the Ford Foundation to the Carnegie Corporation of New York, and found that their total support of research in education averages less than $40 million annually. Even then, the study implied strongly, the money isn't always money well spent. "Increasingly, foundations and corporations have funded bold and large-scale demonstration projects that make no attempt to provide objective research-based determinations of success and failure. Most disturbingly, several major champions of research have completely withdrawn their support for research in favor of a plethora of widely heralded but quickly forgotten 'action projects.'" Universities play only a small part in funding, usually by granting faculty members time to conduct research or giving them small stipends to help cover costs.

In addition, education research is starved for more than just money. In any kind of research, talent and prestige follow funding. Theoretical inquiry in education, chronically short of financial support, has also suffered from a shortage of the vigor and attention that come with research money. As a result, the field has been tainted by methodological weaknesses and a tendency to let ideological fashion color the direction and results of investigation. Although such flaws aren't as glaring as critics often proclaim, the field's feeble reputation is, to a significant degree, self-sustaining.

In addition, education researchers can't extricate their work from controversy. It's hard to find any aspect of education—intelligence testing, the balance between independent study and structured class-work, the relative roles of drill and conceptual understanding in sub-ject mastery, or virtually any question of reform—over which partisans haven't long since squared off. Blurring the lines of objectivity even more, the federal government's main agencies of educational change have long been notable political footballs. Members of Congress have criticized the National Education Institute and its successor, the Depart-ment of Education's Office of Educational Research and Improvement (OERI) for selecting research subjects that advanced presidents' social agendas more than they did educational progress. For example, some claimed that President Carter's appointees to the agency thwarted re-search on the educational impacts of dual-earner families because the results might have provided ammunition to critics of women's wider work opportunities. Others accused Reagan-appointed agency man-agers of ignoring possible remedies for the well-documented "gender gap" between boys' and girls' performances in science and mathe-matics.

Teachers pay almost no attention to such controversies, though, because they pay almost no attention to education research. A thirteen-school survey conducted by the National Education Association's Mas-tery In Learning Project in 1988 found that 85 percent of the teachers responding said they didn't have time to keep up with research literature; 54 percent complained that research topics often didn't have much to do with the "real world" of the classroom, and the same proportion found the research papers they did read larded with inscrutable jargon and undecipherable statistics.

"Much of what we hear from teachers about research . . . is true," Dan Lortie writes. "Little educational inquiry is rooted in a concern for the actual difficulties facing classroom teachers." But he also finds another missing link between classroom teachers and education research: aspir-ing teachers aren't trained to use, or even to value, research as an instrument of ongoing personal improvement.[16] Writing in *Teachers and Research in Action*, published in 1989 by the National Education Associa-tion,[17] language-arts teacher Susan Walters reminds us that "a defining characteristic of a profession is the use of a technical knowledge base to solve problems and inform decision making." Yet an essay by Georgia elementary-school teacher Jimmy Nations in the same book notes that "teachers are unaccustomed to using educational research as a source of data for making decisions about problems and issues that affect their daily lives."[18]

Because teaching isn't seen as a complex body of proven skills to be refined and expanded, says Lortie, "teaching has not been subjected to the sustained, empirical, and practice-oriented inquiry into problems and alternatives which we find in other university-based professions. The preparation of teachers does not seem to result in the analytic turn of mind one finds in other occupations whose members are trained in colleges and universities." The case histories that law students absorb and the integrated framework of experimental results in scientific fields—the frameworks of technical cultures—"allow new generations to pick up where earlier ones finished. Research in education . . .—a small-scale affair—has concentrated on learning rather than on teaching. . . . A teacher today can be considered outstanding by those who are familiar with his work without being thought to have made a single contribution to knowledge of teaching in general."[19]

A 1992 report by the National Research Council's committee on the federal role in education research (of which Kenneth Wilson was a member) describes the void bluntly: "Whether or not the judgment is justified, research in education is more likely to be dismissed as trivial or irrelevant than it is to be considered a fundamental ingredient in understanding how children learn and in improving how they are taught. Teachers commonly indicate that they do not use research [to enhance their classroom techniques] and do not see its connection [to] what they do on a daily basis."[20] Complicating the issue further, teachers not infrequently hear programs touted as effective that later are found to show either modest or ambiguous results. "Many of the innovations presented to teachers have been 'fuzzy,' lacking in a clear rationale, without specific procedures, and without convincing evidence as to their effectiveness. Others have been so specific—in an attempt to be 'teacher-proof'—that they have demeaned the teachers and undermined their talents and skills." Not a good way to woo customers to your product.

The Gap Between Research and Action

The disjunction between research results and classroom practices is only the first of several missing links that mark the teaching profession. In industry, development engineers turn the promising results of research into products. In education, there's no corresponding band of trained specialists to test new ideas in practical ways, no process that tells innovators what steps to follow in transforming ideas into programs. "Instructional design" isn't a profession that has been legitimized by a particular field of study, credentialed by university degrees, or even acknowledged within the education community. Its practitioners are usually self-appointed and become "certified" only through the success of the innovations they create. The lack of development specialists deepens the void between promising research results and innovative school programs.

The Gap Between Teachers and Education Research Generally

Lack compounds lack. In industry, the connection between research and product development is followed by another connection that moves an innovation from developer to user. But educational innovation lacks any equivalent of marketing or sales campaigns; there is no direct path by which promising innovations move into classrooms. Reforms conceived at universities sometimes can cobble together enough grants from public and private donors to move programs from test-site schools into wider use, but such funding is tenuous at best. For example, the Success For All restructuring program—developed under the direction of Principal Research Scientist Robert Slavin at Johns Hopkins University's Center for Research in Effective Schooling for Disadvantaged Students—succeeded in Baltimore, and school districts in fourteen other states gathered local grants to import it. But even as that marketing effort was in progress, the OERI abruptly ended its financial support for the research center for innovation in elementary- and middle-school education that Slavin headed. "It wasn't as though there was a competition for the grant and we lost," Slavin says. "The money didn't go to someone else doing the same thing. They just told us, 'We're not going to do that anymore; we're into something else now." The money follows fads rather than serious, long-term commitments."

Perhaps the saddest contrast between industry's and education's approach to change lies in a tiny Department of Education agency called the National Diffusion Network. The NDN is the only national agency whose job is specifically to monitor education reform and innovation around the country, evaluate initiatives, and disseminate the most promising of them nationwide.

It's an agency dwarfed by the scale of its own mission. In essence, the NDN is a marketing office whose "customer" is the $200 billion-a-year U.S. schooling system. According to the American Marketing Association's most recent figures, U.S. commercial firms spend an average of 8 percent of their yearly sales on marketing. No comparable figures are compiled for education. But we would argue that if programs were developed that doubled the number of U.S. students succeeding in serious academic programs, U.S. schools might be persuaded to set aside 10 percent of their budgets—totaling $20 billion nationally—to refine and implement those programs, including the cost of disseminating them to schools across the country. Programs showing such results would easily save schools that proportion of their budgets by eliminating the cost of "reworking" failed students through remedial programs. Within this $20 billion budget, an 8 percent marketing outlay would be about $1.6 billion. Instead, the NDN, the only agency devoted to just that kind of effort, limps along on an annual budget of just $15 million, less than 1 percent of what American industry would consider adequate to accomplish the job. With such a small purse, the NDN can field only one "facilitator," its equivalent of a marketing representative, in each state to counsel schools in selecting and adopting NDN programs.

The Gaps Among Education Researchers

The NDN also is only loosely connected to the scattered education architects and designers whose products it markets. The agency does subsidize efforts by the designers of some of its approved programs to take them to schools by underwriting designers' publicity and teacher-training projects. Eight or nine programs a year are each granted aid averaging $75,000 annually for four years, a total of about $2 million—far less than could be used to good effect by one reform program, let alone several.

But more significantly, the network fosters none of the links between designers, or between designers and teachers, that are necessary to make an educational design process effective. The missing links among designers leave innovators in the same situation that airplane builders were in before the Wright brothers stayed aloft at Kitty Hawk. A century ago, people making airplanes were usually solitary, self-taught visionaries or eccentrics following their own theories and hunches. They lacked a good deal of basic information about aerodynamics, they were in touch with each other informally if at all, and they didn't pool ideas to speed the pace of successful flight. One tinkerer might hit on a better wing shape, and another might come up with stronger wing bracing, but the two didn't pool their advances to create one significantly better airplane. They continued to work separately, often unknowingly crossing and recrossing each other's tracks, unable to take advantage of or build on each other's successes. In aeronautical design, this chaotic and inefficient approach to innovation was abolished only when the aircraft industry institutionalized a formal process of change. Large, rapid, and widespread gains in U.S. educational achievement will be possible only when individual school reforms leverage their individual powers by integrating themselves through a process of design and redesign.

The Gaps That Isolate Teachers from One Another

The teaching profession's final missing link exacerbates the effects of the rest: teachers are isolated from one another in a crucial way. Specialists in professions nurture their common bonds as a way to improve the field's collective wisdom and expertise. Scientists, engineers, marketing executives, and countless others from purchasing agents to police chiefs congregate in professional societies and relate and analyze the meaning of their experiences through journals, local chapter meetings, and regional and national conventions. But a teacher typically pursues excellence alone according to personal intuition, not as part of a group of trained experts pursuing common goals in coordinated ways. (The proportionately few teachers who do attend meetings of professional groups such as the National Council of Teachers of Mathematics rarely go expecting the meetings to give them hands-on help in polishing their pedagogical techniques.) Lortie calls it the "egg crate school," in which teachers are closeted in separate rooms where they are expected, and expect, to spend their time teaching and working alone. Most teachers virtually never have the kind of opportunity to watch one another work that Reading Recovery routinely provides.

Implicit in all of these missing links is the problem of quality. At a time when U.S. industry is undergoing a "quality revolution," U.S. education still hasn't tackled the sizeable problems of quality control—problems attributable in part to the lack of a robust research and technical culture. The same National Academy of Science committee report that decried the OERI's feeble funding also accused the OERI of certifying programs as being effective on the basis of too little proof. The report complained of "evaluations in only a handful of sites, on only a few outcomes, and with no follow-up assessment one or two years after" students left the program to see if they'd retained what they'd learned in it. Evaluations were muddied further by the lack of objective and independent testers. The reports on programs' effectiveness are virtually always made by the program designers themselves, using their own data. "The kinds of evaluations behind these programs were often very poor," Slavin confirms. "For a time, any program that met the national average for educational improvement was certified [for NDN sponsorship]." Other innovators have delivered programs to the NDN that were clearly effective under their own supervision but failed to produce equivalent results in other schools.

Unfortunately, the NDN's lack of a systematic way to judge educational quality is only symptomatic of education as a whole. In a profession that defines its essence as individualistic, expressive, and possessing no technical culture, the concept of a common quality standard is absurd—as absurd as attempting to enforce common aesthetic standards or working methods among all poets or painters. Collective standards can't be effective until they're rooted in a collective paradigm, a common notion of what professionalism in education is.

WISDOM OF THE EAST

The egg-crate school and the missing links that have created it are central to the traditions of American education. Recently, though, a study has finally offered evidence that a paradigm of the teaching profession that differs radically from the prevailing American model might well be far more beneficial for students and teachers alike. The study surveyed the structure of the teaching profession in parts of Asia: China, where few teachers spend more than three hours a day instructing children; and Japan, where laws limit the time teachers spend in front of their classes to no more than four hours daily. Up to 40 percent of the balance of teachers' workdays is spent in crafting more effective lessons and studying to become more effective instructors.

The consequences of these and other practices were analyzed by psychologists Harold Stevenson and James Stigler in their 1992 book, *The Learning Gap: Why Our Schools Are Failing and What We Can Learn from Japanese and Chinese Education.* The authors found that not only do Asian teachers spend less time teaching, but they also teach bigger classes—up to fifty children at a time. Although this violates the U.S. teaching profession's fundamental precepts of limited class sizes and long hours in class, Asian teachers seem able to teach their students far more effectively than do their American counterparts.

"By having more students in each class but the same number of teachers in the school [as in the United States]," Stevenson and Stigler write, "all teachers can have a lower teaching load. Time is freed for teachers to meet and work together on a daily basis, to prepare lessons for the next day . . . and to attend staff meetings. Although class sizes are large, the overall ratio of students to teachers within a school does not differ greatly from that in the United States." The two also found that Asian teachers spend an average of more than nine hours a day at school, while American teachers average barely seven. "This does not necessarily result in a shorter work week for American teachers," they write. It simply means that American teachers who work after class do so at home, alone, and not at school where they can study with, help, and be helped by colleagues.[21]

In contrast, during those extra school hours Asian teachers often work in groups to become better teachers. In Japan, teachers meet regularly to discuss teaching techniques and hone their classroom presentations. "A whole meeting might be devoted to the most effective ways to phrase questions about a topic or the most absorbing ways of capturing children's interest in a lesson," Stevenson and Stigler note. Teachers often watch each other work, sometimes traveling to other schools to do so, and then critique each other's performance and suggest improvements. Also, each Japanese school reserves a large workroom for teachers' exclusive use. Each teacher has her own desk in the room, away from students, where she corrects papers, prepares lessons, and has daily opportunities to interact with other teachers. In addition to meeting daily in each school, Japanese teachers also gather informally in districtwide study groups. Professional study and training is a permanent part of their workday. "American teachers, isolated in their own classrooms, find it much harder to discuss their work with colleagues," the authors point out. "When we compare the . . . nature of the teaching profession in American and Asian societies, it quickly becomes clear that . . . American teachers are inadequately trained. . . . In the United States, training comes to a near halt after the teachers acquire their teaching certificates. . . . The real training of Asian teachers occurs . . . *after* graduation from college."[22]

This seems to have dramatic impact on students. During the 1980s, Stevenson and Stigler devised and administered a series of intelligence and skill tests for children in the first and fifth grades. They tested randomly selected school classes in Minneapolis (known for its superior school system), the Japanese city of Sendai, and Taiwan's capital city, Taipei. Their approach was scrupulously crafted, and used the advice of psychologists from each country to ensure that the exams weren't culturally biased to favor any one group. The results indicate the power of a new paradigm of teaching rooted in a technical culture.

The study's results contradict a common U.S. assumption that Asian children are simply smarter than their U.S. counterparts. The American and Asian children performed similarly in intelligence tests. Social and personal factors also were roughly balanced. For example, the proportion of children tested whose mothers worked full time outside the home was about the same from culture to culture, as was the number of intact families and students' distribution across social classes. But the differences in skill-test scores were stark.

In a first-grade mathematics test, American first-graders as a group ranked slightly below the 38th percentile. In other words, 62 percent of the students taking the test did better than the average U.S. first-grader. The Japanese children's mean score reached the 53rd percentile, while Chinese students as a whole almost reached the 60th percentile. By fifth grade, though, the highest-performing American school group did less well on average than the *worst*-performing class in either Sendai or Taipei. American children barely cleared the 30th percentile in mathematics; their relative scores fell throughout elementary school. Chinese students' results also fell, but only to the 55th percentile. Japanese children, on the other hand, improved their mean score, which climbed to the 65th percentile. Reading tests of children in Chicago and in Beijing, China, uncovered similar, although less drastic, differences. Among U.S. fifth-graders tested, 31 percent were reading at only the third-grade level, while just 12 percent of Chinese students surveyed performed that poorly, even though reading Chinese requires that students learn to recognize and combine more than three thousand written characters.

Contrary to another common Western assumption, Asian students aren't always taught merely to follow instructions and deliver answers. As Stevenson and Stigler make clear, children in Asian elementary-school reading and mathematics courses are given a far better grounding in higher-order skills than U.S. children are. That contrast is made vivid in the differences between the ways in which Asian and Western teachers use questions. U.S. teachers usually ask questions that can be answered quickly, without slowing the class pace or risking more than a momentary detour from the lesson's narrow path and quick pace. The questions serve primarily as quick, random checks to find out who isn't paying attention or hasn't done the homework. "Three times two is what?" or "What's an isthmus?" or "The Declaration of Independence says all people are entitled to what three things?" are typical of the depth and searching quality of the questions with which American teachers pepper their students. "In the United States, the purpose of a question is to get an answer," Stevenson and Stigler write. "In Japan, teachers ask questions to stimulate thought." One Japanese teacher told them that a good deal of the time teachers spend working together "is spent talking about questions we can pose—which wordings work best to get students involved in thinking and discussing the material. One good question can keep a whole class going for a long time; a bad one produces little more than a simple answer."

As part of that approach, the pace of a typical Japanese lesson is slow, the researchers say, with teachers sometimes lavishing weeks on a single topic—"but the outcome is impressive. Japanese teachers want their students to be reflective and to gain a deep understanding. . . . Thinking takes time, and Japanese teachers strive to allow their students time to think. . . . There is time for the kind of discussion that transforms the solution of problems from something that must be memorized to something that is understood."

While Stevenson and Stigler are quick to acknowledge that other factors play a part in boosting Asian children's achievement, they attribute the differences in learning in no small measure to the differences in the teachers' schedules. "What has impressed us in our personal observations and in our data is how remarkably well most Asian teachers teach," they write. "It is the widespread excellence of Asian class lessons that is so stunning." The American result is quite different. "Lacking the training and time that are necessary to prepare lessons and the opportunities to share experiences with one another, American teachers find it difficult to organize lively, vivid, coherent lessons. Preparing well-crafted lessons takes time. Teaching them effectively requires energy. Both are in short supply for most American teachers. In the face of the limitations in time for preparation and consultation and a heavy teaching load, it is surprising that American teachers teach as well as they do." Their conclusion: "Surely the most pressing challenge in educating . . . children is to create new types of school environments . . . where great lessons are . . . commonplace. . . . In order to do this, we must ask how we can institute reforms that will make it possible for American teachers to practice their profession under conditions more favorable for their own professional development and for the education of children."[23]

THE KEY TO REFORM

As research for his book, *The New Meaning of Educational Change*, Michael Fullan studied the process of school reform in the United States and Canada and surveyed the parts played by everyone from students to government officials. Among his principal conclusions: "Educational change depends on what teachers do and think," he says. "It's as simple and as complex as that."

The statement is straightforward in its logic: if students become educated in school, they do so primarily through the efforts of teachers. If teachers are to be willing to work earnestly to find ways to improve those interactions, they first must change how they think about what they do—in other words, they have to exchange old paradigms for new ones. But the idea is hugely complex in practice: the teaching profession, by its internal norms and structures, doesn't provide the technical culture by which antiquated paradigms can be exchanged for more effective and efficient ones. No matter how sincerely teachers try to improve their techniques and materials, they remain trapped within a profession that in its essence remains entirely unequipped to change. Before teachers can discard education's old paradigm and adopt its new, more useful one, the framework of their profession must be rebuilt to let them.

Stevenson and Stigler's findings support Fullan's contention that educational improvement depends on teachers' abilities to conceive and do things in new ways. Asian societies understand that if teachers steadily gain new insights into classroom lessons and techniques—if their professional paradigms permit regular, positive, incremental change—teaching and learning become steadily more effective and efficient. The lesson for the West should be clear: if we're to reform our schools, teachers must be given the tools to dismantle outworn paradigms of schooling and construct new ones in their place. But unless the teaching profession restructures itself as a collaborative, unified endeavor—a technical culture linked at all its points, from research labs and university-based teacher-preparation programs to networks of working teachers themselves—our struggle to reshape our schooling system faces a potentially devastating obstacle.

Stevenson and Stigler's work also reveals indirectly the energy and imagination that teachers can call up when their work is acknowledged to be a higher-order skill—something to be studied, practiced, and refined continually. In that way, the new paradigm of teaching-as-technical-culture draws on the strengths of the redesign process: a steady flow of new insights yields new approaches and techniques to be tested, evaluated, and refined as part of a continuous, integrated process of improvement. The most effective teachers will be involved in a process of continuous innovation, which won't be possible in U.S. schools until teachers are granted the time, support, and psychic and material resources necessary to carry it out. If U.S. schools are to innovate, U.S. teachers must be permitted to adopt the balanced schedule that Asian teachers use to steadily improve their own proficiencies.

But that step toward structural change can't be taken in isolation from other elements in a process of guided change. As powerful as the Asian process of teacher study and collaboration seems to be, it still doesn't fully embrace and integrate the steps of research, development, marketing, and redesign. If North American schools adopt a process of teacher development similar to Asia's but embracing a genuine technical culture rooted in the full process of redesign, our schools can begin to close the performance gap that stands between them and world leaders in education, such as Japan. However, taking that decisive step requires more than just a scheduling change for teachers. It also requires a cultural change in the larger society's concept of the nature and purpose of school itself. Until we make that change, our schools will not be able to meet society's demands for a different kind of teaching—or of learning.

5
The Culture of the School

Educational Politics and
the Problem of Change

When Joseph Fernandez arrived in January 1990 to be the new superintendent of New York City's schools, he was hailed as a savior. In his previous job as head of Miami's school system, he had dismantled bureaucracies, given teachers and principals power and control over educational matters, and raised student achievement. Now he was to do the same for the nation's largest school district. He attacked New York's educational problems with such force and zeal that within months of his arrival people were touting him as the city's next mayor. Three years later, he was out of a job. Ostensibly, the school board voted him out because it disapproved of his decision to make condoms available in the city's high schools and of his new elementary-school curriculum, which would have taught tolerance of homosexuals. But the reasons ran much deeper.

Few dispute Fernandez's achievements. He won a hard fight to end "building tenure," the practice of guaranteeing that junior- and senior-high principals with five or more years in a school could never be transferred out, regardless of their performance on the job. He led the successful campaign to abolish the district's Board of Examiners, a notoriously stodgy lot whose job was to certify prospective employees' professional fitness. (It once refused to offer a job to a nationally regarded, innovative principal because he did poorly on the board's antiquated exam; similarly, it denied a junior-high mathematics teaching job to a woman who'd graduated summa cum laude in economics from Stanford, saying that her economics training couldn't have properly prepared her to teach junior-high mathematics.) Fernandez also created thirty "theme" high schools similar to magnet schools, raised graduation requirements in mathematics and science, and launched a pervasive program to wrest an array of powers from central management and turn them over to front-line educators.

Few dispute that such programs were necessary to free New York's schools from the grip of fossilized and outworn structures. Fernandez's problem lay elsewhere. "Joseph Fernandez came ... as an outside reformer with a mandate to shake up the system," a former New York City school-board staff member told the *New York Times*.[1] "But his failure to develop a cadre of field generals and troops who supported his ideas and were willing to put themselves on the line to see them to fruition was a sure-fire prescription for disaster." Fernandez's real failure, the *Times* went on to point out, was that he hadn't infused his own convictions into the ranks of New York's teachers and administrators. In short, he failed not for policy reasons but for political ones. Joseph Fernandez was defeated by the culture of the school.

EDUCATIONAL POLITICS

As Fernandez's fate makes clear, reconfiguring educational practices means changing policies; just as much, though, it means changing minds. In any society, education is unavoidably political.

Similarly, the political is also cultural. The tendrils of our schooling system reach deep into our concepts of ourselves as individuals and as a society, and efforts at reform and change are inextricably bound up with issues of cultural identity and social ideology. Any diverse group of people will disagree somehow about what children should learn, what they should be protected from knowing, and how they're to be taught. The ongoing flap over the teaching of Christian theology's "creation science" in public schools is an example; so is the question of sex education or the practice of making condoms available in schools. Parents transfer their children from one school to another, people campaign for election to school boards, and principals, administrators, and even superintendents are hired or fired over such issues.

To illustrate the political dimensions of educational reform, there's no better example than Chicago's struggle to recast the governance of its schools. The struggle was led by the city's business leaders, who in the mid-1980s responded to two alarms. First, it became clear that local schools were not adequately educating tomorrow's workers and that area employers faced a future shortage of capable employees. Second, Chicago schools were spending more and more money turning out graduates with fewer and fewer skills. The city's business leaders took their concerns first to the top of Chicago's sprawling, centralized educational bureaucracy. The system's executives were sympathetic but hamstrung: the city's school system housed 16,700 administrators and managers supervising the work of 23,700 teachers. Programs and projects were legion, each creating its own bureaucracy, constituency, and vectors of influence and political power. Bureaucrats do not surrender turf without a fight; overworked and underpaid teachers, for reasons already detailed, are often equally reluctant to embark on unproven innovations. Changing minds, habits, and structures by working within the city's schools demanded either a miracle or irresistible intervention from outside.

Choosing the second option, Chicago's business elite took its case to the Illinois state education office. There it found an ally in Theodore Sanders, a creative and energetic state superintendent. Backed by legislators sympathetic to the cause, Sanders introduced a bill in the 1988 state legislature mandating that Chicago dismantle its centralized school-management system and surrender vast decision-making power and control to individual schools.

An array of interest groups took up arms against the bill. The school district's administrative bureaucracy opposed it because it would vaporize thousands of middle-management jobs and dismantle hundreds of bureaucratic power bases. Teachers' union leaders opposed it, knowing that a centralized power structure would be easier to influence and negotiate with. Teachers opposed it, fearing that pressures to cut costs would jeopardize the quality of their work and results. Members of other unions—cooks, custodians, and so on—opposed it because those same cost-cutting pressures would threaten their wages and jobs. Some leaders of the city's black community spoke out against it, even though minority children populated the worst schools in the city; they worried that job cuts resulting from the plan would fall hardest on minorities, parting them from some of the best-paying opportunities open to them. With such formidable opposition, the bill faced defeat. Just before the legislature was to vote, Sanders and sympathetic politicians organized a lobbying blitz by the chairmen and presidents of some of Chicago's largest corporations. Thanks to their forceful arm-twisting, the Chicago School Reform Act of 1988 became law.

In the first five years of the plan, more than 25 percent of the district's middle-management jobs have disappeared, saving millions of dollars annually. In each school, a Local School Council made up of parents, community leaders, teachers, and the principal hire and fire, set policy, and allocate budgets. Studies in a number of the schools show that parents feel better about their schools' ability to educate their children effectively, that teachers have begun to embrace change and take a leading role in making innovations work, and that in subtle ways students' attitudes toward school are beginning to perk up. According to John Godbold, a professor of education at Illinois State University and a consultant to several Chicago schools working through new approaches to education, "This level of change would never have been possible without a state law. If you're talking about a policy change that stretches across an entire school district, then change is always political. Race, cultural identity, money, jobs—there's too much at stake for it *not* to be. The only way to minimize that is to put real power and the control of change into the hands of teachers and principals."[2]

Internally, the education community itself is no less partisan. Educators derive their livelihood from their particular expertise—reason enough to battle change that threatens a particular program or field. But many also find in their careers a large portion of their personal identity and sense of self-worth; their mastery defines their role and place in life and frames for them some basic truths about life itself. Educators, like other professionals, cling to paradigms. Deep cultural change cannot be effected by policy edicts alone, even in relatively superficial ways.

Consider the surprise of a New England elementary-school principal who set out to introduce hand-held calculators into his school's mathematics lessons. "You know—those cheap little solar-powered things that banks give away," he says. "They have the power to absolutely revolutionize mathematics teaching in elementary school." When the principal began teaching elementary grades in the early 1960s, mathematics lessons were about arithmetic facts: five plus four is nine; three quarters minus one half is one quarter; four into three won't go. "Now that every child can own one of these little calculators, we don't have to spend hundreds of hours over six years teaching these kids mathematics facts," he says with passion. "The calculators can show them the facts. We can spend our time teaching kids math *concepts*—teaching them to think mathematically, not just to calculate like a machine. There are new curriculum materials out there that support that approach. We just need to decide to do it."

The principal met with his teachers to talk up the idea. To help induce them to try it, he even bought a few dozen of the calculators himself and distributed them to some of his teachers. Many welcomed them; others had a quite different reaction. "There is a significant minority that won't use them," he fumes. "They say, 'Well, what if these kids have to solve an arithmetic problem some time and they don't have a calculator?' Or they say, 'Well, learning arithmetic tables helps teach children to think logically and in an organized way.' If some of them were telling the truth, they'd say, 'Well, this is the way I've always done it and I'm too tired or too scared or too busy to have to think about learning something new.' So now we have some kids in this school who are beginning to see mathematics in a whole new way, and others in the same school who are sitting in class reciting, 'Two times three is six.' "

It's easy to forgive the principal his pique, even if he did—like Joseph Fernandez—help to bring on his troubles himself. Industry's redesign process is structured to effect change in an orderly and continuous way, even when people within it bridle at the prospect of something new. But because schools lack the orderly pattern of change that the redesign process structures and coordinates, educational innovation is buffeted by the subjective agendas, desires, and political maneuvers of every individual and interest group taking part. That those cheap calculators have for years been ubiquitous everywhere *but* in classrooms is a good measure of just how cautiously schools approach new ideas.

In fact, the principal's initiative is a typical example of the way a new idea makes its debut in a school. He had a good idea, perhaps even a great one. But he did no extensive diagnoses to define the problem his idea was meant to solve. He could offer no research to convince teachers that using calculators boosts children's mathematics achievements. He didn't look for a similar program in another school that could provide a convincing example for his teachers to review, nor did he attempt to establish a pilot program within his own school to provide measurable results that his teachers could observe and critique. To make things worse, the principal neglected the political skills and techniques of inclusive leadership that effective educational change demands. Instead, he attempted to impose on his teachers a product of his will instead of working with them to develop a consensus about just what needed to be changed and how.

Finally, and perhaps most important, the principal didn't understand the real nature of the change he was asking his teachers to make. He thought that he was simply suggesting that they use calculators in class. Actually, he was suggesting that teachers transform the basic nature of their work. In a traditional classroom, the teacher is chiefly a source of factual information. His or her job is to communicate to children that five plus three is eight. The principal proposed giving that job to a calculator and leaving the teachers instead to deal in concepts—the broad web of systematic and philosophical principles that explains, for example, *why* five plus three is always eight and never nine. Teachers' training and experience, especially at the elementary-school level, has done nothing to equip them with the expertise necessary to teach as coaches instead of as the purveyors of facts. It's no surprise that a significant number of them felt threatened by the principal's suggestion. He thought that he was proposing a new electronic technology, but he actually was proposing a fundamental new way for teachers to do their jobs. Some disagreed with the philosophical assumptions underlying the change; others felt unsure about their own abilities to adapt to the new system. In either case, the principal didn't understand that his policy initiative couldn't keep from becoming a political and cultural one as well.

A reform idea so narrowly conceived goes unarmed into battle. Because the traditions of the teaching profession grant each teacher a large measure of professional sovereignty in her own classroom, many wield that freedom politically, to subvert or simply disregard changes that threaten or don't inspire them. Because the principal offered no proof that his idea would benefit the school's children, his teachers had no compelling reason to accept it. Because he didn't involve teachers in the idea's development, he invited their resentment at being treated as foot soldiers to be commanded rather than as colleagues to be consulted. He lost the battle over his idea before it began because he tried to impose reform on his teachers from above instead of planting it to grow from within their own ranks.

At first, schools' cultural resistance to change might seem paradoxical. After all, no institution confronts change more often than a public school. New textbooks and resulting alterations in curricula, experiments in classroom technique, teacher workshops, alternative disciplinary approaches, new regulations, and so on flow through schools like water through a pipe. Despite that constant flow of changes through them, however, *schools in their essence have changed very little in the last eighty years.* The reasons, many of which the principal encountered, coalesce into a formidable barrier to education reform: politically and culturally, public schools, as they're traditionally organized and operated, are endemically inhospitable to change.

That lesson has been paid for with decades of reforms that failed— because, to a greater or lesser degree, their designers didn't grasp or acknowledge the need for an orderly process of change. "The number and dynamics of factors that interact and affect the process of educational change are too overwhelming to compute in anything resembling a fully determined way," the University of Toronto's Michael Fullan observes in *The New Meaning of Educational Change.* "People do not understand the nature or ramifications of most educational changes.

They . . . experience ambivalence about [their] meaning, form, or consequences. It isn't that people resist change as much as they don't know how to cope with it."[3] In industry, change is a familiar part of the routine. The people involved may not always welcome it, but they expect it. They've lived through it before, they know their respective roles in the process of change, and they understand that change brings benefits. Educators as a group have no such experience. Change in schools is still seen largely as alien, threatening, and chaotic, a risk to order and outcome that offers no clear benefits to offset the necessary struggle and disorder involved.

Seymour Sarason, a retired professor of psychology at Yale and an educational consultant, shares Fullan's conclusion. In his 1991 book *The Predictable Failure of Educational Reform*, he notes that "in too many cases, where new ideas deserved consideration, the processes through which they were implemented were self-defeating . . . the process of implementation requires an understanding of the settings in which these ideas have to take root. That understanding is frequently faulty and incomplete."[4]

Predictably, if the process by which schools try to innovate is chaotic, random, and inconsistent, the innovations carried into schools in such flawed ways won't fare well. In his landmark 1972 book, *The Culture of the School and the Problem of Change,* Sarason offers what he considers to be a typical example of the way change is brought to schools: "The new math is quintessentially representative of how change takes place in a school culture."[5] It's not a sunny story.

In 1958, the Soviet Union launched the Sputnik satellite, the first permanent human-made object in space. U.S. policy-makers panicked. They were convinced that the Soviet Union, the nation's Cold War archenemy, was surpassing the United States in scientific and technological innovation and skill. The obvious response, they decided, was to direct legions of American students into technical careers. But there was a problem.

It was the prevailing mathematics curriculum, students' traditional gateway to careers in the sciences. Experts agreed widely, if not publicly, that the conventional materials for and approaches to teaching mathematics didn't entice students more deeply into the subject; instead, it snuffed out what interest most of them had. The American technical and political community reasoned that because mathematics was the basis of scientific and technical literacy and success, the shortcomings of the mathematics curriculum had disastrous consequences for our national future. The answer was to have mathematics experts fix it. Some argued for new textbooks to solve the problem, others for teaching teachers to coach mathematics as a thinking skill instead of as a process of information-transfer to be mastered by pencil-and-paper drills. Sarason writes: "I'm not aware that anyone at any time viewed the problem in terms of . . . a diagnostic process requiring a description of symptoms, possible alternative explanations, and investigative procedures to gain new information that would support the diagnostic formation. The decision to change the curriculum did not reflect . . . awareness of these processes."

Instead, university mathematicians and educational psychologists launched a crash multiyear program. Classroom teachers weren't involved in designing the curriculum or consulted about how such novel material might best be presented to their students. The new math wasn't "marketed" to teachers in any attempt to win them to the program's cause or convince them of its benefits. It wasn't tested in prototypes, critiqued by the "customers," the teachers who would use it; it wasn't forced to improve as a result of early problems that would have cropped up in trials. Indeed, there were no trials. Instead, teachers were introduced to the program in five-week summer workshops held shortly before the new program was premiered in schools in 1962.

Sarason reports that the workshops "took place in an atmosphere of tension and pressure." The program experts who explained the curriculum and its methods to the teachers showed little concern for their plight: having to unlearn a career's worth of methods, vocabulary, and patterns and replace them in five weeks with a wholly new and alien understanding. "The more anxious they became, the harder they worked," Sarason says, "all the time asking themselves that if *they* were having difficulty, what would their pupils experience?" The workshops ignored the teachers' own acute case of new-math anxiety. "The teachers perceived themselves as pupils whose job it was to learn what the teacher was presenting, and the workshop teachers perceived themselves as imparters of knowledge and overseers of skill training," Sarason finds. "Both teachers and pupils in the workshop implicitly agreed that personal attitudes and feelings, as well as the nature of the relationship between pupil and teacher, was not an inevitable part of the educative process and, therefore, had little or no claim to workshop time."[6] Predictably, the workshops also made no effort to alter the teachers' styles of instruction. The program's designers seemed to assume that a revamped curriculum would simply inspire teachers to adopt new, more effective classroom styles. The workshops made no mention of—and so offered no guidance in—new teaching techniques or approaches; the teachers, steeped in traditional habits and practices, clearly were overwhelmed by other, more immediate concerns.

The same lack of planning and deliberation was apparent after the program was launched. There were far too few supervisors to visit all the schools in which teachers had questions, confusions, or needed more training—much less simply to see how the program was going. In short, the teachers had no positive stake in the program's success, they were badly and inadequately trained in it, and were given no moral or technical support as they tried to make it work. The implementation of new math became yet another of the recurring disasters of American education reform, lingering on to alienate an entire generation of students and educators.

The story of new math makes such a good object lesson in how not to reform schools because it did so many things in classically ineffective ways. First, it was introduced in a way that ignored the prime principle of educational innovation: change takes root and flourishes only when teachers desire it and the culture of the school accepts it. In this case, teachers and principals weren't asked if they wanted a change, if they wanted this particular change, or even how the change could be most effectively implemented in their classrooms. Designers assumed that the new material would be taught effectively without showing teachers how that was to be done and guiding them as they adopted innovative methods. Teachers were given no help in adapting to the innovation or in learning to use it, their training was short and superficial, their use of the program was unsupervised, and the program itself wasn't systematically monitored and measured to gauge its effects. As a result, there also was no explicit, reliable base of data and experience that could be used to figure out how to improve the program after it had begun.

By the late sixties, as the program's spectacular failure became clear, it took on new political dimensions. "It is not surprising . . . that the teachers were the chief recipients of blame," Sarason says. Among students, parents, principals, administrators, and others involved, "teachers were in the center of the stage." Few critics and commentators reached Sarason's broader conclusion: that the program failed "as a consequence of processes taking place in and characterizing a particular social organization, or as reflecting conceptions (implicit or explicit) about the nature and structure of the settings that determine how the change process will be effected."[7] Because they ignored those cultural components, new math's boosters created a disaster instead of a renaissance.

Since the dark days of new math, U.S. education as an institution has learned little about the process of change in schools. The problem has been studied, but, as we've seen, the insights those studies offer rarely make their way to teachers and administrators, who in turn are left to cope with change as periodic spasms instead of as a continuing pattern of professional skills to be perfected. With so many innovations following such a suicidal route, partially or totally, it's no wonder that few reforms survive to make a lasting difference. Often, one of the strongest impressions they do leave behind is a wariness toward change itself.

It's not hard to see why. As in the case of the new math fiasco, most failed reforms ultimately scapegoat teachers. Any educational innovation ultimately succeeds or fails by what happens in classrooms, and classrooms are places that teachers nominally control. If the change doesn't work, "the teacher did it" becomes an easy explanation for others seeking to fix, or avoid, blame. The psychological effect on teachers is as devastating as it is pervasive. In *The Predictable Failure of Educational Reform*, Sarason relates a conversation he had with the leader of a teachers' union. The school superintendent in the union's district had proposed to grant local teachers the unprecedented power to make whatever changes they thought would improve their schools, as long as they didn't violate existing budgets. The teachers' initial wave of enthusiasm had faded before a series of planning meetings was even finished. When the two officials asked what went wrong, they found the teachers unable to trust—to believe that what had been promised actually would be delivered. "I really didn't comprehend the depths of the distrust that teachers have," the union official told Sarason. "Everything in their experience taught them two things: Don't believe the sincerity of what you're told, and don't allow yourself to hope that a real change is possible because you'll be disappointed. But there was another factor at work, and that's that if they exercised the new power we were giving them and things didn't work out well, they [believed they] would be clobbered."[8]

Teachers can't be blamed for being human. In his 1974 U.S. Department of Education study *The Politics of Educational Innovation*, reform pioneer Ernest House comes to a conclusion that is no less true today: "The personal costs of trying new innovations are often high . . . and seldom is there any indication that innovations are worth the investment. They require that one believe that they will ultimately bear fruit and be worth the personal investment, often without the hope of an immediate return."[9] That kind of experience breeds a cultural climate that sees change—especially change imposed from without—as an enemy. Eventually, giving comes to an end. House concludes that "the amount of energy and time required to learn . . . new skills or roles is a useful index to the magnitude of resistance."

Michael Fullan expresses a similar outlook: "Grappling with educational change in self-defeating ways has been the modal experience over the last thirty years," he notes. "The response of many has been to redouble their efforts. For those in authority, this has meant more advocacy, more legislation, more accountability, more resources. For those on the receiving end, the response has been more closed doors, retreats into isolationism, or out of education altogether."[10]

Obviously, teachers are the chief gatekeepers of change in schools. Without their support, change doesn't happen. But it's equally clear that explaining innovation's failure as the failure of teachers, while politically expedient and thus tempting for many, is plainly wrong. Just as crack front-line troops can't save a general staff's flawed battle plan, teachers' efforts to reshape their classroom practices won't succeed if they're denied any portion of the full array of broader cultural support they must have to make change work. Most teachers don't balk at the idea of innovation; on the contrary, as we've seen, when teachers are given the genuine power to create genuine change, educational results surge. But teachers rightly resist reforms that demand change from them *but that don't demand correspondingly deep changes in the inherent culture of the school.* The dominant culture of education—not the teachers, administrators, parents, or students enveloped by it—remains the real barrier to systemic (and systematic) educational change.

Like every complex culture, that of schools evolved not by plan but by chance. As a result, the individual threads of school culture have become entangled: one can trace individual strands, but it's maddeningly difficult to separate one from another unless one is prepared to unravel the entire skein. In fact, possibly the only thing more difficult would be to change some aspects of the tangle while leaving others intact—to pull out old threads or weave in new attitudes and approaches without altering the relationships of those already there.

Schools are among our few social institutions that have yet to adopt a reliable process of change that can weave new ideas into those kinds of dense cultural fabrics. Consequently, national education reform can't succeed until educators confront the social, institutional, and organizational obstacles that block it—obstacles buried deep in school culture. "Reform is not putting into place the latest policy," Fullan says. "It means changing the cultures of the classrooms, the schools, the districts, the universities."[11]

First Premises

Two decades of research into education's political and cultural resistance to innovation reveal that the U.S. schooling system carries in it a collection of unconscious assumptions and innate biases that shape our cultural approach to education and learning. Some of those assumptions and biases sprout from our larger national culture, others are purely organizational, and a number, as we've seen, are built into the teaching profession itself. But no matter where they've come from, they work together formidably to smother educational innovation.

First, Americans reflect the view that schooling isn't any more important in a child's life than any number of other activities. Asian children are in school more days than not, while American children attend school for an average of barely 180 days—fractionally less than half the calendar year. Asian parents also encourage and discipline their children to excel in school, while U.S. parents worry about children who sacrifice play time to study. Japanese parents spur their children by reminding them of the legendary peasant boy who did his farm chores with one hand while holding an open book in the other. In this country, students devoted to their studies are labeled "nerds" or "grinds"—hardly terms of approbation. During the round of school budget cuts that plagued the United States in the early 1990s, plans to cut sports programs routinely drew more passionate opposition from both students and parents than proposals to curtail academic offerings. (Perhaps the most controversial aspect of Texas's comprehensive school reforms during the 1980s was the rule that students failing classes wouldn't be allowed to play football until they raised their grades.) Asian parents expect their children to excel in school; U.S. parents want their children to be "well rounded."

The assumption that schooling is of no more importance than many other ways to spend time feeds a second cultural assumption that thwarts educational excellence: the long-standing cultural assumption that academic success is a matter of inborn ability rather than diligent effort. That notion, as fundamental in U.S. schools as it is damaging, not only is unsupported by fact but also is contradicted by other nations' results. The damage it does is easier to recognize in contrast with Asian cultures, which assume the opposite: that academic achievement is a matter of hard work and not a lucky accident.

In *The Learning Gap*, Stevenson and Stigler compare Asian attitudes about the importance of academic effort versus innate ability with Americans' assumptions. Fifth-graders in Sendai (Japan), Taipei, and Minneapolis were asked to indicate on a scale of one to seven how strongly they agreed or disagreed with the statement "The tests you take can show how much or how little natural ability you have." A score of seven meant "strongly agree" and one meant "strongly disagree." The responses from children in Japan averaged less than three, a rather strong repudiation of the proposition. Taiwanese children as a group were virtually neutral in their reaction. But American children averaged a response close to five, agreeing with the statement as strongly as their Japanese counterparts disagreed. "Chinese and Japanese children were less likely than American children to accept the proposal that tests can reveal natural ability," the two researchers conclude.

Stevenson and Stigler also asked mothers in the same cities to rank effort, natural ability, luck, and difficulty of the task by their degree of influence on children's school performances. Ability and effort were ranked first and second by all groups—but with important differences. Japanese mothers gave effort twice as much importance as ability, with Chinese women rating them almost as disparately. Among American mothers, effort and ability were rated as virtually equal factors in academic achievement. Piecemeal reforms are no match for such a deep-seated cultural bias.

"No matter how we asked the questions or to whom we directed them, the answers were consistent," the two psychologists state. "Americans were more likely to assign greater importance to innate ability than were Chinese and Japanese." To test that conclusion, later in their work the researchers posed the same mathematical problem to classes of Japanese and American children. The problem was literally impossible, one having no solution. American children gave up after a while, but most Japanese children couldn't be persuaded to stop hunting for the answer. This contrast in their efforts illustrates a significant difference between Japanese and American attitudes. Japanese children, taught that effort will bring success, have a natural incentive to pursue problems to a correct solution. American children, taught that natural ability is the key to academic success, seem to believe that "either you get it or you don't." One U.S. mathematics teacher told Stevenson and Stigler that American children appear to believe that if a mathematics problem can be solved, it can be solved in fewer than ten minutes. "The unfortunate result," the psychologists note, "is that American students are likely to give up before they reach genuine understanding."[12]

These assumptions about effort versus ability lead to another contrast that heightens the difference between Asian and American students' academic accomplishment. When an Asian child enters school, its parents commit themselves to a concerted effort to urge and support the child toward academic success. Many American families, assuming that ability and a competent teacher will take over the job, reduce their involvement in their children's learning when the children begin formal education.

To be sure, factors other than national attitudes about academic achievement may contribute to Stevenson and Stigler's results, but the two psychologists argue that "the relative importance people assign to factors beyond their control, like ability, compared to factors that they can control, like effort, can strongly influence the way they approach learning. Ability models subvert learning through the effects they have on the goals that parents and teachers set for children and on children's motivation to work hard. . . . Effort models offer a more hopeful alternative by providing a simple but constructive formula for achieving . . . improvement: Work hard and persist."[13]

U.S. schools carry the ability model's implications to extremes. One result has been what a growing number of educators deride as the "shopping-mall high school." Students are allowed to fulfill graduation requirements not by taking mandated courses in basic subjects, but by enrolling in courses that appeal to them. Students meet requirements in the arts by critiquing television shows; others earn English credits by reading science-fiction novels. Statistically, Illinois's schools have been typical of those in virtually every state; when surveyed in 1977, 741 of its high schools were offering a total of 2,100 different courses. At the same time, national achievement test scores were falling along with student enrollments in basic academic concentrations such as English, mathematics, science, and social studies.

Another consequence of overemphasizing ability has been the widespread U.S. practice of "tracking," or sorting students into ability groups, usually at the end of elementary school. Because academic success is a matter of talent rather than ability, the argument holds, a school should not press a child to meet high academic standards in all areas—especially areas that a child finds difficult—since studying won't help much anyway. As a result, children who are strivers usually are assumed to be college-bound and are tracked into, or assigned to, academically more rigorous classes. Students whose performances indicate a lesser future are consistently guided toward less demanding classes with names like "practical math" or "business math" or vo-tech training. Tracked children may be less likely to face the embarrassment of having their shortcomings exposed in class, but they're also less likely to be challenged or inspired. "Once [children are] categorized as slow learners, a vicious cycle begins," Stevenson and Stigler warn. "They are placed in slower tracks; teachers hold lower expectations for their possible accomplishments, and thus expose them to lower levels of material than they do the more able students; the students come to believe that they indeed are incapable of higher levels of achievement."[14] They quit trying—or even quit school. The principal of a "trackless" school is more blunt. "It makes kids feel like they're dumb," she says. "Labeling is a killer."

Tracking also skews the real measure of students' abilities and achievements, since most teachers grade on a curve. "It's as easy for a general-track student to get a B in business math as it is for an honors kid to get a B in calculus—maybe easier," a Massachusetts high-school teacher told us. "One is taking near-college-level math and the other is doing glorified sixth-grade arithmetic. But both parents look at the report cards and say, 'Hey, my kid got a B in math.' "

Tracking may shield children's embryonic egos from risk, but at the same time it denies them key experiences that can strengthen their sense of self. Stevenson and Stigler point out, "Many Americans place a higher priority on life adjustment and the enhancement of self-esteem than on academic learning"—another indication of our national reluctance to strongly value scholarship. "They assume that positive self-esteem is a necessary precursor of competence. They forget that one of the most important sources of children's self-esteem is realizing that they have mastered a challenging task."[15]

In their 1991 book *Making the Best of Schools*, teachers Jeannie Oakes and Martin Lipton emphasize the damage tracking does not just to children but to a society that depends on them for its future. Tracking, they write, "poses a major impediment to improving the educational experiences of all children. Tracking can be a self-fulfilling prophecy that prevents schools from expecting success of everyone. It teaches children that if the school does not identify them as capable in earlier grades, they will not do well later. Few students or teachers can defy those expectations."[16] The practice institutionalizes mediocrity throughout society—not just in social or economic underclasses—and biases schools against attempts at excellence for all by assuming that, by definition, excellence is exclusive to a few. Tracking not only reflects social traditions and beliefs about human potential, Oakes and Lipton note, but is so pervasive that "even in the suburbs, schools with largely homogeneous populations of white, middle-class children also subject children to needless differences in educational quality."[17]

Again, Asian schools offer an unsettling but revealing contrast. Their students, who have never been tracked, not only show no damage as a result, but also consistently outperform U.S. children academically. According to Stevenson and Stigler, in Japanese and Chinese schools, where students must "adapt to the unwavering standards of excellence of demanding academic curricula, rapid learners practiced their new skills by helping their slower peers and the motivation of slower learners was strengthened by the enthusiastic encouragement of other members of the class. The net effect was that although individual differences among members of the class remained, the overall level of performance of the class was raised."[18]

THE MARCH OF TIME

As if our cultural assumptions didn't create enough troubles themselves, they combine with time's constant urgency to compound the barriers to innovation. The most destructive pressure of time in the school is one that we've already noted: the assumption that a teacher not teaching is a teacher not working. In Asia, the teaching profession by custom and, in some cases, by law reserves a portion of the school day for teachers to study and to improve their professional competencies. But in the United States, the universal demand that teachers devote all of their energies and time to dealing with the immediate demands of children effectively denies teachers the time and resources, both personal and professional, needed to fashion, implement, test, and refine innovation in their own classrooms. Until that temporal tyranny is vanquished, U.S. education will improve only marginally.

The demands of time rule our schools in other, more subtle ways. Consider teachers' staple practice of asking questions. In several studies, researchers have counted the number of times in a normal classroom hour that teachers and students ask questions. Consistently, they find that teachers normally ask a hundred or more questions during an hour of classroom presentation. Students as a group ask an average of two questions during the same time.

There are several explanations, and many point to the pressures of time. "While children remain question-asking organisms," Sarason says, "they are learning that asking questions is not an especially rewarded behavior." Questions demanding lengthy or unstructured answers take precious class time—time the teacher needs to cover material that all students in the class must be exposed to before advancing to the next lesson, which is usually scheduled for the next day. The same studies show that most questions that U.S. teachers ask require only a quick answer based on recall. Typically, teachers also exhibit little patience in waiting for an answer. If a child doesn't produce the intended response within a few seconds, the teacher abruptly moves on to one of the other individual children competing to recite. A question that invites speculation or debate takes the class pace and agenda out of the teacher's hands and leads it in uncharted meanders away from the lesson plan. Children also have a habit of asking questions to which adults don't always know the answer—an event that teachers may regard as an embarrassing loss of authority and legitimacy with their students.

In much of Asia, as we've seen, teachers consider questions that provoke a quick response to be poor questions. Often, entire lessons are built around a single complex or multifaceted problem. Stevenson and Stigler cite the example of a fifth-grade teacher in Taiwan who showed a drawing of a six-sided figure to her class. She asked them to spend the class period working in groups to devise as many different ways as they could to measure the figure's area—not to actually measure it, but just to come up with different ways of structuring the task. After the children had proposed various approaches, the teacher closed the lesson by saying, "We have to remember that there is not only one way we can solve each problem." Such a "pointless" lesson that imparts no specific data or polishes no academic skills—such an indulgence in sheer creative thought—remains a rarity in American classrooms.

Teachers, trapped within the bounds that the school culture has laid down, can't be blamed for their behavior. In fact, Sarason tells of a group of teachers who, when confronted by the results of the question-asking study, began asking more probing questions in their classrooms. Unfortunately, says Sarason, even teachers willing to experiment run "smack into the obstacle of another characteristic of the school culture: there are no vehicles of discussion, communication, or observation that allow for this kind of variation to be raised and productively used for purposes of . . . change."[19]

Teachers have to fit their academic sessions around constant interruptions, from collecting permission slips for field trips and announcements over the schoolwide loudspeaker system to fire drills and disciplining disruptive children. It's rare for a teacher to cover fully in a day the lessons she'd planned. "For most teachers, daily demands crowd out serious sustained [reforms]," Michael Fullan says. "The circumstances of teaching . . . ask a lot of teachers in terms of daily maintenance and student accountability, and give back little in the time needed for planning, constructive discussion, thinking, and . . . composure"—the time to improve the processes of teaching and learning.[20]

TOO MANY CAPTAINS

When it comes to deciding the course of education, everyone wants to put a hand on the tiller. The resulting contest for control usually plays out in political arenas. State governments, for example, have always insisted on a voice in deciding what children within their borders will learn. California is only one state among many that once decreed that its schools should teach students to be kind to animals. Texas once passed a law mandating schools to set aside ten minutes a day for instruction in "intelligent patriotism," while Wisconsin's legislature once determined that students in its schools should be taught the value of dairy products.

States may change their curricular priorities from time to time, but they rarely ease their grip. As Fullan notes, "The biggest development on the educational scene in the last five years has been the increased presence and activity of the state." In response to the alarms sounded in *A Nation At Risk*, state governments boosted their education budgets by an average of 21 percent between 1982 and 1983 and again between 1986 and 1987. With more money came more state and federal mandates and regulations, and under that control education took on an increasingly political cast. Similar forces are at work in Canada. Michael Fullan reports that "nearly every province has taken to defining the curriculum more carefully over the last 15 years. Guidelines typically include a list of objectives, topics and content to be covered, and ideas and resource suggestions for teaching activities." U.S. states are equally vigilant. Many now determine which textbooks their school districts may choose among, mandate course content, and conduct their own standardized tests. The school district spreads another layer of control, shaping courses and charting curricular paths in detail. In that kind of multilevel hierarchy, innovations that challenge mandates sent down from above face an uphill fight for life.

So, often, do innovations that might require new forms of grading and evaluation. Those who don't know schools intimately might logically assume that tests are determined by what is taught. All too often, the reverse is actually the case: a curriculum is frequently shaped by the test that waits at the end of it. Teachers whose students don't perform well on standard national or statewide exams might find their professional fitness questioned, as do principals whose schools fall short. Some legislative reforms now propose to deny money to schools whose students underachieve according to broad-based norms. As a result, "teaching to the test" is a common, if subtle, form of political and cultural coercion on teachers when they plan their lessons. If there's class time left *after* a teacher has covered material that will appear in standard exams, then the teacher often will enrich the course with material of his or her own choosing. The reverse is seldom true. Until education hierarchies are more open and more flexible in their ideas of measuring the progress of learning, innovations routinely will be expected to fit neatly into existing testing patterns. Those that fail to do so will be too easily dismissed as vague or impractical.

A swarm of less obvious but no less insistent controls dictates the structures of teaching and learning. A single, outdated textbook can anchor a curriculum for years. Often such books have been specifically designed to exclude material that any interest group could find offensive. A new edition of a textbook can cost tens of thousands of dollars to create, millions to publish, and millions more out of school districts' perpetually strapped budgets to buy. A district, like a publisher, expects its investment in materials to last for years, a budgetary necessity that can freeze a curriculum in place until the textbook that defines it is revised or replaced.

By definition, a curricular innovation requires teachers to do something different in their classrooms. Because teachers are rarely given enough time or support to master new techniques and materials, they often ignore them in favor of methods and materials they know well and feel that they use most effectively—another source of curricular inertia. Not infrequently, an innovation rides into a school or district on the shoulders of a new superintendent or principal who champions the change and inspires (or orders) those lower in the chain of command to adopt it. But, far too often, that crucial advocacy quickly disappears. One study found that superintendents commonly leave one school district for another every three to five years. Often, a superintendent's tenure on the job is inversely proportional to his or her zeal as a reformer. A new administrator can slash funding for a predecessor's pet project or simply let it die from neglect. Any innovation not widely embraced by teachers and administrators has dangerously shallow roots.

SIX FALLACIES OF REFORM

The culture of the school isn't contained by the buildings' walls. It becomes a part of all of us who've spent time in traditional schools. During our formative years as students, most of us absorb the attitudes and assumptions of traditional education along with our spelling lists and multiplication tables. Like teachers, we still harbor those unconscious notions and apply them, unaware, as a sort of template to tell us what schooling should be like. Sarason emphasizes the monumental difficulty of escaping from the beliefs that one slowly, unconsciously, and therefore uncritically accumulates during those early years. Those assumptions can keep us from realizing that there can be valid alternatives to even the most basic norms of conventional education.

Reformers are no less human. Their efforts typically grow out of assumptions that hamper or even are antithetical to their objectives. As a result, reform suffers from innate cultural liabilities of its own, and innovations frequently fall victim to at least one of six fallacies all too common among reformers:

- ▸ *Reform begins in the classroom.*
- ▸ *Reform has to show results right away.*
- ▸ *Reform can't work unless we reduce class size.*
- ▸ *We can't afford it.*
- ▸ *Continuing education for working teachers is too expensive.*
- ▸ *Scores on standardized tests offer the best gauge of effective reform.*

Fallacy No 1: Reform Begins in the Classroom

Too many reformers have a limited idea of what education reform really means. Many who want to improve education in general don't understand that their first effort should be to improve their own knowledge and understanding of the reform process itself. We have encountered a surprising number of would-be reformers who haven't read the basic literature of school reform—the books by Sarason, Fullan, and others who have studied patterns of largely unsuccessful innovation in schools and have suggested ways to make change smoother and more effective. This is like someone wanting to become a successful architect without realizing that to do so one must understand in detail how sound buildings are constructed. Innovators who have struggled to "unlearn" their own lifelong assumptions and replace them with broader and more accurate ones will gain additional credibility and leverage in effecting reforms. By understanding what they're asking administrators, classroom teachers, and students to go through, they'll be able to structure and implement their innovations more knowledgeably and effectively than reformers who haven't experienced the personal turmoil of deep change.

That particular limitation stems partly from a broader assumption that's common not just among reformers: the idea that, while everyone else's education is shot full of flaws, one's own schooling has been first-rate. That premise feeds the widely held conviction that our education system used to be better than it is now. After all, if my education was good enough and my child's now isn't, schools must have deteriorated since I was in them. In truth, our schools aren't necessarily less effective than they used to be *in carrying on the kinds of teaching and learning they were established to do.* The problem is that we're now demanding that our schools educate every student in ways they haven't had to before.

It's not just a matter of teaching disciplines as higher-order skills. It's also the new urgency about integrating what's learned. Traditionally, as children progress through successive grades, knowledge and skills become increasingly compartmentalized. In science classes, students don't write; they solve equations. In English courses, students write essays about literature, not about mathematics. But, as the world becomes more complex and the pace of change quickens, graduates need to be able to coordinate an ever-expanding base of knowledge and skills. Research scientists must be able to explain their work plainly and clearly to public-interest groups. Journalists must be able to report accurately about the details and implications of complex technological change. Managers and technicians must be able to communicate and think through solutions to their common problems, whether they're about technical processes or policy issues.

Ironically, reformers themselves still tend to remain locked in a specialty instead of reaching beyond their disciplines to form networks that could sustain widespread innovation. Breadth and integration are no less crucial to education reformers than to research scientists, journalists, and managers. Too few reformers realize that schools will become steadily more effective only as isolated reforms are integrated into coordinated structures of linked, wide-reaching improvements.

Fallacy No. 2: Reform Has to Show Results Right Away

Many observers argue that our schools are in such desperate condition that we must initiate reforms that will deliver dramatic results right away—that we can't afford to deal in incremental change. That fallacy leaves educators, parents, and taxpayers prey to the Magic Bullet Syndrome, the idea that there's one "right answer" to school failure—bigger school budgets or parental choice, for example—that will, by itself, transform schools into institutions of excellence in short order. In reality, our schools' current shortcomings grow out of an intricate combination of several complex factors inside and outside of schools that have been decades in the making. Each of those factors needs to be addressed if all are to be changed. This can't be accomplished suddenly, nor by the rigorous application of a single idea.

Again, reformers who have struggled to overcome their own inherited assumptions about the nature of school and learning will be far better equipped to understand what others keep failing to grasp: that political and cultural barriers within education will always blunt the thrust of magic-bullet reforms. As Fullan and Sarason have shown, educational change is a process of cultural change, something that happens from the bottom up and not from the top down. It can be done, but it takes time and has rarely been accomplished effectively. Of course it's urgent to begin the process of reform. But the only truly effective reforms will be those that set out to reverse the continuing *long-term* decline of U.S. students' learning compared to the ever-changing and increasingly complex demands of the world in which they will live. That will be done most effectively and efficiently by a process of redesign and not by instant solutions, whether they come from within schools or from without.

Fallacy No. 3: Reform Can't Work Unless We Reduce Class Size

As one prominent U.S. innovator told us, "Everyone who knows what they're talking about [in education reform] says that you can't continue to have adult-student ratios that are around forty to one, as they are now in California. You just can't do that." Yet Asian schools do it all the time, and teach large groups of students far more effectively and efficiently than we teach small ones.

Our problem isn't simply that classes are too big. It's that we haven't mastered the teaching and learning techniques that allow larger-size classes still to be effective environments for learning. In U.S. schools, class sizes grow not by design but by accident—usually as a dreaded consequence of budget cuts or teacher shortages. In those circumstances, complaints that huge classes hamper learning are entirely accurate and justified: teachers aren't equipped with the resources and techniques that would allow them to turn large classes from disasters into opportunities to learn through new methods. An array of resources—including cooperative learning groups, certain applications of electronic technologies, and even parent volunteers and students themselves serving as co-instructors—can help teachers extend their reach and impact over larger classes, as we'll see in a later chapter. As part of a school-based redesign process, researchers must design, test, and perfect these and other methods of instruction that would allow larger classes to be just as effective learning milieus as smaller ones. Once teachers and administrators have proved tools to boost learning even among large groups, the issue of class size need no longer place limits on our concepts of reform.

Fallacy No. 4: We Can't Afford It

School boards and administrators too often see reform only as an immediate expense rather than as a source of long-term budgetary efficiencies and resulting savings. Education is now subject to numerous individual innovations, many of them worthwhile in some way, and each vying for a share of shrinking educational budgets at all levels. Instead of expediting comprehensive reform, such competition paralyzes it, for most individual reforms address only a small part of the overall problem in schools. One targets the middle-school science curriculum, for example, while another directs high-school English students to write more. Because each of those reforms is isolated and small in scope, logically each is entitled to only a small share of the scarce resources available to support reform—far less than each needs to grow and succeed.

There are two ways to escape this dilemma. One is to channel vast amounts of additional money into education reform. Given the condition of the U.S. economy and taxpayers' state of mind, that's not a politically realistic solution. The alternative is to develop a framework of reforms that can ultimately free more resources than they consume. Those newly freed resources can in turn support additional reforms.

A process of redesign can be the mechanism that creates these progressive efficiencies, as it does in industry. But the means will be distinctly different. Industry gains efficiency through standardization, mass production, and an increasing reliance on electronic technologies. Education will begin to gain efficiency as more effective methods of teaching and learning gradually supplant techniques that are less effective and currently leave too many students confused, untouched, or in need of remedial help. As educational redesign evolves, students also will benefit from teachers' growing assortment of resources and techniques, including students' ability to teach themselves and each other.

Those efficiencies will accelerate as redesign integrates the power of individual innovations. At first, the redesign process can develop ways that allow teachers to use specific types of reforms as elements in a single, coordinated structure of learning instead of piecemeal, as is now usually the case. As the process develops, it will integrate not just techniques, but also disciplines. For example, in science classes students might encounter a new emphasis on investigation and problem solving. That new emphasis would draw them deeper into mathematical calculation and reasoning. They might then be assigned to write an essay explaining the procedures they followed to reach their conclusion—in French. As more effective techniques intertwine, educational efficiencies will increase in tandem with students' achievement levels.

Fallacy No. 5: Continuing Education for Working Teachers Is Too Expensive

The fifth fallacy is coupled with the fourth and is common among administrators who hold the public purse: the notion that schools can't afford to pay for working teachers' ongoing professional study and improvement. The deep-seated cultural assumption underlying this fallacy is that properly structured professional development is an expense that's superfluous to effective reform instead of an investment essential to it. As the structure and results of Asian education indicate, though, investing in teachers' professional development is among the most cost-effective uses that schools can make of public money—one of the surest ways to use reform as a tool to free existing scarce resources for continuing innovation. Teachers who are always learning more effective ways to teach become steadily better able to teach more effectively and efficiently. Such teachers can work with larger groups at a time while still leaving fewer behind who require the expense of special help (or who drop out and thus waste many of the resources that schools have already expended on them). Unfortunately, so little attention has been paid to effective professional development for working teachers that few people or organizations know how to go about it. With the exception of the best workshops on cooperative learning, virtually no offerings now show teachers how to make the best use of the resources they already have.

Fallacy No. 6: Scores on Standardized Tests Offer the Best Gauge of Effective Reform

The final fallacy is less common among reformers than among the general public. It is easy to become trapped in the belief that standardized tests measure schools' effectiveness and that small changes in those scores have meaning. An educational consultant told us of attending a recent school board meeting at which an official touted as a "significant improvement" a two-point increase in high-school seniors' Scholastic Aptitude Test scores. Not only was the change actually insignificant in statistical terms, but also there was no evidence that the increase was part of any multiyear pattern. The consultant said that this board member "has enough background in statistics to know that. In part, he was playing up to the hopes and expectations of the board and the public."

Overemphasizing the significance of scores from standardized tests creates three problems. First, changes in the scores themselves offer no detailed clues to the problems that cause poor results or the practices that improve them. Instead, they divert attention from the classroom processes in which problems originate and through which they ultimately must be solved. Second, playing up the tests' importance stresses rote learning and test-taking skills, such as memorization, at the expense of the higher-order abilities that are far more important to learn but that are developed and measured through very different means. Third, the scores ignore the global context in which our graduates must compete. These tests tell us nothing about the performance of our students in relation to those of other countries with which we compete for scientific discoveries, patents, commercial technologies, or investment funds. Rising scores can too easily be taken to mean that our schools are improving in healthy and fundamental ways. They don't.

Taken together, these six fallacies form a hidden "culture of reform" that thwarts its own professed aims. No less than the traditional culture of the school, these unconscious assumptions have to be confronted openly and vanquished before meaningful, comprehensive reforms can progress.

THE KEY TO REFORM

The six fallacies are only some of the assumptions, common to educators, that stand in the way of genuine innovation. Each of those notions underscores a common point: schools don't naturally repattern themselves when they confront change. On the contrary, they tend by instinct to ensnare innovation in a cultural and political gridlock. That response, reflexive rather than calculated, is a form of self-defense, even self-preservation; as we've noted, culture is about continuity, not change. But these days, our schools need to be about change rather than tradition— the kind of change that a process of research, development, and redesign can build into schools as the framework for a system of continuous innovation. It's the only system of orderly change that confronts and transforms culture.

A school traditionally has been an uneasy federation of small, independent sovereignties, each wielding a measure of political power over educational structures and processes. Government regulators and local school boards have the power to lay down rules that school districts must obey. District administrators set policies that tell local schools how those rules are to be accommodated. Principals may choose to aid, resist, or disregard those directives—often in addition to making their own for teachers within their own schools to adhere to. Parents press demands of their own, from detailed ideological agendas to special privileges for individual children. Teachers, frequently granted tenure by law and unobserved behind the closed doors of their classrooms, can promote, resist, alter, or ignore virtually any change they choose as long as they don't actually violate laws. This long and unrelenting channel of political and cultural cross-currents awaits any innovation entering a traditional U.S. school.

The system of research, development, and redesign that industry relies on is a defined, orderly, institutionalized pattern of progressive change that routinely overcomes subjective and unpredictable human resistance to the new. When one searches for a comparable process in education, one finds only isolated pieces of it. Educational research is underfunded and often aimless or inexpert. Promising research results have no ranks of educational architects and instructional designers waiting to turn them into better classroom materials or techniques; instead, educational innovation remains a cottage industry of lone tinkerers—some highly skilled, some far less so—who work in isolation, too rarely communicating or collaborating to build on each other's progress. The only established marketing or technical-support agency waiting to transfer workable innovations to interested schools is tiny and fragmented. The overall result is a process of educational innovation and school reform that is random and chaotic, operating more by chance than by method. It shouldn't be a surprise to anyone that renewed pressures for change in our schools have led only to turmoil.

In part, that's been due to a power struggle. Some people, like the principal with his calculators, have tried to impose top-down change on teachers without giving them a role in planning. Teachers' resentment of that approach can color their attitude toward the reforms themselves. On the other hand, teachers who propose classroom reforms to administrators often find the same kind of resistance—a reluctance to disturb present routines and to make an investment in something untried and unproven. The knack of the redesign process is to defuse that struggle. When the process is fully developed, it draws everyone into a comprehensive approach to necessary change. Those involved have experienced the process of regular innovation, they expect it, and each person understands the specific role he or she is to fill in effecting it. They know that change means work and some difficulties, but they also know that redesign improves patterns and results enough that the work and trouble are more than justified by the effort's result. They also know that the redesign process itself will help them work through the trouble that accompanies change.

In education, such a redesign process can become the entryway for innovation backed by research. It would assemble, test, and refine successful experiments into comprehensive educational systems that schools and teachers could adopt knowing that the methods and results have been tested and proved. By acknowledging and addressing educators' complaints about previous designs, a system of redesign not only would improve educational quality, but would also give teachers a vital stake in guiding innovation and making it work. If a design doesn't meet their needs, the innovation's developer will be forced to redesign it in a way that makes it more useful and gives educators even fewer reasons to resist it. The process of research, development, and redesign can equip the conflict-ridden and change-averse school culture with a way to confront innovation without fearing it. When that culture adopts a proven system of change that doesn't threaten, progress finally becomes not only possible but assured.

6
Measuring Up

Assessment and Evaluation
in Educational Redesign

In the 1920s, pilot Wesley Smith wedged a half-full whiskey bottle on its side between his airplane's instrument panel and windshield. By flying the plane in a way that kept the liquid level along the bottle's length, Smith knew that he was keeping his plane's wings roughly parallel to the ground—information vital to a pilot's spatial orientation. His crude improvisation was one of the first cockpit instruments to measure an aspect of how a pilot and plane perform during a flight.

Now, to all but the trained an airliner's cockpit is a bewildering place. Dozens of gauges, dials, and videoscreens monitor the plane's cabin temperature, electrical functions, compass heading, altitude, exterior barometric pressure, and scores of other systems and factors moment by moment. In Boeing's 747 jumbo jet, cockpit instruments monitor more than 150 different variables at once, each with its own dedicated indicator. None is superfluous. A slight change in wind direction outside the plane demands a corresponding change in heading to keep the craft on course. A malfunction, even a small one, in any single subsystem could lead to disaster, either during the current flight or a later one. By spotting small problems and discrepancies as they occur, the plane's crew can take immediate corrective action or alert repair technicians later to minor troubles before they grow into major ones.

The specialized, sophisticated instrumentation that enables such close and constant scrutiny serves an equally crucial purpose in airplanes' progressive evolution: it separates genuine improvements from mere change. For example, suppose that an aircraft engineer has designed a new shape of wing that he says will allow planes to fly faster while using less fuel. Another engineer argues that it won't. The only way to find out who's right is to make exacting measurements—first through a series of complex calculations, and then by mapping the ways in which air flows over and around scale models of the new components in wind-tunnel tests. Finally, if a full-size prototype of the new design is built and flown, the ultimate proof is made aloft. The argument's final arbiters are the plane's airspeed and fuel gauges—more measuring devices.

Although that example is simplistic, its point is valid. In an effective redesign process, only changes that show measurable improvement over previous versions are embraced; proposed changes that are merely new without being better are shelved. Measurements and the instruments that make them are indispensable to the process of drawing those distinctions and are therefore indispensable in any process of continuous innovation.

Educators, too, must be able to make deft use of two complementary kinds of measuring devices: evaluation and assessment. The first, like an airplane's instrument panel, monitors the processes of education as they occur to determine if they're working as intended. The other, like an inspection after landing, assesses how well children have learned as a result of those processes. Without the first, innovators can't be sure that classroom processes are being carried out as intended; without the second, they won't be able to verify the processes' effectiveness and efficiency. By auditing process and result together, educators can gather the data that will allow them to invest consistently in improvement instead of squandering personal and public resources on the merely different.

It's important to recognize that assessing students' learning and evaluating classroom programs and techniques are halves of one whole; without the other, each loses much of its value as an indicator. Harold Stevenson and James Stigler demonstrated the relationship in collecting data for their book, *The Learning Gap*. Using carefully designed comparative tests, they were able to prove that Asian students consistently outperformed U.S. children in mathematics. But the tests didn't indicate why. To find out, they had to visit and observe Asian classrooms to see what processes were at work there that were missing from U.S. schools. Only when they'd witnessed those processes could they begin to draw preliminary conclusions about the relative value of different approaches to teaching. Conversely, if Stevenson and Stigler had only observed Asian teachers and noted differences between their approaches and those of U.S. educators without measuring results, they would have had no way of knowing whether those differences mattered in students' accomplishments. The moral of their method is clear: tests rarely disclose the reasons for their results and, similarly, no classroom observation can properly measure the effects of a given classroom process on learning. Only the two used together can do an adequate job of guiding the process of redesign.

Unfortunately, at a time when educators need new and better ways to assess learning and evaluate competing ideas, most of their measuring instruments remain about as subtle and sophisticated as Wesley Smith's whiskey bottle. They're also far more politically charged. A process of educational redesign will succeed only if it evolves subtler and more precise measurement tools while it evolves more effective and efficient approaches to learning.

TESTING, TESTING . . .

Currently, U.S. educators rely largely on a single, primitive implement to assess learning as well as to evaluate programs: the standardized multiple-choice test. It's a seductive tool—inexpensive for educators to administer and easy for regulators, funding agencies, and the public to use as a measure of educators' relative competence and students' year-by-year performances. As a result, such tests' use has more than doubled over the past decade as the public demands greater accountability among educators for children's learning, and they now cost U.S. schools more than a half-billion dollars each year to buy and process.[1] Experts estimate that the typical U.S. school child takes between two and three standardized tests every year, in addition to the parade of classroom exams that mark the end of learning units or textbook chapters—tests that often are closely patterned on standardized versions.

Ironically, as standardized tests have become more pervasive, they've also become far less meaningful. In the evolving process-oriented classroom, standardized exams are about as useful as Smith's old spirit level: they measure the kinds of knowledge that are becoming steadily less relevant to our new definition of education. The most widely used conventional standardized tests continue to measure fact retention and the isolated performance of rote skills. Most have not yet acknowledged the need to measure students' growth in the creative application of knowledge, or figured out how to do it. As a result, the tests that educators rely on to measure the effectiveness and efficiency of teaching and learning can't provide the very information they must have in order to make real improvements.

Although most educators admit the weaknesses (some would say the uselessness) of the form, its results continue to dominate the decisions they make. Largely on the basis of such results, students may be labeled as gifted or slow and tracked into limited or expansive programs; teachers may be singled out for leadership roles or their contracts may not be renewed; principals may be replaced or promoted; and schools or even entire districts may gain or lose a reputation or needed government funds. The enormous and often decisive power the tests wield in determining the shape of U.S. education is out of proportion to the little real learning they measure. *The Influence of Testing on Teaching Math and Science in Grades 4–12*, a 1992 Boston College study outlines the extent of the damage. "The tests most commonly taken by students— both standardized tests and textbook tests—emphasize and mutually reinforce low-level thinking and knowledge, and were found to have an extensive and pervasive influence on . . . instruction nationwide."[2]

The survey, funded by the National Science Foundation, categorized the questions on six standard, nationally administered mathematics and science tests published between 1984 and 1992 according to the kinds of thinking and knowledge being tested. It also scrutinized tests published as part of the most widely used U.S. textbook series in the subjects and found them "similar to standardized tests in content, format, and types of thinking [tested]." Its findings were unequivocal. In the mathematics tests, 97 percent of all questions tested what it called "low-level conceptual knowledge"—things like repeating memorized definitions or identifying concepts from a list of choices. Furthermore, 95 percent demanded only low-level thinking skills, such as remembering equations. Finally, between 87 and 92 percent of the questions were found to tap only low-level procedural knowledge, including solving problems using standard formulas and recognizing which operations to use in which circumstances. High-level knowledge and skills—reasoning, explaining procedures, creating examples, using models, or making judgments, for example—were targeted in 5 percent or fewer of the questions.

Science tests were found to be more demanding, but in only two of the three categories. In standard exams, 23 percent of the science questions tested higher-level conceptual knowledge, while 8 percent of textbook final tests did. Higher-order thinking skills occupied 27 percent and 10 percent of the questions respectively. But 92 percent of the questions in standardized tests and 95 percent in textbook finals didn't test procedural knowledge—an understanding of how science is done—at all.

"These tests do not meet current recommendations of science and math curriculum experts nationwide," the study reports. "[E]fforts to raise standards for math and science education *for all students* will be impeded unless serious efforts are taken to update [testing methods] in order to bring them in line with current recommendations."[3]

As part of its study, the group interviewed two hundred mathematics and science teachers and their principals in six different school districts. Often, half or more said that their students' scores on mandated, standardized achievement tests were "very important" tools used to assign students to academic tracks, judge their readiness for promotion or graduation, and to rate teacher, school, and district performance. Scores also become political capital; more than two thirds of those interviewed by the survey team reported pressure from district offices to ensure that students performed well on those tests. For example, in one district a certain proportion of students in each school must perform above a fixed level on a standardized test. If even one school's group doesn't, the district faces a state takeover. The district has been close to failing for several years and the pressure on teachers to guarantee student performance is overwhelming. However, nearly two thirds of the teachers queried believed that mandated testing programs have a negative effect on what they teach and on how well students learn. An elementary teacher said, "Lots of the time we're teaching to the test and students don't necessarily learn what they should because we're concerned with getting a certain score and a certain amount of money [from government funding agencies, on the basis of test scores]." The survey concluded, "Interviewees' remarks indicate that they experienced *conflict* between pressure for [high] test scores and their own ideas about tests and good educational practice."[4]

The custom of "teaching to the test" is pervasive. One fifth-grade teacher told researchers that "eighty to ninety percent of time in math is based on preparation for proficiency tests. Testing restricts my teaching to a narrow range of objectives. The exercises and tests are dull and unimaginative and do not encourage thinking or doing." Another fifth-grade teacher complained, "I'm working on a strict timetable to cover all of the objectives [represented in the standardized test]. . . . If I didn't have the strict schedule for the test I would stick with an area until the students got it." Almost half of the teachers interviewed reported that they teach material they wouldn't otherwise handle in class simply because upcoming standardized tests include the material, or that the tests determine the relative emphasis they place on some things. The same proportion also admits taking time away from substantive coursework in order to teach test-taking skills.

The damage wrought by pervasive standardized testing is even worse in schools with high proportions of minority students. The survey found that teachers in such schools are far more likely to teach to the test and drill students in test-taking skills than are teachers in schools with white student majorities. "Between the first week in January and the second week of March when the test was given, I and most other teachers *suspended* our curricula and prepared for the test," reports one inner-city elementary-school teacher. Ironically, the push to improve minority students' test scores actually can deny them the remedial help they need to succeed academically. "Kids in the seventh and eighth grades have very limited skills and definitely need basic skills [instruction]," a junior-high teacher said of her minority students, "but because they've been crammed and prepared, their scores [on mandated standard tests] are too high and therefore they're not eligible for [extra help with] basic skills, and this is a tragedy because they need [that help] very badly."[5]

The survey warns of "a gap in instructional emphases between high- and low-minority classrooms that conflicts with our national concern for equity in the quality of education. . . . In other words, the negative consequences that many . . . researchers have found regarding the increasing role, amount, and stakes of standardized testing is significantly worse for minority classrooms."[6] More broadly, they can do no good for any students as long as antiquated forms of assessment are expected to guide new forms of teaching and learning.

TESTING FOR MASTERY

Recently, though, an insurgency has sprung up. Innovative educators are developing new tests that can measure students' ability to think and to apply their skills to real problems. California's statewide twelfth-grade mathematics test asks students to find inaccuracies in equations or diagrams and to explain in writing why they're wrong; a Connecticut exam requires students to design the biggest possible dog pen using eighty feet of fencing and to write a short essay defending their designs. Even the national Scholastic Assessment Test (SAT) taken by college-bound high-school seniors has been redrafted to emphasize reasoning and comprehension and has dropped multiple-choice mathematics questions so students have to create their own answers. "The standardized-test movement is beginning to retreat," says Robert Slavin, the noted educational innovator at Johns Hopkins University who developed the Success For All program. "But it's so far advanced that even in retreat it's far stronger than its opposition. The trend is in the right direction, but it's still comparatively small."[7]

The insurrection is being led by two new forms of assessment. Although they're designed explicitly to gauge students' abilities to think, analyze, adapt, and integrate their knowledge and skills, the new methods also are proving to be a formidable means by which teachers can shape new, more useful ideas of what education means.

Around the country, a number of high schools are beginning to replace their usual final exams with "exhibitions" or "mastery demonstrations" for graduating seniors. The approach has been championed by the Coalition of Essential Schools, an informational network of more than 150 diversely innovative schools organized by noted reformer Theodore Sizer, professor of education at Brown University. The coalition has made student exhibitions, which it likens to music recitals or athletic performances, the capstone of a process it calls "planning backwards."

According to a 1992 Coalition paper "Steps in Planning Backwards," written by Coalition senior researcher Joseph McDonald, when a school begins the process of planning backward, its teachers "[set] aside temporarily [conventional ideas of] what is broadly called curriculum and instead simply imagine the school's candidates for graduation using their minds well. In its mind's eye, the school struggles to acquire a vision of integrated intellectual performance, unfogged by Regents exams, state curriculum requirements, Carnegie units, and SAT formulas."[8] In that vision, one candidate for graduation might field questions from outside experts on a subject the candidate has studied in depth. Another might write a collection of essays about the relationships and meanings of a series of books she's read. "Perhaps they do this in two languages," McDonald writes. "Perhaps they show the sculpture they've created, the boat they've built, the technology they've contrived to solve a problem. Whatever the particularities of the vision, the kids who animate it handle themselves in ways that make their teachers proud."[9]

In most participating schools, a student's exhibition takes the form of an interdisciplinary project similar in process to a doctoral thesis. The subjects are broad; at one school, a senior set out to learn exactly how pure the local water supply was, while another investigated the ways in which local courts dealt with child abuse cases. Others detailed the problem of cholesterol in the American diet, conflicting issues in waste recycling, and the causes and effects of change within a culture. As a final effort, seniors produce an artifact—a written report, a multimedia presentation, an object they've built, a design—and make a presentation about their project to a faculty committee, which sometimes includes subject experts or others from outside the school. As part of the presentation, they're expected to field questions and critiques from committee members.

A school's decision to use exhibitions as a measure of learning becomes a decision to reinvent itself as well. As McDonald points out in his 1991 Coalition paper, "Exhibitions: Facing Outward, Pointing Inward," exhibitions as an assessment tool "provoke healthy skepticism about the traditional means of instruction. If what is wanted is kids who think things through, write well, speak persuasively, act with confidence, work well with others, trust their intuition, and so on, how much practice with these things can they gain by sitting silently in large groups most of their days?"[10] The move to exhibitions typically is followed by a proliferation among the lower grades of interdisciplinary classes and projects, seminars, workshops, group coaching, and other nontraditional teaching methods.

At Hodgson Vocational-Technical High School in Newark, Delaware, a Coalition member, the faculty found that exhibitions "encouraged us to rethink our entire curriculum," a committee of teachers wrote in a Coalition report. "If all seniors . . . must do this exhibition . . . then it makes sense to prepare underclassmen for the demands of long-term research . . . and public demonstration. . . . To this end, starting in ninth grade, we began to ask students to perform tasks—individually and in groups—that require the same skills they will to employ as seniors."[11] Teachers at Thayer Junior-Senior High School in Winchester, New Hampshire, settled on a list of abilities they deemed essential for graduating seniors to demonstrate, then broke apart the traditional subject-defined curriculum and reorganized it around six skill groupings: literacy, expression, ethics and values, personal proficiency, problem-solving, and cultural awareness. Those kinds of changes begin to break down the assumptions that have rendered schools immune to change for so long. "Most significant . . . has been an alteration in the faculty's perception of our students' abilities," Eileen Barton, a teacher at Chicago's Sullivan High School, says in the report. "Prior to instituting the exhibition, we had focused on the differences in [students'] academic preparation and achievement and had assumed that these differences should guide the revision of our instructional program. Consequently, we were tailoring our curriculum to address student weaknesses rather than strengths. In instituting 'Diploma by Exhibition,' we . . . reversed our emphasis."[12] Under an exhibition program, according to Coalition researcher Jody Brown Podl, "Students become more invested in their studies; teachers function more as advisors and coaches than disseminators of information; subject matter is connected to students' lives and its interdisciplinary nature is tapped; [and] schedules become more flexible in order to allow for sustained inquiry and coaching."[13]

Schools inside and outside the Coalition are testing another promising new assessment technique: judging portfolios of students' collected works. Vermont has launched a statewide initiative to grade students by their portfolios instead of by their performances on gang pencil-and-paper tests, while Arizona and other states are developing similar schemes. Among the most advanced portfolio programs in the United States is the one at Central Park East Secondary School in New York City, a school whose students are largely minority and poor.

When the school opened in 1985, the faculty agreed that students' progress would be gauged by their growth in five "habits of mind": the ability to weigh evidence, an awareness of varying viewpoints, the power to discern connections and relationships, the imagination to speculate intelligently about possibilities, and an understanding of personal and social values. Project by project and grade by grade, each student builds a body of work that demonstrates growth in the five habits across fourteen areas of academic and personal challenge. The school assesses student performances using a grid system that translates teachers' judgments of a student's skill and understanding in each area into ratings points. During each school year, those ratings, along with the substance of a student's work, are reviewed and critiqued at two individual conferences that bring together student, parents, and faculty advisor. Ultimately, each senior researches and presents a major interdisciplinary project to a faculty committee.

Like any approach to testing, though, demonstrations and portfolios bring problems that aren't easily resolved. Most schools using the new methods still must translate their subjective judgments into the traditional letter grades demanded by their district or state. Teachers who plan backward argue almost constantly about the fairest and most accurate ways to quantify and systematize their subjective judgments of quality. At the same time, most want to avoid the kind of standardization they set out to escape. "At the committee meetings that evaluate portfolios, how much do you want to know about a kid?" says Paul Schwarz, codirector of the school's portfolio project. "Do you want to know that this is the work of a learning-disabled kid who's been raising his three brothers and sisters in extreme poverty, or that this is an upper-class kid who's had a private tutor all his life? Those are the kinds of issues we spend a lot of hours on. If all you care about is a score of twelve hundred on the SAT, that's easy. But if you care about setting real standards for real people who can do real thinking, you're going to be talking among yourselves all the time."[14]

In doing so, broader questions about the structure and application of standards can spark harsh controversies among faculty members. Jody Podl notes that "schools that plan backwards are constantly in motion, and the motion is not always forward. . . . Planning backwards can be messy, and sometimes even turbulent." Thayer High School committed itself to the idea of a "skills-based diploma" in 1986 and still finds that "many stumbling blocks remain," according to mathematics teacher Julie Gainsburg. The Watkinson School in Hartford, Connecticut, began converting to an exhibition-based curriculum in 1987. After four years of constant work, a 1992 faculty report declared, "We have the framework established. . . . Now, we need to make it happen."[15] Virtually all schools that try the techniques have institutionalized some means, usually special committees or regular facultywide meetings, to monitor the program and make constant adjustments.

Ultimately, that process leads educators to reflect on the effectiveness of their own techniques and processes. One Coalition school requires each student to present not only a final exhibition, but also a portfolio that documents the project's evolution: notes from interviews and readings, drafts of a paper, and so on. "A portfolio of this kind, to be worth the trouble it takes to keep and review, will be more than the documentation of a performance," McDonald says. "It will be the documentation of a *coached* performance—an artifact of teaching as well as learning." Indeed, judging exhibitions and portfolios "is a sort of moment of truth for all parties to the teaching and learning process," notes Linda Darling-Hammond, a professor of education at Columbia University's Teachers College who has followed Central Park East's progress. "There is no escaping what's worked, what hasn't worked, and what needs more work." As a result, the schools' teachers are constantly working together to re-create their curricula, reshuffle academic schedules, groom their coaching skills, and refine their standards. New assessment tools become the tools of collaborative redesign and program integration. McDonald notes that they also can help innovators to answer "two complexly intertwined questions: What can these kids do now that I've taught them? What can I learn from what they show me?"

ONWARD AND UPWARD

Although planning backward engages teachers in a rudimentary process of redesign, it can't dissect classroom processes of teaching and learning with the objectivity and detail of a formal program evaluation. Evaluations are conducted by specialists, usually professors and graduate students from a university. In a typical evaluation, they first interview teachers and administrators at length to learn the aims and goals of the program they're to evaluate as well as the purpose of the evaluation itself. Next, evaluators administer "pretests," sometimes custom-designed, to measure children's understanding and skill in an area they're about to study using the program, technique, or set of materials being evaluated. As the course proceeds day by day, evaluators observe and record events, incidents, and impressions ranging from how children seem to react to different aspects of the material and the way it's taught to how class time is spent. When the course ends, evaluators administer a "posttest," also perhaps custom-tailored, to gauge the impact of the instructional approach under study. They then sift, organize, and interpret the statistical data they have gathered and combine it with in-depth narrative descriptions and their personal analyses of things they have observed. Finally, evaluators meet with teachers, administrators, and other officials to discuss their findings. "When it's done right, the process can tell you a tremendous amount about how well a program meets its objectives," Robert Slavin says.

Most educators believe that program evaluations are done right more often now than they used to be. During the late 1970s and through the 1980s, evaluators began to move beyond the traditionally rigid framework of statistics and scientific method. They began talking with teachers and students, writing narratives of what was happening in classrooms, and paying closer attention to the more subjective aspects of quality. "That's become the standard approach," says Dr. Eva Baker, a UCLA professor of educational psychology and director of the Center for Research on Evaluation, Standards, and Student Testing. "Most evaluations integrate different approaches to data collection. There is interpretive and quantitative information, such as test scores, structured observations, and other data that can be crunched objectively. If a study doesn't have those things, it's considered soft. But we've also become more anthropological—talking with people over time to see how their ideas change, using videotapes, testimonials, and similar things that give human dimensions instead of just abstract statistics."[16]

There seems to be consensus among educators that evaluators' repertoire of techniques enables them to design focused, detailed evaluations and draw accurate conclusions about most aspects of any educational program. "We don't lack evaluation methods," Slavin says. "But are they put into practice? Rarely. Most schools have never seen a real evaluation."

There are three reasons. The first is simply one of cost. "We used to joke about our standard ten-thousand-dollar evaluation study," Baker recalls, "which meant that you bought one arm of a graduate student and a little supervisory time." A thorough study of a single, multischool program by topnotch investigators can take months and easily could cost a school district more than it spends in a year to operate the program itself. "Evaluation is very expensive to do right," Slavin says, "so people often don't do it at all." The second reason, which is political, often renders the trouble and expense of evaluations pointless. "Evaluators are driven by technical concerns and the effort to do a good job," Baker says. "But the people using evaluations' results have more often used them to rationalize whatever political decisions they're making. So—big surprise—the results of program evaluations haven't always been used to formulate policy decisions [that logically follow from those results]. Policymakers begin, continue, expand, or end programs for political and constituency reasons, not necessarily because of the program's effectiveness." Third, while the field of evaluation is rich in theory and technique, it lacks expert evaluators who have been seasoned on the job. Because there's little demand for on-site program evaluations, relatively few people have done many of them—compared, for example, to the numbers of people designing and interpreting standardized tests. As a result, the effectiveness and efficiency of most recent school reforms have never been formally and expertly scrutinized. Testimonials and tales of success might abound for a given innovation, but that only serves to sustain education's chronic assumption that enthusiasm is an acceptable substitute for evidence. "If people are willing to accept poor or no evaluations, as is common in education, then the demand and resources for better evaluations won't be forthcoming," Slavin warns.[17]

MEASURING UP

In traditional schooling, the measurement of learning typically is viewed as yet another isolated event. Tests are given, results are gathered and compared with a few previous years' scores, and alarms or comfort levels are raised. There things usually rest until the next batch of scores is collected. There are no continuing links that join test scores, program evaluations, and the practice of teaching in an ongoing, conscious process of improvement.

In contrast, the redesign process recognizes measurement as a permanent research program that's as vital as a heartbeat. "The development of curriculum . . . should be guided by knowledge of what students know and can do, rather than by assumptions about what they should know and should be able to do," writes Dr. Lillian McDermott, leader of the University of Washington's Physics Education Group, in a 1992 paper, "Research as a Guide for Curriculum Development." "Although short-answer responses can give an indication of how pervasive a particular error may be, they do not provide sufficiently detailed information to be helpful in curriculum development."[18] Redesign's chief task is to test one idea against another and to select those that confer the most effective and efficient results; assessment and evaluation make up the single multifaceted tool that educational redesign must rely on to make those judgments. Unfortunately, our present level of skill in educational measurement is crude compared to the long-term demands that the redesign process will make on it. Consequently, a continuous three-part research program in educational measurement is integral to the success of redesign in education.

First, any such research program will need to forge new techniques to measure subtle differences in quality among varying classroom approaches directed toward the same goal—for example, which ways of teaching mathematical reasoning, beginning reading, or American history are the most effective. That won't be as easy as it might sound. In the aircraft industry, a relatively simple mechanical device tells engineers that one airplane cruises at a steady 600 miles an hour while another can't top 580. There is, however, no device to attach to students' minds that tells educators that one textbook or teaching technique delivers six hundred units of educational value while another delivers twenty fewer units. Nevertheless, the process of progressive improvement in schools increasingly will depend on innovators' ability to recognize and incorporate exactly that kind of small, subtle gain. In the early stages of educational redesign, only sizeable performance gains—perhaps 25 percent or more—will register consistently on our currently primitive educational "instrument panel." If the redesign process is to succeed in education, that low level of sophistication won't be useful for long.

The three-part research program's second facet grows out of the first: evaluators will need to develop ways to measure innovations' relative cost efficiencies. To understand why, consider again that twenty-point difference in airplane speeds. If a design change allows a plane to increase its speed from 580 to 600 miles an hour without using more fuel, it's a gain of barely 3 percent—seemingly trivial. But when the resulting gains in fuel efficiency and travel time are multiplied over dozens or hundreds of planes and millions of passenger flights, the resulting economy becomes huge, and well worth the investment needed to incorporate the design change in future models and give them an added competitive advantage. Similarly, industrial engineers may invest a good deal of effort to figure out how to shave a fraction of a cent from the cost of processing a part without reducing its quality. If that part is to be replicated millions of times—as many auto parts are, for example—a manufacturer is wise to invest a sizeable sum to achieve such an incrementally small savings.

Although such incremental efficiencies can add up to similarly sizeable savings in education, they're harder to create with present tools. If a school shaves a fraction of a penny from a dollar's worth of instructional costs, educators' "instruments" can't measure the saving's impact—if, indeed, there is one—on the quality of teaching or learning. Without sensitive detectors, educators will be far less able to identify those innovations that yield the subtle, progressive cost efficiencies that ultimately will make school-based redesign cost-efficient. Only large-scale efficiencies, such as those that Reading Recovery now affords, show up on today's educational measuring gauges. That may be adequate at the moment, but it won't be later.

The research program's third task is to refine the ability to conduct detailed, internally consistent evaluations of single programs at work in diverse communities and classrooms in hundreds of districts and dozens of states. There's more at stake here than replacing political favoritism or expediency with objective measurement. Redesign's purpose is not only to select the most useful ideas, but also to foster their adoption in all schools that wish to use them *while maintaining a consistently high level of effectiveness and efficiency at all sites*. The greater the number and diversity of the students, teachers, and communities involved in testing an innovation, the clearer the innovation's inherent power, or lack of it, becomes.

As an example, imagine that you have just invented the first thermometer for measuring human body temperature. You slip it under your tongue and discover that your own temperature is 98.6°F. It's a meaningless number because you have nothing to compare to it. You take your lab assistant's temperature: also 98.6°. But there still are too many unanswered questions to allow you to draw conclusions. For example, you're both adult males; perhaps all adult males have a body temperature of 98.6°, but women's and children's are different—or perhaps your temperatures are the same because you've been working closely together and you've both caught the same illness. You find that your parents and your sister have the same body temperature as you, but even then you can't form a conclusion: perhaps temperature varies from one gene pool to another, and the fact that your assistant's is the same as yours means that the two of you are cousins. You take the temperature of everyone in your town—all the same, 98.6°F. But you live in Denver, Colorado, a mile above sea level. What if human body temperature increases or decreases with altitude? To establish the normal temperature of the typical, healthy human being, you'd be obliged to record temperatures among both genders, among different races, among meat-eaters and vegetarians, among the athletic and the sedentary, among the young, middle-aged, and elderly, and so on. To approach validity, your study would have to measure as many people—and as many different kinds of people—as possible, so any anomalies are overwhelmed by the increasingly huge number of similarities. (Suppose, for instance, that altitude *did* affect body temperature. You would still need a large sampling to effectively overwhelm this anomaly and establish it as such.) The larger the population involved, the more accurate the results will be.

Educational measurement poses similar challenges of breadth but far greater ones of complexity. As we have seen, each teacher relies on his or her individual strengths, style, and personality to foster learning in students. One educator might find a particular technique or approach very comfortable, even energizing, while another might find it awkward; their students' learning will rise or fall in some degree as a result. Also, individual students will react in differing ways to the same material, program, or method. Only by surveying large numbers of diverse classrooms can educators begin to measure the effects inherent in a given innovation itself and not merely students' or teachers' reaction to it.

Redesign's power to improve learning's effectiveness and efficiency nationwide rests largely on its power to draw that distinction. For that reason, the more teachers and students are at work evaluating innovations, the faster the power of the redesign process will grow.

THE KEY TO REFORM

Any effective system of redesign recognizes that process is inseparable from result. Consequently, education must learn to measure each as an aspect of the other to calculate accurately the impact of classroom changes. However, it's clear that conventional methods of assessment and evaluation—chiefly standardized tests and costly customized studies—aren't capable of the novel, precise, and sophisticated measurements on which a national process of educational redesign must rely for guidance. In assessment, educators are only beginning to test new tools for judging students' mastery of higher-order skills. In evaluation, too few specialists can expertly compare the subtleties of competing programs against a common quality standard. Besides, a shortage of resources continues to prevent evaluators from using their range of skills to measure differences in quality among the hundreds of classrooms in different districts, states, and regions that adopt a single program.

Because the dynamics of classrooms' changing processes must be scrutinized as often and as closely as their results, a program of educational redesign must include the recruitment and training of a new kind of educational measurement specialist. First, such specialists must be experienced and competent teachers. The most effectively structured student assessments will be designed by people with a deep and intuitive understanding of how teachers, students, and materials interact. Evaluators who have a visceral grasp of the classroom's rhythms and dynamics also will be far better able to interpret and balance the subjective and objective judgments that make up a thorough program evaluation.

Second, those who design the tools of educational measurement must understand that education's effectiveness is swayed strongly by factors beyond the classroom. Students in an upper-middle-class suburb may well respond quite differently to a given innovation than might inner-city minority children. Just as it takes specialists in physics education to evaluate fully the value of an innovative physics curriculum, the best program evaluations will be developed by specialists with intimate understandings of the communities in which those evaluations are being made. In recruiting a new corps of evaluation specialists, education must reach into all sectors of the population.

Third, measurement specialists must work alongside innovators throughout the process of invention. Instead of judging an innovation's efficacy only after teachers and researchers have invested their energy and time to create it, those specialists must weigh and question design choices continually as each innovation takes form. Close collaboration between impassioned designers and cool observers can skirt design problems before flawed concepts waste precious resources.

Finally, educators not only will need to craft precise new ways to determine specific innovations' relative values; they also must devise accurate methods by which to monitor and guide education's approaches to the redesign process itself. Schools' new emphasis on improving educational processes also means continuing to improve the processes of reform.

7

Enacting the New Paradigm

New Structures of the Redesigned School

A paradigm—whether it's democratic self-government, atomic theory, or a new concept of education—is an abstraction. It might be an abstraction capable of changing the world, but it's still an abstraction. Tapping an abstraction's power in ways that make practical differences in people's lives requires building human structures that enact it. In the case of democratic self-government, those structures encompass a written constitution, a body of laws, and a schedule of free elections. The structures that make atomic theory meaningful include a theoretical framework, the body of results from experiments, and a commonly agreed upon set of procedures that allow comparison of the two. In education, we're already beginning to see the structures that can bring a new paradigm to life.

These structures are the handful of reform initiatives that, in a realm where failure is the norm, show early signs of long-term success in changing the ways in which teachers and students work together. They're not part of any broad-scale, nationally mandated programs. Rather, they've been crafted on a smaller scale, independent of each other, each one a particular solution to an individual need rather than as the answer to a multifaceted national problem. But in these cases, small doesn't mean insignificant. The informal evidence that these initiatives work is fourfold:

❶ They improve the quality of life in school for teachers and for students by making school a more exciting, involving place to be.

❷ They seem to make many kinds of learning more effective and efficient and thus raise student achievements in a widely diverse assortment of classrooms.

❸ They thrive and grow, moving from school to school and state to state because educators and students—not just regulators or academic theorists—champion them. (Reading Recovery and its comprehensive, continuous teacher-training process is among the best examples of a reform that meets these three tests.)

❹ They make it possible for teachers to handle larger classes without sacrificing their effectiveness.

These tools can enable teachers to reach more students with a wider variety of learning skills and styles than they have been able to previously.

Even when used separately, each of these techniques brings a new effectiveness to teaching and learning. The processes collectively known as *Total Quality Learning*, or TQL, let students and teachers tailor lessons to students' needs and abilities without compromising course content or student performance, and usually enrich both. *Teachers empowered to work collaboratively* capitalize on each other's creative imaginations and practical wisdom, replacing weaker lessons and techniques with more effective ones learned and developed from their source of choice— colleagues. The insights of *cognitive science* can show educators how to structure lessons and courses that work with, not against, natural mental processes, while capitalizing on students' inherent strengths and pinpointing their weaknesses. *Cooperative learning* lets children teach each other, and themselves in the process, while fostering mutual support and easing the fears and distractions of traditional classroom competition. *Electronic technologies* can give students control of the means of learning, which lets them not only optimize the pace of their own studies but also broaden and deepen their access to diverse sources of knowledge.

Unfortunately, these efforts have no means to coordinate the integrated structures of the new paradigm that needs to rise from their groundwork. One innovation addresses one group of problems in one group of schools, another in another. They're not linked; they have no way to leverage each other's insights and expertise into a coordinated, dynamic, more complex pattern of compound change. But these few exceptional reforms can serve as cornerstones of the foundation on which to begin to build a process of educational redesign. That process can integrate these efforts through the new paradigm's overarching vision and build from them schools in which the new paradigm is made real.

TOTAL QUALITY IN THE CLASSROOM

Candace Allen had good news and bad news about her 1991 ninth-grade world geography class at Pueblo, Colorado, Centennial High School. The good news was that fewer kids were failing her course than were failing most others in the school. The bad news was that nearly a third of her students still weren't making a passing mark. Schoolwide, the students' failure rate was close to half.

Because her students expressed ongoing concern about their grades, she asked those earning steady As and Bs to list on the blackboard the kinds of things they did to keep their grades up—studying a half hour every night, using the dictionary to learn the meaning of new terms, and so on. Using these tips, many of the lagging students turned in better performances for a few days or weeks, but soon they seemed more lackadaisical than before. After talking with a friend who is also an education consultant, Allen decided she'd been pursuing the wrong goal. Instead of focusing on ways to raise students' grades, she decided to concentrate on changing her classroom approach, the actual process of learning, in ways that offered her students a new definition of success.

She began with the assignment the class was working on at the time. They were to use the school library's resources to answer twenty-five questions about Central and Eastern Europe, then use what they'd learned to predict the region's future. When she asked them if they were having trouble with the assignment, the students responded with an emphatic "yes!" She asked them to describe the problems they were having and listed their responses on the blackboard: the library's materials were inadequate, there were too many questions, the assignment itself was overwhelming, and more than a dozen others.

Then Allen made a leap of faith. Instead of just restructuring or abandoning the lesson, she asked the students themselves to figure out ways to improve the course's processes of learning, using this assignment as an example. First, the class broke into committees. One committee worked on ways to address the library's inadequacies, another on the tactical problems created by the twenty-five questions themselves, another on ways to interest students in the assignment. When the class reconvened, Allen and her students haggled at length and finally agreed on a new learning process. Among its components: Students would have a voice in deciding what was to be studied and in shaping their lessons and assignments. Instead of being handed letter grades by the teacher, students largely would set their own measures and standards of performance. Each student's ultimate grade would be determined jointly by the teacher and the individual student, measuring a student's work against standards of quality the students themselves laid down.[1]

The results surprised everyone. "At the end of two weeks, she had students coming to her saying, 'Some of the other kids still aren't getting it; what can we do to help them?' " says Margaret Byrnes, the consultant and former classroom teacher who helped Allen develop her new approach.[2] Her students became so involved in their work that many reported to Allen at the close of the school year that they were sorry to see the class end.

The progress of Allen's students mirrored her own as a teacher. She began the 1991 school year with a grading scale that assigned letter grades on the basis of the percentage of questions a student answered correctly. The next year, her written grading policy stated that "grading and ranking of students will not be a primary activity" and that when evaluation is called for, "student self-assessment is as critical . . . as Mrs. Allen's assessment." Every three weeks, each student assesses his own progress in attitude, working with others, and doing quality work in geography. The student rates his strong and weak points and then sets out a plan for the next three weeks to improve in all three areas. Because the class lives within a school system that still relies on traditional A-to-F grading scales, Allen confers with each student individually to work out a letter grade equivalent to the quality of work the student has done. "A lot of teachers are afraid that if you give students real power, they'll turn on you," Byrnes says. "That, for example, if kids define their own standards, they'll just try to get away with easier work. But that's not what happens. Kids *want* to work, but at meaningful things. When they have input into defining the goals, they buy into those goals."

Candace Allen's class is one among a growing group that has been transformed by the principles of Total Quality Management. In a small but expanding number of U.S. schools, TQM (or TQL, for "Total Quality Learning") is beginning to redefine classroom norms and practices in radical ways. *Beginning,* however, is the operative term. "We're all still in preschool when it comes to TQL," says David Langford, a former classroom teacher who's now a TQL consultant based in Billings, Montana. "But from what we've seen in the schools that have done it well and taken it the farthest, TQL has a consistent power to change teaching and learning for the better."[3]

The fourteen specific concepts and techniques of Total Quality Management were formulated by U.S. engineer W. Edwards Deming shortly after World War II to reduce the number of defective products rolling off assembly lines. Demings's ideas were ignored by U.S. industry, but not by war-torn, desperate Japan. In the decades since, Japan has made TQM a cornerstone of its industrial triumph. Most programs adapting TQM to use in classrooms incorporate all fourteen points, but modify them a bit to make each more relevant and useful to education. To detail all fourteen is beyond our present scope, but most of TQL's key ideas can be grouped under three broad headings. First, the quality process gives students meaningful authority and responsibility to determine the shape and course of their own learning. Second, TQL abolishes the traditional emphasis on outcomes—grades, test scores, and so on—and focuses instead on improving the classroom processes by which learning takes place. When that's done effectively, TQL's disciples say, outcomes will improve inevitably. Third, the technique drives fear out of learning. It deemphasizes competitive grading and testing in favor of new kinds of assessments, which students themselves help to design and which allow all students to succeed in measureable terms.

The first step to quality, power sharing between students and adults, shatters the wall that typically bars teachers and students from talking openly about what goes on in their own classrooms. It's not uncommon for teachers to work in earnest, believing that their students aren't interested in learning, while at the same time their students don't understand the material, why they should study it, or just what the teacher expects them to do with it. Hour after classroom hour is wasted, when an open and continuing dialogue could turn those hours to opportunities for real and enthusiastic learning.

Langford first began to dismantle that wall in a business course he was teaching at Mount Edgecumbe High School outside of Sitka, Alaska. A boarding school for the children of indigenous Alaskans, Mount Edgecumbe quite possibly is the nation's most advanced experiment in TQL.

Langford, credited with initiating TQL at Mount Edgecumbe in 1987, had read about TQM and talked about it with business executives. When his class's performance lagged, he decided to test TQM's efficacy in schools. "I said to the kids, 'look—I've done about everything I can think of to improve this class and it's not working very well,'" he remembers. "I don't know what else to do and I need your help." He explained the quality process to them and said, "We can all learn how to manage this classroom in a whole different way and, by doing so, you can learn the techniques that you're going to need to know when you graduate, because military and business organizations all over the world are turning to this process and you need to understand it." Just as Candace Allen found, the classroom came to life. "We'd have discussions about quality by the hour," Langford says. "The students came in at night, on weekends, using their own time to work on this and figure out how to use it and apply it." In the process, they were gathering and analyzing information, writing, debating, and gaining practice in inventing solutions to real-life problems and shaping change.

A teacher who cedes that kind of genuine classroom power to students is making, says Langford, "a leap of faith that's fundamental to TQL. It was a radical step for me to acknowledge that my students had brains." He is quick to admit the statement's implications: "If that sounds strange, it's because we've set up the entire educational process on the assumption that they don't. We tell them to throw their brains in the trash when they walk into class, sit down, shut up, do what I tell you when I tell you, and everything will be all right. But it's not all right. We end up with five or ten percent of the kids who can do that really well and we waste the other ninety percent. When I opened up these lines of communication and started talking to my students like they were real people, they started giving me real answers and real ideas."

Langford and his students had discovered one of TQL's key points of leverage. When teachers and students share equal power in the pursuit of quality, they also begin to share an explicit common purpose—often for the first time. Conventional classrooms typically are fraught with conflicting agendas. Some teachers see their chief mission as discipline and control; most want to pursue their individual visions of effective teaching; while a few try to get through their days with as little effort as possible. A few students are out to collect straight As, others want to learn what they can, and a handful express contempt or apathy toward everything that "school" represents. TQL has the power to break down those barriers and unite teachers and students in the common pursuit of excellence—a unity essential to innovation's success.

With shared power, though, comes shared responsibility. "When you tell students to pursue external standards, they have no particular reason to be motivated—other than those who are competitive about grades," Byrnes says. "When students develop their own standards, you see two results. First, teachers learn that their students usually have higher standards and expectations for themselves than teachers ever do. Second, when the standards come from the students themselves, students have a stake in the outcome. They're motivated. The class becomes tremendously focused, discipline problems disappear, and kids actually begin to learn things." Adults do, too. "With TQL, my whole job changed," Langford says. "I began to concentrate less on delivering information and more on ways to change the processes by which the class functioned to allow students to take progressively greater responsibility for their own learning."

That concentration on process—the second broad category of TQM's emphasis—is at the heart of TQL. When students and teachers come together in the pursuit of excellence, two procedures usually change drastically and quickly. First, hunches and guesswork about school dynamics are replaced by facts and data. Second, as Candace Allen learned, the standards and methods by which students' work is judged can be reconceived. "As educators, we have a hard time collecting and using data to solve problems," Byrnes admits. "As a group, our tendency is to see a problem and try right away to fix it. Too often, we try to solve problems before we really understand what they are. But, while observation can provide some classroom insights, it can't ever replace an efficient, effective, ongoing data collection process."

In an early data-gathering experiment at Mount Edgecumbe, Langford's students surveyed the school's teachers to learn which three questions students asked most often about classroom processes. "The most frequently asked was 'What are we going to do today?' " he says. "That the students didn't know told us that they weren't deeply involved in the work of the class. The second most-asked question was 'Why do we have to do this?'—which smacked of a lack of clear purpose. The third was 'What's my grade?' They were so extrinsically motivated that their grades were the only outcomes they seemed concerned with."

After the survey, each new assignment in Langford's classes began not with a lecture but with a discussion of purpose. "We'd talk about where the ideas in this assignment could be used beyond school," he explains. "If it was a writing assignment, I might bring in journalists or politicians as guest speakers to talk about the importance of effective writing in their work. Once we'd set a clear foundation for why we needed to do this assignment, then we'd get to work." As TQL took hold at Mount Edgecumbe, Langford found himself regularly measuring an increasing number of indicators. He logged the numbers of students who turned work in late and how often it happened. When the numbers began to rise, he talked about the importance of on-time performance to workplace success and asked students to suggest ways to cut the number of tardy assignments. He kept track of the number of various kinds of errors in the school newspaper and asked the staff to find out what was causing them. He recorded the collective numbers of mistakes in final assignments, asked students if those error rates were acceptable to them under the standards of excellence they'd set, and coached them in their discussions of ways to do better. Some students even began keeping data on themselves in attempts to boost their own performances. One who had assumed he was studying two hours a night found through his own records that he actually was averaging thirty-five minutes.

That kind of data collection is alien to conventional education. "Systems management is based upon fact, not intuition," Byrnes writes with co-authors Robert Cornesky and Lawrence Byrnes in their 1991 book, *The Quality Teacher.* "[TQL] . . . can never be achieved without collecting data. . . . [But] many who work in 'people-related' careers are resistant to the notion that statistics can drive the system better than some 'softer' approach such as human relations." Yet if teachers and students can't measure their performance to begin with, they'll never be able to know if their innovations result in actual improvements. "The use of statistical methods helps to discover . . . how the class is performing. What [becomes] important is the quality you generate because you [are] able to collect baseline data and compare results over time."[4] Margaret Byrnes told us, "For teachers and students willing to use it, that kind of information is invaluable. This is a major paradigm shift in education."[5]

Equally major is the change in approaches to grading students' work. Candace Allen's experience is typical: when students use their shared power to free themselves from the prison of standard grading scales, their interest in learning soars. Of Allen's role, Margaret Byrnes says, "She acts as a facilitator who allows her students to decide what they envision quality to be in a given circumstance. She gets them to bring out the best in themselves." Teachers in quality-based classrooms work with students to define performance standards that will allow them to meet state and district regulations, requirements for graduation, and the external standards that teachers are held accountable for. Beyond that, most TQL teachers let students lead in setting achievement goals. "As they progress in pursuit of the standards they've set, the kids realize with each assignment that they fell short in some way of their ideal," Byrnes says. "They continuously redefine quality for themselves, setting higher and higher goals. Even so, the pressure isn't as great as in a conventional grading system because it's not competitive. By following that process, you really eliminate all need for external motivation. Virtually all kids become internally motivated to do quality work." Under TQL, says Langford, "There's no good and bad anymore—just better."

The pursuit of quality typically forces drastic changes in the methods of assessing students' progress. Langford developed a process that allowed each student to judge his own competency in a given area: "Over a five-year period, we moved to total self-assessment." He coached his students to evolve their own standards and to develop their skill in critiquing their work through successive drafts and revisions. "The more we got students involved in evaluating their own work and observing what was happening while they were learning, the more powerful the learning experience was." There's nothing inherently wrong with the idea of testing, he's quick to add. "But if we're just giving a test to rank students against each other, *that's* wrong. That not only doesn't improve the processes in the system, but it also puts the responsibility for improvement back onto the individual student. Testing should be designed and used to evaluate the system, not the student."

In that way as well as others, the quality process vanquishes fear. Fear, an insidious form of waste, is pervasive in conventional schools. Children sit in silence when teachers call on them for fear they'll offer a wrong response and embarrass themselves in front of their peers. Each time that happens, a learning opportunity is missed. Students dread tests because they might get a low grade. The consequence: they often drill or memorize in high-pressure cram sessions aimed at earning a short-term grade instead of gauging their own mastery—another learning opportunity wasted. Girls in particular often turn away from advanced mathematics and science classes explicitly because they fear that the work might be too hard and spoil their grade-point average. Where there's fear in school, there's waste. "In the conventional A–F grading system, when somebody wins somebody else loses," Byrnes says. "It sets student against student, and in subtle ways it can set student against teacher. It tells kids at the top of the grading scale that they don't have to exert themselves any further, and it tells kids farther down that they're not quite good enough. It's an invitation to boredom and frustration that demoralizes everybody and leaves everyone absolutely no hope." She describes the TQL ideal. "When you have a classroom committed to a common goal of quality, then everyone is committed to helping everyone else achieve it. It's not enough anymore for Joe to be a good student. If he has some degree of expertise, Joe also takes responsibility for helping other kids to achieve quality." In Allen's class, students critique each other's work and suggest ways to improve it. They learn quickly that constructive suggestions and moral support are returned, and all learn to work together for everyone's success. In Byrnes's experience, when teachers ease the fears surrounding traditional letter grades by emphasizing the processes of quality, "academic achievement rises so sharply that you wonder why everyone doesn't do it. Everyone who's done this has the same experience."

One reason why everyone doesn't do it is that implementing the quality process well is an arduous job. Partly because of that, fewer than a hundred of the nation's fifteen thousand school districts have experimented with TQL. Virtually all that have are still so new to the process that they have no firm numbers to prove that the technique consistently boosts student learning. But in almost every school that has used TQL effectively, the reports are consistent: students and teachers become engrossed in their work. Students take responsibility for their own learning, motivated by challenge and curiosity rather than by the external spur of competitive grading. Learning loses its rote character and becomes a steady march toward mastery as students practice higher-order skills. Along the way, they also gain experience in planning and guiding change, a skill that will be critical to their success in the workplace. TQL's ability to engage teachers and students as equal partners in genuine learning earns it a central place among the practical structures of the new educational paradigm.

FROM TOP-DOWN TO BOTTOM-UP: EMPOWERING TEACHERS

The second structure helping to enact the paradigm frees the collective wisdom and creative imagination of experienced teachers and principals. Such "teacher power" underlies many of the most promising reforms that are restructuring today's schools. Robert Slavin's Success For All project (developed at Johns Hopkins University), the School Development Program (pioneered by psychiatrist James Comer at Yale University's Child Development Study Center), and the Accelerated Schools Program (ASP, a project of Stanford University's Center for Educational Research with the School of Education and directed by professor of education and economics Henry Levin), are just three of the most effective examples. All aim to rescue disadvantaged kids from educational failure, but not by conventional means. Instead, they give teachers the power to use their own experience and judgment to enrich teaching and learning in ways that will abolish failure. As these programs demonstrate, the success of any major change in schooling depends on two things: giving the power to initiate, shape, and steer innovation to those responsible for making change work; and bringing teachers together to leverage one another's hard-won experience. The reason is basic. The success of public education depends on what happens between student and teacher in a classroom. As three decades' worth of failed reforms have proved so graphically, simply telling teachers to change their professional patterns and attitudes is futile. Teachers will fully invest themselves only in the changes that they believe in, and those prove to be the ones that give them the power to use their imagination and skills. If our schools are going to change in fundamental ways, teachers must make those changes happen—not alone, each following his or her own peculiar vision, but in collaborative settings that liberate their energies and judgment to drive innovation from the bottom up.

San Francisco's Daniel Webster Elementary School, a pilot school for Henry Levin's Accelerated Schools Program (ASP), runs on that kind of teacher power. "Traditionally, teachers just stay in their classroom and do their thing," says the principal, Willie Santamaria. "Here, teachers own the organization and are responsible for the implementation of new ideas."

It didn't used to be that way. In the late 1980s, Webster's test scores ranked it sixty-ninth among the city's seventy-two schools. It was simply another failing inner-city school in a crime-ridden area, three quarters of whose students came from welfare families. Then Webster volunteered to become a pilot school to test Levin's concept.

When a school joins Levin's program, its district must allow the school to cut itself free from the normal bureaucratic controls and dictates and to pursue its own collective vision of excellence. One principal says: "Everything that isn't against the law is on the table for negotiation." Teachers aren't simply involved in the program; it's up to them to make it work. The teachers and principal at each accelerated school must articulate in detail their vision and goals for the future of their institution. They decide which specific problems to target for improvement—from student failure or a dilapidated building to absenteeism or the lack of geography classes—and in which order. They also devise their own approaches and solutions in pursuit of those goals. The work is done in committees that research and recommend comprehensive answers to specific problems, such as parent apathy or fights in the lunchroom. "It's not a prepared program," Santamaria explains. "Rather, it's a philosophy that we can bring back here and develop on our own." At Webster, teachers voted to jettison most lectures and worksheets and replace them with more complex, practically oriented problems and hands-on experiences. They also worked together to develop lessons that crossed conventional dividing lines between subjects. In the process, the teachers began to change their beliefs about children who many had assumed were born to fail. One teacher says, "We went from negativism to positivism."

Their students changed, too. In two years, their scores on standardized tests (the only citywide measure of improvement at the time) moved from sixty-ninth place among San Francisco schools to twenty-third, the largest gain of any school in the city. "Most times, teachers talk about [things like] how to organize the ditto room," Levin says. "Accelerated schools are getting them to talk about things that matter."

That deeper level of communication opens the door to a treasure-house of professional experience that hasn't been available to them before. They begin to trade tips and ideas that let students blossom. When each teacher in a school shares the techniques and approaches that have benefited learning in her own classroom, all begin to collaborate and replace their less-effective and less-efficient methods and habits with more useful and powerful ones. Penny Brockway, a teacher at the five-grade Hollibrook Elementary School, an ASP school in one of Houston's Hispanic barrios, says, "There's a lot of power in this building because the teachers work so closely together. You can't say, 'I'm going to accelerate my own classroom.' It doesn't work that way. You have to use every idea of every teacher and every student in every classroom to help you. It's the group vision, everybody working together to make each other better and stronger, that makes this work." Leslie McIlquham, a teacher at the ASP Fairbanks Elementary School in Springfield, Missouri, describes her experience: "There's a synergy that comes out of it. When three people are contributing ideas to a single plan, you don't just get the sum of three sets of ideas. You piggyback off each other's ideas, and the result is something that grows almost geometrically."

Teachers' newfound freedom and community not only ignite a new love for their work, but also fight the fearfulness and competition that so commonly cloud a school's atmosphere. One Fairbanks teacher describes what happened after discipline problems in her sixth-grade class left her "in tears." The principal and other teachers met with her informally to offer suggestions and moral support. "They didn't make me feel like I was doing something wrong. They gave me suggestions and encouragement. In the old days, teachers with that problem would have felt that they were completely on their own—fearful of admitting there was something they couldn't deal with because it might have seemed like a reflection on them." Fairbanks principal Joyce Creemer explains that "no teacher is held completely responsible for the total success or failure of any one child. When you understand that, it becomes quite all right to talk about the problems you're having. Each child's success is a group responsibility." McIlquham says, "We compete against ignorance, not against each other."

Roy Ford, Hollibrook's principal, watched the barriers fall between teachers as the Accelerated Schools Program transferred power to the school's instructors. "They thought, 'I'm finally being heard,' " he recalls. "When teachers have the power they need to take charge of kids' educations, they become very responsible—and that means always searching out new ideas, better ways to do things. You can't do that by yourself." Ford identifies the individual strengths of each teacher in his school and encourages the teachers to share their expertise. "You can't help but want to work in a situation where you're appreciated for your strengths instead of hearing about what you *can't* do," he emphasizes. Penny Brockway says, "Here, we're hired as professionals. That's what we are and that's how we behave."

The transformation in teachers' attitudes toward students, their profession, and themselves has been noted in study after study. In her 1989 book *Teachers' Workplace*, the late Susan Rosenholtz, a professor of elementary education at the University of Illinois, notes that effective schools link professional development with mutual effort. "[I]mprovement in teaching is a collective rather than individual enterprise," she writes. "Analysis, evaluation, and experimentation in concert with colleagues are conditions under which teachers improve."[6] Another 1989 report on school cultures in England says that "[teachers] are happiest in a social environment characterized by mutual dependence in which 'sharing' is the norm and individuals do not feel ashamed to admit to failure or a sense of inadequacy." According to the University of Toronto's Michael Fullan, studies of school reforms regularly find that changes go more smoothly when "teachers interact with each other and [with others capable of] providing technical help. Virtually every research study . . . has found this to be the case."[7]

Collaboration and empowerment change the character of teaching in a school, and Hollibrook is no exception. "We got rid of the drill-and-kill, the worksheets," says Brockway. "There are a lot more hands-on activities, and the teacher has become more of a facilitator." If a pair or group of teachers chooses to, they can team-teach to capitalize on each other's strengths. Students can order their day's studies according to their interests at a given moment. For example, says Hollibrook teacher Stephanie Vaughn, "Reading doesn't end when the lesson plan says, but when the children want to stop reading. If they're enjoying themselves in learning, we want to take advantage of that—not put a stop to it." Typical of accelerated schools, the teachers also plan extensively together. In 1992, for example, the teachers in all of the school's five grades worked together to hatch a cross-disciplinary study of the Summer Olympics. The event shaped classes in art, science, history, language, and others.

Clearly, pooling the energy and ideas of the teachers within a single school can set off an explosion of creative innovation. But that's only a first step. If twenty or thirty teachers working together can boost the interest and ability to learn in one school, what would result if dozens, hundreds, or even thousands of teachers with diverse experiences and ideas contributed to a common pool of professional knowledge and technique? An essential structure under the new paradigm will be a repository for those ideas and experiences, a common body of professional knowledge on which all teachers can draw, similar to the compendiums available in Japanese schools.

A number of individual restructuring programs address that need. Schools affiliated with Levin's Accelerated Schools Program are grouped by areas or states and send representatives to regular regional meetings where they swap newfound know-how and ideas. Between meetings, a quarterly newsletter tells the stories of individual ASP schools, how they have dealt with particular challenges, and offers pointers on overcoming barriers to innovation. Schools that have joined Success For All also share a newsletter, but the program's originator and director, Robert Slavin, sees the need to do more. "There are a lot of things going on at schools in our program that other schools never get to hear about," he says. "One of the major tasks before us is to make educators in the twenty-four school districts in which we're working into a group of professionals communicating with each other." He hopes to accomplish that in part by using teachers from member schools to train colleagues in schools new to the program. "The trainers see how other places solve common problems as they work with these schools over time. It's a cascading effect."[8]

One of the most effective ways to unite teachers separated by distance—whether or not they're involved in specific innovative programs—seems to be to link them electronically in computer networks. The National Education Association's "Mastery In Learning" Consortium has joined its eleven member schools in what it calls a School

Renewal Network, a computer-based forum that unites teachers and researchers in the pursuit of excellence. According to an article written by consortium officials Gary Watts and Shari Castle in the May 1992 *Phi Delta Kappan* magazine, "Problems exist . . . in sharing the largely uncodified wisdom of practice," but the network has shown "the power to change not only the user but also the environment in which the user works."[9]

Robert McClure, the consortium's director, offers one example among many. "A fourth-grade teacher in one of our schools noted that kids appear to learn a skill, but when you check back a few months later they seem to have forgotten it. The teacher sent a query out over the network for suggestions he might use to make skill instruction stick."[10] Other teachers on the network seconded the question, while still others shared their own methods to address the problem. An educational psychologist cited research studies that indicate children master skills more effectively when they demonstrate and perform those skills publicly. "Another researcher got on-line and said, 'I think he's onto something; let me tell you what we've done that's similar in a couple of our experimental schools.' Then other teachers joined in with examples of what they were doing and asked if those were the kinds of things the researchers were talking about." The "conversation" took place over nearly three months. Finally, the teacher who had asked the original question rejoined the exchange to detail a number of steps he'd taken in his classroom to solve the problem.

"Teachers on the network moved from isolation in classrooms to collegiality with other networkers to collaboration on issues of substance," Watts and Castle write. "A synergistic knowledge base, greater than the sum of its parts . . . has been the result."[11]

Some restructuring initiatives expand that pool of expertise to include areas other than classroom teaching. Success For All provides its member schools with a three-hundred-page family-support manual that enlists educators as social workers by giving them practical, specific knowledge and techniques to combat the social and family ills that stand between inner-city students and effective learning. By equipping teachers with the specialized knowledge they needed beyond their own discipline, the program seeks to make their in-class time far more productive. Comer's School Development Program (SDP) groups educators into teams, each of which deals with particular problems: the mental-health team might work with students causing discipline problems in class, while the student-services team might help a failing student find a good tutor. Sometimes, though, the techniques aren't so complex. The SDP program, for example, urges counselors, psychologists, and social workers serving the same schools to meet together for an hour or two each week to pool their views about problem students and patterns of trouble in that school. "Each one has a different angle on a situation because of their different expertise and experience," a program official explains. "It becomes a matter of just coordinating their schedules so they can sit down and talk."

Successful restructuring programs work in school after school because they offer not pat solutions to problems but new patterns by which problems can be addressed. Although they encourage educators to change, most refrain from telling them why or how, preferring instead to offer a framework within which teachers and administrators can search out the innovations that fit their unique needs. The power to change is the power of choice, and the programs that work leave that power in the schools. Levin uses an analogy to explain why. "When a doctor determines that a patient needs an appendectomy, then of course we'd want that doctor to know precisely how to do it. But if the doctor decides to take out the patient's appendix just because the patient has an abdominal pain, that troubles us. Typically, that's how schools work. If the kids aren't doing well in math, for example, the solution is usually to look for a new textbook, a new technique, a new package. In fact, those kids might not be learning math for a lot of reasons that have very little to do with the math curriculum: parents might not be involved, school may be a very unexciting place in general, there might be language difficulties. But teachers won't discover those things if they start out with the belief that every child with a stomach pain requires an appendectomy. Too often, schools never ask the right questions, find out what the problem is, ask what evidence there is, and choose an appropriate response. They just buy a new package. We're trying to move schools away from the package mentality."[12] School Development Program officials are equally reluctant to have the program become a wholesaler of change.

"Teachers can't call us for a catalog of solutions to their problems," says SDP communications director Cynthia Savo. "The program isn't prescriptive. It's up to a school to assess the specific needs of that group of kids and then choose the right ways to meet them."[13]

That kind of "hands-off" approach has regularly produced dramatic results. Over its twenty-five years, the School Development Program has logged consistent gains in student learning of up to 20 percentile levels in a single year. Between 1982 and 1985, schools in Benton Harbor, Michigan, under the plan saw student suspensions fall 19 percent at a time when suspensions in the district as a whole rose by more than a third. SDP schools in the city also abolished corporal punishment, while its use declined by only 35 percent in Benton Harbor's other schools. Better still, tests revealed that SDP students show more self-confidence and self-respect than children in similar social circumstances whose schools haven't followed Comer's ideas. Before it joined the Accelerated Schools group in 1988, Fairbanks was able to move fewer than 20 percent of its remedial students each year back into the mainstream regular classes. That figure is now approaching 40 percent. Hollibrook joined the ASP program a year earlier, when the Iowa Test of Basic Skills indicated that the school's typical fifth-grader was entering sixth grade with the average academic skills of an advanced third-grader. Fully 60 percent were below their proper grade levels in some way. But 1991's tests showed that 80 percent of the school's graduating class is now at or above grade level. "Our kids are averaging mathematics scores equivalent to children more than halfway through the sixth grade," boasts Hollibrook principal Roy Ford. "That's excellent, considering that nine out of ten kids come to this school not speaking English."[14] In fact, it speaks so well for the program that middle-class Anglo families nearby now have begun transferring their own children to Hollibrook.

Such gains are common when teachers, given the power to make real changes, pool their creativity and experience. Kristine Estrada, head of the humanities department at San Jose's public Burnett Academy middle school, which also is part of the ASP program, says, "You continue your own education by working with other people. Helping each other helps the students." It not only makes learning more effective and efficient, but also shows students how exciting it can be.

COGNIZANT OF COGNITION: HOW CHILDREN LEARN

Third among the structures giving shape to education's new paradigm is the web of fundamental new understandings about the ways in which people actually learn. It's too soon to know what effects these discoveries might ultimately have on curriculum and materials design or on teachers' classroom approaches. But the new concepts have already begun to guide educators toward more effective and efficient techniques of teaching and learning.

During the past two decades, the study of cognition, generally called cognitive science, has gradually supplanted behaviorism as the dominant force in psychological research. Behaviorism, which ruled American psychology from the 1910s into the 1960s, was an attempt to bring the objective rationalism of physical science to the understanding of the human psyche. Orthodox behaviorists dismissed as irrelevant such concepts as knowledge, thinking, or motivation because these mental phenomena defied numerical measurement.

Behaviorists conceived of education—of all learning—as resulting from stimulus and response: an external prod is applied to a subject and repeated until, through observation or simple trial and error, the subject happens on the right response. A laboratory rat is run through a maze until it can make its way to the cheese at the end without running up any blind alleys; a student is shown the problem "$2 + 3 = ?$" and is corrected in his responses until he consistently returns the answer "5."

The influence of behaviorism over American psychology was all-pervasive during a time when the United States was enthralled by science, order, system, and rationality—the same period during which the current structure of public schooling evolved. The stimulus-and-response notion of learning, in fact, lends support to the "empty vessel" approach to schooling that still guides much of what happens in American classrooms. The approach assumes a student's mind to be an empty vessel, which teachers stock with facts, formulas, and other knowledge. When a student responds mostly correctly to a series of homework problems and a test, she has demonstrated that she has "acquired" the knowledge in question. From that point on, when the now-educated student needs a fact or formula, she will be able to delve into her brimming vessel, choose and retrieve the relevant bit of knowledge, and put it to proper and effective use.

Drawing on the work of Swiss developmental psychologist Jean Piaget and incorporating insights from computer science, cognitive theorists have evolved a view of learning as uniquely subjective and personal. Their ideas, collectively known as constructivism, are being corroborated by ongoing experimental work worldwide.

Constructivism holds that learning is anything but passive, as behaviorists contend. Instead, a person learning something new brings to that experience all of his previous knowledge and present mental patterns. Each new fact or experience is assimilated into a living web of understanding that already exists in that person's mind. As a result, learning is not passive or "objective"; it is an intensely subjective, personal process and structure that each person constantly and actively modifies in light of new experiences. (Constructivists would argue that, by definition, a person who is truly passive is incapable of learning.) In school, each child structures his or her own knowledge of the world into a unique pattern, connecting each new fact, experience, or understanding to the growing structure in a subjective way that still binds the child in rational and meaningful relationships to the wider world.

The "whole-language" approach to reading is one reform among several that rests squarely on the constructivist idea. In a whole-language classroom, first-graders "write" a story on their very first day of school. Many just scribble; others incorporate what few letters or words they know. Then each child "reads" his or her story to the class. Of course, each child performs successfully because the story is simply a platform for imagination rather than an intimidating test of unfamiliar skills. Children continue writing in class, gradually learning to spell and to structure sentences as a self-paced natural process unclouded by abstract rules of language. "It's similar to the way children learn to speak," says Fred Hechinger, the retired president of the New York Times Company Foundation and the paper's former education columnist. "Children learn to speak not because they memorize rules of speech and grammar, but because they hear it and pick it up naturally. A three-year-old may say, 'I goed home' instead of 'I went home,' but you don't worry about it because you know that, over time, the child

will naturally learn the correct way to speak."[15] Whole learning has no
lack of critics; not everyone is ready to take such a casual approach to
the teaching and learning of crucial skills. But the approach links new
scientific understandings with classroom techniques in a way that
promises to leave fewer children behind in basic skills than conventional methods often do.

Another of cognitive science's major discoveries has been the pervasive persistence of what Howard Gardner, an educational psychologist at
Harvard University and a MacArthur Foundation "genius grant" winner,
calls the "intuitive theories" of childhood. Gardner details the concept in
his 1991 book *The Unschooled Mind*. He contends that deeply held,
unconscious misconceptions about the world, usually formed long before a child enters school, persist into adult life in a great many areas:
"These very early and deeply entrenched understandings form the basis
of robust theories that emerge during the following years, and these
theories, in turn, are the views with which formal education must contend if disciplinary understandings are ever to supplant intuitive ones."[16]

Gardner notes a number of examples: Until they are taught differently, children usually assume that because dolphins and whales are
shaped like fish and live in water, dolphins and whales must both be fish.
They also assume that parakeets and penguins are so different that both
can't be birds.[17] In an often-repeated demonstration, a child, usually of
preschool age, is shown a wide, squat glass full of milk. As the child
watches, an adult pours the milk from the short glass into a tall, narrow
glass. The child will generally conclude that the second glass now
contains more milk because the column of liquid stands so much taller
in it than it did in the shorter glass.

Such misunderstandings aren't surprising in young children. But
cognitive scientists have found these same sorts of misunderstandings
endure, subtly and unconsciously, not only among older children but
also even among educated adults. Study after study has found that high-
school and college students who have taken and passed courses on a
subject frequently have a hard time applying the principles they have
studied and mastered in classrooms to real-life events. The largest collection of evidence comes from physics and mathematics, where problems
and answers can be crafted and judged with precision. Gardner cites

several examples that he calls "quite typical of what is found when students with training in physics or engineering are posed problems outside the strict confines of class." In one case, engineering students were asked to imagine a coin being flipped and then to describe the forces acting on the coin as it reaches the peak of its flight. The answer is gravity alone (apart from the minor effects of air resistance). But 90 percent of engineering students who hadn't studied mechanics and 70 percent of those who had argued that, in addition to gravity, "the original upward force of the hand" still influenced the coin's motion. According to Gardner, "Most people, whether or not they have survived a mechanics course, are not able to comprehend that an object can continue to move in a given direction even though the only force apparently operating on it is exerted in the opposite direction."[18]

Such misconceptions aren't confined to science. People taking a test were told of a medical treatment that saved the lives of two hundred sick people out of six hundred. In another context, they learned of a medical treatment for the same illness under which four hundred people died out of six hundred afflicted. Although the statistical results were identical, most people said they would opt for the former treatment. "Students may learn to give 'proper' interpretations of historical events or proper readings of classic novels or plays when they are under the guidance of a teacher," Gardner notes. "They can adopt subtle [learning strategies] that will help them succeed in formal examinations. But when they are asked about the same types of events or characters some time later, they may well regress to the earlier, more entrenched, and more stereotypical ways of interpreting human behavior."[19] For example, people may learn as students that World War I was caused by a confluence of complex events that culminated in the assassination of Archduke Ferdinand—not by the assassination itself. But the same people might unconsciously attribute the cause of a race riot in Los Angeles to the jury's verdict in a single police-brutality trial.

On the basis of such findings, Gardner and other constructivists argue that the old behaviorist format of lecture, recitation, and rote drills leaves far too many students incapable of bringing useful knowledge with them from the artificial setting of the classroom into the real world. Schools intent on seeing students master higher-order skills must explicitly confront and destroy the simplistic intuitive theories that linger from childhood. Otherwise, those covert notions will remain—often undermining the results of a typically superficial classroom education.

One research project at the University of Washington at Seattle has taken on that task directly. Rooted in the insights of cognitive science, the research group's mission is to develop more effective ways to teach physics. As an integral part of that effort, for more than two decades the group has been teaching working and prospective teachers who, because of their own weak backgrounds in science, hesitate in or simply avoid teaching science to their own students. The group has put together a laboratory-based curriculum under the name Physics By Inquiry, that lead present and future teachers through basic experiments in electricity, motion, light, magnetism, and so on. But the lessons do so in ways designed expressly to bring people into confrontation with their own misconceptions about science and to force them to scrap false "intuitive understandings" in favor of conscious, accurate ones.

Most science courses outline a general rule or principle, then walk students through a laboratory experiment demonstrating the rule that's been taught. The Physics By Inquiry lesson materials work in an opposite way. The course's text is skeletal: each lesson poses a series of experiments. Students work in groups to carry out the experiments, while the teacher acts as gadfly and coach. When each experiment is concluded, students attempt to answer a series of open-ended questions that draw them into a search for explanations of the experiment's results. Ultimately, they attempt to formulate a general principle. Concepts—whether as familiar as "velocity" or as abstruse as the work–kinetic energy theorem—are named not at the beginning of a lesson, but only after students have experienced a phenomenon and been able to articulate their experience's larger meaning. In his 1990 book *A Guide to Introductory Physics Teaching*, physicist Arnold Arons, who originated the teacher education program, explains why:

"Few students, even at college level, [understand] how words acquire meaning through shared experience. They tend to think that words are defined by synonyms found in a dictionary and . . . are completely unaware of the necessity of describing the actions and operations one executes, at least in principle, to give these terms scientific meaning."

The precise scientific meaning of words like *force*, *velocity*, or *acceleration* can be quite different from their more vague and casual everyday meanings. "The students remain unaware of the alteration [in meaning] unless it is pointed to explicitly many times—not just once. Students . . . must be made to tell the 'stories' involved in . . . velocity, acceleration, and so forth in their own words."[20]

Consequently, Physics By Inquiry insists that students draft their own "operational definitions" of concepts before labels are applied. That leads students not to memorize a superficial explanation but to find out *why* something is true—"consciously raising the questions 'What do we know? How do we know? Why do we accept or believe? What is the evidence . . . ?' " It demands "understanding where [a statement of fact] comes from or what underlies it . . . and also involves the capacity to use, apply, transform, or recognize the relevance of . . . knowledge in new situations."[21] Such skills are integral to a person's success in a quality-based workplace driven by the search for creative solutions instead of by conformity to rules and commands.

Students often find that Physics By Inquiry's methods make them uncomfortable. The course strips them of their dependence on memorized abstractions and shreds their unconscious assumptions about the physical world. But that discomfort, constructivists would argue, is essential to real learning and ultimate mastery. "Instead of memorizing a rule or definition and not understanding why it's true, they experience the concept for themselves," explains Suzanne Lea, an associate professor of mathematics at the University of North Carolina who also teaches courses using Physics By Inquiry materials. "That makes it no longer an abstract concept, but a part of their own experience."[22]

The course structure is guided by the project's own first-hand research and development, a painstaking process spanning decades and demanding patience as much as it does scientific and pedagogical expertise. The work, which was begun under Arons, continues under the program's current director, Lillian McDermott. She and her teams of student and faculty investigators interview teachers and students to discover which basic concepts in science they misunderstand and to isolate the specific principles of which they're ignorant. The researchers then devise, test, and refine lesson materials that will most forcefully and directly contradict the false ideas students typically hold and will lead to real understanding.

In one of McDermott's studies students were shown two steel balls rolling in parallel tracks. The first track was flat and the ball rolled along it at a uniform speed. The second track was sloped slightly uphill. The ball in it started out faster than the first ball and passed it, then slowed as it climbed the incline; finally, the first ball retook the lead. Students were asked if the balls ever had the same speed. Many of them, including 60 percent of the elementary-school teachers who participated, identified the moment when one ball passed the other as the instant at which their speeds were the same—not when the balls maintained a constant distance between themselves.[23]

According to Arons, students relied on their own experiences of riding in cars to make the judgment: the car behind is slower than the car in front, the car in front is faster than the one behind, and the speeds are the same when the cars are "neck and neck" for "a while." "The association of 'same speed' with 'passing' or 'same position' was persistent and symptomatic and not idiosyncratic." After gaining some skill in measuring and graphing data, students were led back to the rolling balls. As they graphed the balls' positions at different instants, they were brought face to face with the inescapable fact that their first conclusion had been wrong. Then they were asked to explain in writing what they'd learned. "Our students do a lot of writing, because our tests and quizzes ask them not just to give an answer but to explain their reasoning," Lea says.

The course makes students confront their false ideas, repeatedly bringing them back to the same hard-to-grasp concepts in gradually more sophisticated contexts as their understanding increases. Arons explains that even though students have been told something or given a formula for it, "the idea has not registered because it has not been made part of the individual student's concrete experience, and they have never had the opportunity to articulate the idea in their own words. Such exercises should be repeated still later. . . . It is only such recycling of ideas over fairly extended periods of time, reencountered in increasingly rich context, that leads to a firm assimilation in many students."[24]

A cognitive approach to learning can make that kind of mastery possible in any subject. Cognitive-based research can find the quickest paths to understanding by discovering how people learn; it also can let educators flag a subject's inherent chasms and then equip teachers and students with the tools and materials they need to span them. Learning, like education reform, is a sort of ongoing paradigm shift. As we've seen, that process is most effective when those responsible for the results have the tools designed specifically to ensure success.

COOPERATIVE LEARNING: ALL FOR ONE, ONE FOR ALL

"No! It's like this," says the third-grade girl, reaching out to the boy across from her. She takes a small green wooden triangle from his hand and picks up a red parallelogram lying on the desk of the girl next to her. "See?" She holds their edges together and studies the result, which doesn't seem to be what she expected. "Um . . ." The other boy in the quartet picks up two similar triangles from his desk and holds them up to hers. "What if we do like this?" he says. As he sets them edge to edge beside the parallelogram, the other three children lean forward to watch.

The four are team members of the Care Bears, a learning group whose desks are joined, facing each other, like the quadrants of a square. This morning, the teacher has passed out colored shapes made of wood—rectangles, hexagons, and triangles of different sizes in addition to squares and parallelograms—to each of the six learning groups in his class to help demonstrate the concept of fractions. After a minute's trial and discussion, the Care Bears arrange three triangles in a way that matches the shape and size of the parallelogram. "Yes!" says the first boy. The Care Bears give each other high fives all around.

In more and more schools around the country, groups like the Care Bears are replacing the solitary child as the focus of instruction. Cooperative learning, the fourth structure supporting education's new paradigm, is displacing the old solitary-competitive model as the new standard of classroom structure—for good reason: it fulfills two criteria of the evolving paradigm mentioned on page 157 of this chapter. It extends a teacher's reach and impact, and educators learn the approach through formal training programs conducted by researchers and seasoned teachers who are masters of the method. The technique isn't yet well integrated with other reforms, and teachers are often inadequately taught to make the best use of it, but cooperative learning is no fad: since the 1930s studies have shown that students learn more, learn better, and develop more useful social skills and attitudes when they cooperate, rather than compete, to learn.

In basic ways, cooperative learning challenges the classroom ideal most of us grew up with: children quiet, all facing the teacher who is the source of knowledge, each listening or working in silence as a self-contained learner. First, cooperative classrooms are noisy. In Success For All elementary-school students read to each other in pairs. The atmosphere can be cacophonous, but each student does much more actual reading than would be possible if pupils took turns in a conventional round-robin reading group of ten or fifteen children. Second, in a cooperative classroom the teacher doesn't control, and so can't evaluate, each individual learning transaction. Instead, the students challenge or correct each other's responses. Because friends are usually less intimidating than teachers, and group exchanges less daunting than individual recitations in front of an entire class, children find it easier to debate, question, and revise ideas in pursuit of solutions to problems. In addition to leveraging a teacher's time by deputizing each student as an instructor, cooperative learning also eases the fears and distractions sparked by the competition of student against student. It also cultivates higher-order thinking and teamwork skills.

Typically, a group of children organized as a cooperative class will divide into groups of four or five who share responsibility for one another's learning. Combining children of different ability levels in each group offers children what research has shown to be the most effective setting for learning new concepts in deep and lasting ways: small interactive groups. Small groups also multiply the power and reach of the teacher's instruction: as bright children tutor slower ones, quicker students are forced to construct and articulate the concepts they're studying in more explicit and detailed ways than they would if they were learning silently by themselves. Slower learners benefit from hearing information and ideas explained many times by different team members, each with his or her own approach to and construction of the material.

As they explain things to each other, and as they challenge and defend different ideas, children cooperating spend more time working actively on new material than do individual or competing learners. Also, researchers say, repeating new knowledge out loud aids the mind in incorporating that new knowledge into long-term memory. By cooperating, children help themselves to learn while helping each other.

Cooperative learning doesn't necessarily eliminate the competitive element from the classroom, but the technique is flexible enough to allow teachers to manage and direct competition toward positive results for all children in the class. Cooperative learning classes and competition can be structured in various ways. Most often, competition is channeled toward grades and test scores. Some teachers give and grade tests individually even though the learning was done in groups. Others give the same grade to all members of a learning group, which motivates each member not only to learn well but also to make sure that teammates do too. Group scores also prod slower learners to take greater responsibility for mastering material so they don't let down the other members of their teams. Teachers may yoke children's competitive and cooperative energies by averaging an individual's grade with that of the worst-performing member of that child's team, and learning groups may compete with each other for class prizes and honors.

Regardless of the particular structure of a cooperative learning class, the boons to learning seem consistent. David Johnson and Roger Johnson are codirectors of the University of Minnesota's Cooperative Learning Center, which has imparted the method to thirty thousand teachers. They have conducted more than twenty-six studies of cooperative learning's effects—on boys and girls from all social and economic classes, from various ethnic and minority groups, from grade school through college, and across a range of subjects from geometry to physical education. "We have found considerable evidence," they report, "that cooperative learning experiences promote higher achievement than do competitive and individual [ones]."[25] In sixteen of twenty-one studies designed to measure overall achievement, cooperative learning yielded clear gains, with two studies showing inconclusive results and three no difference. The method also resulted in gains among different ability groups. Of four of the Johnsons' studies measuring the learning gains of high achievers, three showed that bright students who cooperated with slower ones learned more than those who competed. In twelve of thirteen experiments, academically handicapped students achieved more in cooperation than did those in traditional schemes of classroom organization. "Currently, there is no type of task on which cooperative efforts are *less* effective than are competitive or individualistic efforts," the Johnsons report. "On most tasks (and especially the more important learning tasks, such as concept attainment, verbal problem-solving, categorization, spatial problem-solving, retention and memory, motor, and guessing-judging-predicting), cooperative efforts are more effective in promoting achievement."[26]

In addition, the Johnsons and other researchers consistently report that cooperation in learning fosters friendships and trust among children working together—even across ethnic and racial boundaries—far more easily than do competitive arrangements. Similarly, physically or mentally impaired students consistently seem to improve their academic achievement and social skills, as well as their acceptance among unimpaired students, through cooperative work in mixed-ability groups. In addition, surveys among children find that a student working cooperatively is more likely to feel liked and accepted by other children and to feel supported in his or her studies. The surveys also note that children learning cooperatively like their academic subjects better, feel more positive about studying, and like school more in general than those in other structures. "Rather than fostering dependency on the group," one teacher notes, "cooperative learning actually seems to empower each child."

Clearly, cooperative learning's success carries implications beyond school. More and more adult workers find themselves in teams, working together to identify and solve problems and accomplish mutual goals. Solutions to social problems—achieving racial and gender equity, resolving tensions between industrial needs and environmental protection, strengthening families—increasingly demand the same kinds of group-oriented, cooperative skills. Cooperative learning in schools today might well be laying a foundation for social and economic strength tomorrow.

Like most successful innovation in schools, though, effective cooperative learning programs aren't accidental. Children must be taught to work together productively and manage controversy and disagreement in positive ways. At the same time, students have to believe that grades are computed accurately and fairly to reflect individual accomplishment; otherwise, cooperative arrangements fall apart. Research isn't yet complete, either; educators still are trying to find out just why cooperative learning works, for whom it works best, and in what forms it's most productive. As important as those questions are, though, they are only details. Cognitive science and classroom experience have firmly established the broader point: that cooperative learning aids mastery by empowering students, just as collaboration empowers teachers and leverages their individual effectiveness and efficiency.

Group learning seems to work equally well in a somewhat different form, commonly called peer tutoring. In the past, teachers have often used peer tutoring not only out of necessity but also because it seemed effective. Recently, independent research has proved it to be. Dr. Martha Rekrut has seen the approach work in the schools of Warwick, Rhode Island, where she teaches high-school English. Rekrut reports that younger students, even those hostile to their own classroom teachers, look up to older students who tutor them in the way that children often respect a more knowledgeable or experienced older sibling. A student-to-student tutoring program can sidestep personal or psychological issues that grow out of a school's usual structures and power relationships and that thwart learning.[27]

The tutors—particularly if they're average or below-average students—usually learn at least as much as the children they're helping. In one study, Rekrut divided a class of tenth-graders into three groups. The class studied the structure and interpretation of short stories. One group practiced by themselves the techniques learned, the second group didn't practice at all, and students in the third group tutored elementary-school children in reading comprehension. Later, Rekrut tested the three groups' skills at framing stories' meanings and subjected the results to statistical analysis. She found that the students who had tutored younger children performed "significantly better" than those in the other two groups.[28]

The outcome was typical. "When I ask kids [who have never tutored other kids] what good readers do to read well, they talk about rereading or following the text with their finger," Rekrut says. "Kids who've tutored other children come up with a whole galaxy of ideas—looking at any pictures for clues, sounding out words, picturing the scene in your mind, and so on. They've learned more about it because they've had to become more resourceful as they've tutored other children."

There are several explanations. Tutors have to go over material several times if they're going to teach it successfully to others; that repetition probably helps them learn more than they would in just one reading. They also have to organize and structure the material they're going to teach, a process that takes them deeper into the realm of a subject's concepts and broad principles. "It also could be an ego thing," Rekrut muses. "The tutor doesn't want to make a fool of himself in front of another child, so he figures he'd better really learn this stuff. It's hard to tease out any one factor, and I'm not sure it's important to do that. The fact that it works is what matters."

COMPUTER-BASED LEARNING TECHNOLOGIES

The fifth building block of the new educational paradigm is a partnership between humans and hardware. Electronic learning technologies, which made an awkward debut in U.S. schools during the 1980s, are beginning to earn a place for themselves in the practical foundation of education's new structure. After years of false starts and dashed hopes, educators finally are learning two hard basic lessons about what computers can and can't do. First, computers are never panaceas. The arrival of hardware in a classroom isn't necessarily the beginning of a learning renaissance. Electronic learning aids, equipped with well-designed software, can tutor children individually, helping each student progress at her own pace and freeing teachers from rote drill to use their time and expertise more effectively; but a computer still cannot carry on a decent conversation, which is the essence of good teaching. Second, although computers can extend a teacher's reach and multiply his effectiveness across a larger number of students, they do not replace him. Computers serve learning best when they link teacher, student, and information in new, more effective ways instead of simply supplanting teachers or textbooks.

Still, the role of electronic technologies in school classrooms remains a prickly subject. In less than a lifetime, computers have taken over offices and factories and reinvented everything from warfare to buying groceries. It's too easy to assume that computers have the innate power to make everything easier, faster, and more efficient—including learning. It's a short leap from that conclusion to the corollary idea that electronic learning technologies can vault us over the confines of traditional schooling. Why bother to tackle the massive effort needed to reconfigure the human structure of education when computers can render it obsolete with the tap of a few keys?

Like so many other aspects of computers' potential, their power to teach has been overestimated and oversold. Schools learned that lesson the hard way in the 1980s. Spurred by an eagerness to prove themselves relevant in changing times, public schools began buying desktop computers faster than they could figure out what to do with them. Schools installed the machines before deciding proper roles for computers in their classrooms. Limited equipment budgets were invested in hardware before there were adequate supplies of low-cost, effective software or knowledgeable consultants to show teachers how to make creative use of the power inherent in their new tools. As a result, the first wave of computers in schools served mainly as expensive drill sergeants—leading students through sets of arithmetic tables, mathematics problems, and language exercises.

Now, educators are finally learning that computers can be their liberators—can free them to become the "learning coaches" that most want to be. Bob Brown, Institute Professor of physics at Case Western Reserve University in Cleveland, has discovered that something as relatively simple as electronic mail can make that kind of difference. He began using e-mail as an aid in his freshman physics courses in 1988, when the university installed fiber-optic communication networks in student dorms and offered students long-term, no-interest loans to help them buy computers. Brown's students now use e-mail to ask him everything from questions about homework ("I think Problem 4 violates the Second Law of Thermodynamics") to permission to take a test late when a football game interferes. Being able to establish a personal relationship with Brown through e-mail—whether about physics or about less scientific issues—seems to make students feel generally more comfortable with what can be a daunting subject. What began as a convenience, the professor believes, has boosted students' ability and motivation to learn.

"It's been my experience that students in the course are learning more physics with the e-mail system than they did without it," Brown says. "We used to have about thirty entering freshmen interested in majoring in physics. By the end of the sophomore year, we'd lose eighteen or twenty of them to other disciplines. Since we began using e-mail, if we start the year with thirty interested freshmen, we'll keep just about all of them."[29]

In his introductory physics course, Brown normally lectures to an auditorium of 120 students three times a week, and there used to be complaints about the large class size. The course also used to include a weekly workshop in which students could seek help individually with homework problems. Electronic mail has not only made students comfortable with the large class size, but also has let Brown eliminate the weekly workshops except during exam weeks. "I pass out questionnaires partway through the course to get student feedback on how it's going," Brown explains. "Out of a hundred twenty, only one or two wish they were in a smaller class. Thanks to e-mail, each student can have a personal relationship with the teacher and get individual help when needed." Instead of waiting for a workshop class once a week, students now dispatch their questions and concerns to Brown's electronic mailbox as soon as problems crop up. Brown sits down at his computer three times a day to read his mail and respond on the spot. When he has a classwide announcement, such as correcting a mistake he made in composing a homework problem or offering aid for a particularly difficult exercise, he posts the notice on the course's electronic bulletin board.

He often turns his messages into individual tutoring sessions—catching and correcting students' individual misconceptions before they fester. "Students don't sit and stew and get hung up for days," he says. Many students who think they're "clueless" about a problem, or have followed a long calculation to a dead end, simply need a mathematical mistake pointed out to them or a few additional words of explanation. "A lot of the questions just take a few words to answer," he says. "The advantage of e-mail is that I don't have to sit in some room to make myself available where students would come and have to wait around for me to get free."

The system's advantages flow in both directions. Two years ago, for example, Brown was barraged by students' electronic protests early one semester. "I realized I'd jumped too quickly into a subject and had to refigure my approach," he recalls. "In a lot of regular classes, the teacher can be sailing along thinking everything's fine and it isn't until the exam that he finds out that he and the class were completely out of sync." Similarly, students who might be embarrassed to ask a question in front of other students for fear of "looking dumb" seem to lose their shyness in e-mail. With the privacy offered by their computers, they're less restrained in admitting confusion or in speculating about broader issues raised by the material. ("If time is the fourth dimension," mused one, "why isn't it measured in meters like the other three?") Some even share poetry with Brown or make him privy to their romantic entanglements. The daily coaching and constant interaction between students and teacher does more than build trust and free students' intellects, though. It also allows Brown to cover textbook material about twice as fast as he used to. That opens a number of the class sessions for discussions of special subjects, such as chaos or global warming, or presentations by guest lecturers.

"Teachers have been afraid to be in too-close contact with students because they're frightened to death that the students will take all their time," Brown notes. "The lesson I've learned from e-mail is that it doesn't. I can answer the nine or ten messages I get every day in a total of about a half hour. It actually can save teachers time because you don't have to repair things that went awry while you were out of touch—and that can make the difference between a good course and a really bad one. I don't know of any subject or grade level that couldn't benefit from this."

But effective learning technologies don't always come in big packages. For almost two decades, Ohio State University mathematics professors Bert Waits and Frank Demana have been showing that the use of common handheld calculators can bring about sizeable gains in learning.

During the 1970s, Waits and Demana found that too many Ohio high-school students coming to the state university as freshmen weren't ready for the rigors of elementary calculus, even though many had taken four years of mathematics in high school. To prepare future freshmen, Waits and Demana decided to create a new approach to high-school mathematics. They had made calculators part of a successful remedial program they'd put together for college freshmen, so they decided to use the same tool for the new effort. Their "Calculator and Computer Precalculus Project," known as C²PC, has been changing students' minds about mathematics since 1989.

"A mathematical relationship called a function is important in all kinds of mathematics," Waits explains. "Algebra and calculus are really the study of different classes of functions. Often, especially in calculus, we have to draw those functions as graphs. A lot of mathematics is very visual, and a lot of students are visual learners. But we haven't made much use of that in the past because obtaining that visualization has been a complex, tedious, and boring process due to the pencil-and-paper computation involved." Computers can make those computations instantly, and now so can a variety of calculators. "They have standard computer processors, display screens, built-in graphing software, and they're fully programmable," Waits says. "With calculators, we can visualize functions very quickly, easily, and accurately, then use algebraic equations to study them."[30]

Waits and Demana began by introducing C²PC slowly into a few high-school courses in 1986. In a 1990 paper, the researchers wrote that after a year or so, a number of the teachers involved "said it became 'fun' (their words!) because they felt confident enough to move ahead and take 'ownership' of the course and to incorporate more types" of calculator-based approaches in their teaching. When the calculators were used in cooperative learning groups, "teachers reported that students' interest in mathematics and mathematics communication skills increased. Talking about mathematics became common!"[31]

The professors can be forgiven a few exclamation points. Waits told us, "I see kids and teachers getting far more excited about using a technology-enhanced approach to doing mathematics than I've ever seen—and I've been teaching mathematics for more than thirty years." Their calculator-based approach is now part of the curriculum in as many as one thousand high schools in forty-six states, and the number of schools adopting it is now growing by about 20 percent annually. Waits estimates that more than fifty thousand students have been through the program. He's quick to point out that C²PC's results haven't been evaluated formally or objectively; but he notes, "We have a lot of informal evidence to suggest that, in the long run, we're doing these kids a lot of good." Teachers in the program tell of high-school students who've first taken a calculator-intensive precalculus course and then taken advanced high-school calculus. "Even though they're not allowed to use graphing calculators on advanced-placement exams [for college entrance], they've done as well or better than students with conventional backgrounds," Waits says. Similarly, high-school students who have used calculators tend to score better on the Scholastic Aptitude Test. "Teachers using graphing technology are able to ask more higher-order thinking-skill questions," he says. "Teachers who use technology appropriately can ask kids to think more often about what they're doing and about its connections to other things."

Waits and Demana see no particular urgency to verify the accuracy of those anecdotes with a battery of formal tests. "Do C²PC students do better on traditional paper-and-pencil . . . exams? We really don't care. Exactness is overemphasized in school mathematics." Instead, they say, "We see students learning to value mathematics in ways we only dreamed of in the past. We see [that] a technology-enhanced approach can be used to mathematically empower more students. Students who are empowered with technology can solve problems that other students could never touch."[32]

Teachers at the Saturn School in St. Paul, Minnesota, take a similar view. Technology and master teachers collaborate at the school, which opened in 1990, in what Saturn calls a "high-tech, high-teach" approach.

At Saturn, computer-based technologies have abolished grade-level grouping and most regimented, class-wide instruction. Instead, each student works with his parents and instructors to fashion a "personal learning plan" and works at his own pace to fulfill it. There are required courses in mathematics, language skills, science, and social studies, but the technology allows each student to optimize the curriculum's pace. A student with language skills well in advance of his age can whiz through individual computer-based texts and writing assignments without drumming his fingers while slower classmates catch up. The same student struggling with long division can take as much time as he needs to master it without facing humiliating competition common in standardized group mathematics lessons.

Saturn may let technology make learning more effective and efficient, but the term "high teach" indicates that the school doesn't allow computers to isolate students from each other, from teachers, or from the world beyond. Children collaborate daily to research and write reports, produce videotapes, and carry out other group projects. They often visit area museums and libraries. Teachers, liberated from lectures and group drills, have time to work with students individually—coaching them in meeting their learning goals, challenging them with broad, probing questions, and designing new lessons and projects. Saturn's faculty still struggles with the same issues most teachers do—how to design effective tests, for example, and how to keep parents involved. But the school's technological aids allow them the time and psychic energy to tackle those issues in creative ways. "Technology, when it works right, can do some things that can be very difficult for a human being to do," says Saturn school director Tom King. "But we're not taking the teacher out of it."[33]

Actually, Saturn's technology yields very human benefits. "It motivates the students because it invites them to take control of some major tools of teaching and learning," explains Mark French, Saturn's associate teacher for science, mathematics, and technology. "Once we've involved them in the technology, it's a lot easier to make subject-matter and curriculum-content connections with them because content comes to them through a medium that has their interest." In addition, mastering technology raises students' confidence and self-esteem. "There's no way that I can know all the technology," French adds. "But students who find a specific interest area become expert in it and even become assistant teachers in certain classes."[34]

It's not just a matter of being computer-literate, French points out. Saturn's electronic teaching machines also provide practice in the higher-order skills the future will demand of students. "They get stuck, hit a wall, or find bugs in the technology, and they spend some time as a group working out solutions to those problems," he says. But, beyond that, they also routinely gather, analyze, and organize information, present it to others, and work in groups—"all of which our instructional technology encourages them to do. It gives them skills that take them beyond school."

THE KEY TO REFORM

These five structures helping to support the new educational paradigm are still being built. They're strong enough to carry the weight of a new, broader, and more complex approach to learning, but they'll remain separate frameworks until skilled architects and builders shape and integrate them into a unified system of support for what is to come. That task remains to be tackled by a process of redesign in education.

Even without being linked together, the five building blocks also can slash the huge amounts of wasted energy, time, and resources that pervade conventional schooling. The tools of TQL can show teachers how to substitute relevant, challenging lessons for those that bore or bewilder their students. In TQL classes, students learn more in less time because they're engaged instead of bored, cooperating with the lesson instead of resisting or ignoring it. Through collaboration, teachers replace less effective, less efficient techniques and lessons with those that teach more students better in the same amount of class time. Cognitive research can help teachers to fashion lessons that avoid problems inherent in learning before they can impede students' progress. Cooperative learning can multiply a teacher's reach and impact by turning each student into an assistant instructor and giving each more practice in using what they're learning. Used wisely, new electronic technologies also can serve as surrogate instructors in a number of circumstances, freeing teachers to work individually with students in ways that make the greatest differences for each one. All five approaches let teachers teach more effectively and efficiently, and students learn more and better in less time and with less wasted effort than before.

They also offer benefits beyond classroom effectiveness and efficiency. Courses such as Physics By Inquiry can polish students' skills in organizing, analyzing, and reasoning from information, in diagnosing causes, and in using experience and information in place of labels or unexamined assumptions. Understanding the processes of Total Quality, being able to work smoothly and effectively in groups, and knowing how to use technology all prepare children for productive places in a twenty-first-century society and workplace.

This new universe of effectiveness, efficiency, and quality is possible only if schools fashion a process that will allow educators to refine, develop, and integrate these and other foundation stones of the new paradigm. Exactly how these separate reforms will evolve and combine most effectively is a question that only a process of redesign can answer fully. But, as we've noted, U.S. education has yet to decide to begin such a process. Edward Fiske, the former *New York Times* education editor, noted the effect of that indecision in *Smart Schools, Smart Kids*, his 1991 survey of U.S. school improvements: "The problem is that most [innovators] are working in isolation. No one has put together a whole package. It's as if a dozen people were trying to modernize an old car. One person is streamlining the hood. Another is converting the engine to fuel injection. Still others are working on the wheels or finding a place for air bags. But we still haven't reached the point where all these changes are put together so that we can say we have a new car. . . . How do we put enough of the pieces together so that we can say we finally have a totally different system of public education?"[35]

Reformers must combine their individual successes for the same reason that carmakers want to put fuel injection, better wheels, and a streamlined hood on the same car: each improvement increases the effect of others, making the whole car more efficient. When experienced teachers are working together to design lessons, the lessons become more effective. When those lessons are designed according to the new insights of cognitive learning mechanisms, they become even more so. When students work on those lessons collaboratively, they learn them more quickly and thoroughly. Electronic learning technologies optimize the pace and complexity of skill training and fact learning so no student need be bored or left behind—a vast saving of time and resources for students and teachers alike. Through it all, the processes of Total Quality can keep everyone involved in education focused on continued integration, leverage, and improvement.

The more the structures can be combined to support and complement each other, the more rare educational failure—the dropout, the functional illiterate, the child who "just doesn't get it"—will become. Each integrated reform offers a "fail-safe" mechanism to the others. Children who struggle to learn under one approach may thrive in another; the weaknesses of one technique may be balanced by another's strengths. If students learn effectively in less time, teachers can be freed to spend a meaningful amount of time every day advancing their skills, consulting with colleagues, and designing better lessons. But the benefits extend beyond school. If students learn to think creatively, to work in groups, to use technology and the mechanisms of Total Quality, our emerging national labor force will develop the competencies it needs to compete effectively with the Asian and European workers who now outpace it.

The result can be a more effective, efficient society in which no citizens are unemployable, unproductive, or need a lifetime of public assistance. In the final chapter, we'll show one way in which Fiske's question—how do we put the pieces together?—might be answered.

8

The Key
to Reform

The Systems Redesign School

A number of separate reforms underway in U.S. schools already incorporate individual aspects of the redesign process. The preceding pages have detailed several. Reading Recovery was developed through original research and equips its teachers with a repertoire of proven techniques. Physics By Inquiry is redesigned constantly in response to classroom-based research and experience. By giving teachers collaborative control over curriculum and other decisions, projects such as the Accelerated Schools Program and Success For All have begun the de facto integration of effective classroom methods and techniques.

These reforms are chipping away at the traditional isolation of both teachers and programs that has robbed education of the power to effect systemwide structural reform. But the scale and pace of these efforts are no match for the underlying task. No manufacturing company could bid for leadership in its industry if each of its workers was busy designing and building his own product instead of contributing specialized skills and experience to a common result. Similarly, innovators working alone can't muster the resources to design, implement, and guide a new national pattern for U.S. schooling. A team of specialized researchers can spend more than a decade perfecting a single program such as Reading Recovery; Physics By Inquiry still considers itself a research project after more than twenty years in development. Innovators can make systemwide changes only when they pool their individual expertise in pursuit of a common goal.

The challenge to U.S. education is to fashion a process that combines isolated experiences and innovations into new, integrated systems of teaching and learning. For reasons already discussed, we know that it also must be a self-improving system, one that can determine when structural changes are needed and then make those changes without precipitating turmoil. Finally, as we've seen, such a process will work only if it's controlled by those responsible for making it work. The only framework of change in industry and technology that has consistently met those tests over time is the system of research, development, marketing, and redesign that impels continuous, self-compounding innovation.

Educators rightly point out that our schools' problems won't surrender to purely industrial or technological solutions; but, as we've noted in earlier chapters, the redesign process in its essence isn't about machinery or products. Although it has been used almost exclusively in those settings, its meaning and power grow from the ways in which it focuses and propels human energies toward an evolving vision of excellence. In adapting the principles of the process to education, however, we do need to alter a term's definition. In commerce, *marketing* describes the informational campaign aimed at winning consumers to products. In education, such campaigns are no less important, but to be most effective they must take a somewhat different form. In a process of educational redesign, *mentoring* replaces marketing.

Marketing works best to sell products, not to foster the changes in personal beliefs and behaviors that a process of systemic reforms requires of teachers. The benefits of a new product are "built in" at the factory; people who buy the products automatically acquire their benefits. But processes like teaching and learning are more similar to plans for a product than to the product itself: the benefits of a new educational process or concept can only be suggested by its design. They depend at least as strongly on how well teachers and students carry out the processes that the design indicates.

Decades of failed reforms have taught us that imposing established programs "off the rack" on skeptical, unprepared teachers frequently creates more friction than motion. In contrast, mentoring offers a framework oriented less toward selling projects and programs than toward collaboration in forging effective classroom processes. Through mentoring, designers and teachers can collaborate to create and test their own reforms in pilot programs or other small settings, evaluate the results, and then share the results with colleagues. This is the approach to educational change that's proving most effective in individual reforms already underway.

That point is crucial. These goals and frameworks aren't distant ideals; in rudimentary and incomplete forms, they're already changing what happens in classrooms. But those changes are isolated and small. To realize their potential, education must combine and expand them, which can be done most quickly and effectively in an institution designed for this purpose, one we would call the Systems Redesign School (SRS). As we propose it, the Systems Redesign School would be able to direct the same explosive power to education reform that has institutionalized technological revolution in industry.

A Laboratory of Educational Change

A laboratory's work is about processes as much as results. In fact, processes often *are* its results. The Systems Redesign School can function as a laboratory, uniting skilled and willing teachers, able researchers and designers, students of diverse backgrounds and abilities, and classroom innovations, all working together to improve each other. The SRS will give education a place and a process through which it can develop the ability to plan, refine, and integrate continuous improvements. The SRS's role in education is similar to that of companies like Boeing or McDonnell Douglas in the aircraft business: to foster, refine, coordinate, and integrate the innovations that bubble up not only from their own ranks but from other inventors within the industry, and to meld those innovations in ways that improve products' quality, usefulness, and reliability while reducing costs.

Each SRS must volunteer for its special role; the task is too large and too unsettling to be taken up by any school not prepared for it. Because each SRS will be a crucible in which the old cultures of teaching and schooling are broken down and new ones forged, they are best drawn from the most successful of those already participating in restructuring programs such as the Accelerated Schools Program and Success For All. These reform frameworks already are helping member schools to reinvent themselves and put teachers at the helm of change. Schools that have cracked their old cultures are more likely than conventional schools to be able to accept and assimilate thoroughgoing reform. Schools that have adopted these programs often house the most disadvantaged students—those struggling to learn amid poverty, social chaos, and poor health. Innovations that show success amid conditions so adverse to learning should succeed at least as well among students whose concentration is less threatened by deprivation.

In addition to an openness to change, schools hoping to become Systems Redesign Schools must show four qualities. First, they must house a cadre of teachers with a record of working together in ways that increase genuine learning among their students as well as themselves. The redesign process demands cooperation, and those who have worked their way from isolation to collaboration will be best able to tackle the challenges of redesign immediately and directly. Second, teachers in candidate schools must be eager to test new ideas. It's not enough that they be willing to take on the tough problems in education; SRS faculty members must be those who actively seek them out—immersing themselves in competing ideas and techniques to winnow the most effective and efficient. Third, SRS teachers and students alike must understand that their role is to serve as well as to experiment. They must be ready to work with other educators and students as exemplars and mentors. An emphasis on service will smooth the transfer of the reform process from school to school, speed the cultural redefinition of teaching as a collaborative and not an isolating profession, and help prepare students to take their places in an increasingly group-oriented workplace. Fourth, an SRS must maintain close communications with the world beyond the school. The problems in education that each SRS will address will be defined by the needs, demands, and realities of the adult world—not by academicians alone.

Many schools might be exhilarated by the prospect of becoming an SRS, but not all will have the right constellation of people, attitudes, resources, and experiences to do the job well. Each school seeking the role perhaps would submit a proposal—in effect, an application—that inventories its teachers' skills and strengths and details their experience with successful collaboration, innovation, and changing educational cultures. The proposal also might define the problems and detail the projects that the school hopes to take on through the redesign process. State or federal education agencies could convene panels area by area to judge the proposals and select the schools that will become SRSs. To do so, the panels could recruit front-line educators, university researchers, business leaders, government officials, community leaders, and others who know their regions intimately.

In keeping with the principles of the redesign process, the first SRSs should be few in number and serve as prototypes. We suggest an initial corps of thirty nationwide—ten each among elementary, middle, and high schools. The number is large enough to allow a diversity of locations and a variety of experiments, yet small enough to keep initial costs affordable. Larger investments will be prudent only after the system of organizing and operating a process of educational redesign has been debugged, a task that should be expected to take at least a decade. Cultural change within any profession is gradual, and among teachers and administrators now at work only a handful have ever experienced it. U.S. education must be granted time to accustom and attune itself to the processes of change. If educators are unwilling to commit at least ten years' effort and resources to developing that process, they should not begin it.

Because workable reforms must be designed and tested in the real world, each SRS will remain responsible for educating its usual complement of students. To accomplish that mission while freeing teachers from their classrooms to pursue innovation, the SRS will need to do two things. First, it must tap the power of cooperative learning, enlisting students to teach and learn from one another and thus to ease the burden of time and psychic demand on teachers. Second, it must increase the size of its faculty—in the thirty pilot SRS schools, probably as much as doubling it. The additional teachers will come from the ranks of experienced educators who have shown a deep personal commitment to positive innovation. To provide them, an SRS's "client" school districts—those hoping to make use of the reforms proven valuable at the SRS—can grant a distinguished teacher a year's leave to work at the SRS. The SRS will have been endowed with enough money to "buy" those teachers' contracts for that year and thus reimburse client districts for the cost of replacing teachers on leave.

Client districts will have a strong incentive to aid their local SRSs. When their tours of duty end, visiting teachers will return to their home districts to share what they have learned. If their home districts choose to adopt any of the ideas, approaches, and techniques developed during their year at the SRS, these teachers will serve as mentors and facilitators in implementing those innovations. Change thus will come to client schools in the most effective way—through their own designated teachers rather than through outside experts and policy-makers.

When students are helping to teach and a larger faculty shares the remaining work, each of the thirty initial SRSs will confront the most urgent task in the process of reform: to perfect approaches and techniques by which every school can halve its own teachers' classroom workloads and free faculties for the professional growth and training needed to make the best use of innovations developed in Systems Redesign Schools. But there's a catch: the new schedules can't demand additional or substitute teachers, and they mustn't compromise, even in the short term, the quality of students' education. SRS faculties might test more elaborate ways to put students in charge of instruction, or they might construct intricate schedules by which teachers move between classrooms and professional study sessions. They might develop electronic mail systems that would let teachers attend more closely to students' individual questions and needs; they might work to draw parents and other volunteers into the schools to take over classes while teachers study. There will be no single "right answer" to the challenge of freeing teachers' time for continuing professional improvement—only the firm requirement that it be done.

When SRSs have designed new scheduling patterns that free teachers' time without shortchanging students, they'll be ready to test them—at first, probably for only a single day. Client districts' teachers working at the SRS will simply observe for that day while the SRS's regular teaching staff conducts classes according to the new structures and strategies. After the test, teachers and students will dissect the experiment's results to determine how well the approaches balance the quality of learning against the amount and value of teachers' freed time. After problems have been pinpointed and the designs refined, the revised patterns can be tested again. Once the patterns work smoothly over the course of a single school day, they can be tested for a week. The longer experiments probably will highlight new faults needing correction, and the redesigned patterns can be tested again for a week. When those patterns succeed, they can be tested for two weeks or a month. Eventually, SRSs will arrive at scheduling patterns that permanently free a portion of teachers' time while sustaining the quality of students' education.

With workable new scheduling patterns in place, SRSs can assume the ongoing work of educational innovation and integration. Their teachers will commission, evaluate, refine, and combine a stream of new approaches, techniques, and materials for teaching and learning. They'll test new ideas, methods, and technologies in their classrooms, differentiate those that show promise from those that don't, refine the best, and integrate them into a structure of educational excellence that steadily advances the effectiveness and efficiency of learning. For example, at one SRS a group of teachers might experiment with integrating computer software and the techniques of cooperative learning in ways that enhance each other's strengths. At another, teachers might offer a chemistry course in French and evaluate its effects on learning in both subjects. At a third, instructors might compare different assessment methods in evaluating the effects of a new course combining physics and calculus. The strengths of each SRS faculty and its other resources will determine its emphasis. Possibly, teachers themselves will specialize in certain areas of innovation—using their new study time to become subject specialists, research analysts, or master teachers.

As we've noted earlier, an effective redesign process demands specialization that necessarily begets new professions. As SRSs evolve, new specialties and professions will emerge in education. Educational architects—innovators similar to Robert Slavin and Marie Clay—will specialize in designing schooling's broad structures, such as new time-management or classroom-organization patterns. Instructional designers will devise and structure thousands of individual learning experiences for students as well as for teachers engaged in career-long professional improvement. Exemplary teachers will work as "teacher-leaders" who coach their fellow instructors toward excellence (as they now do in Reading Recovery). "Change facilitators" will coordinate the school- or systemwide implementation of experiments and innovations, while "systems integrators" will blend individual innovations into orchestrated patterns of change. Within each group, program evaluators and assessment designers will refine their existing techniques and develop more effective ones as they help other specialists measure the results of their work. Each SRS will serve as both a laboratory for innovative programs and a training ground for new professions within education.

Still, systems redesign schools will be integrators first and foremost, not lone reformers. As we have noted, profound innovation demands more time and specialized expertise than most working teachers have. For that reason, SRSs must rely on independent suppliers for most of the individual innovations that become part of the educational systems they devise, just as manufacturers rely on specialized outside suppliers for the parts that make up their products. SRS suppliers may be university-based researchers, as were those who created Reading Recovery and Physics By Inquiry; they also may be individual entrepreneurs or profit-seeking corporations. Their form is unimportant; the quality of their creations is what matters.

Although they'll work in small groups on a variety of projects, SRS teachers and suppliers also will be contributing to a crucial common enterprise. Gradually, SRS teachers and designers will amass the body of tested knowledge, established techniques, and proven materials that will enable each school and teacher to draw on the profession's collective expertise—the hallmark of an effective redesign process.

These goals and frameworks aren't vague ideals. They represent the logical and necessary integration and culmination of initiatives such as Reading Recovery already underway in a number of U.S. schools. These projects demonstrate that teachers are able and ready to work with independent suppliers to create new curriculums, to use resources more efficiently, and to bring to schools the processes of deep, long-term change. A closer look at two such programs glimpses both the promise of the Systems Redesign School and the kinds of problems it can solve.

LEARNING BY DESIGN

"Paper or plastic?"

The middle-school science teacher holds a brown paper grocery bag in one hand, a plastic one in the other. On slips of paper, her students list the reasons why they'd choose one or the other at the supermarket and drop their slips in the bag of their choice. The class tallies the choices and analyzes the reasons behind them.

Over the next month, as the class investigates the role of plastics in the environment, students discover the chemical structure of polymers. They look into the amount of energy used to make plastics and other kinds of materials, weigh their advantages against their drawbacks, and may finally consider ways to make more judicious use of plastics in their own homes.

The class is using a "learning module" developed by the Chemical Education for Public Understanding Program, known as CEPUP—one of the best American examples of educational design. The program develops its modules through a small-scale version of the redesign process, from tracking basic research in education and testing prototypes in real classrooms to integrating innovations and mentoring teachers. In 1992, CEPUP's success in structuring learning experiences in chemistry for elementary- and middle-school students earned it a four-year, $3.2 million National Science Foundation grant to expand its work to science in general. As a result, CEPUP is now SEPUP, the Science Education for Public

Understanding Program, headquartered in the University of California's Berkeley campus.

SEPUP's director, Herbert Thier, a former junior-high-school science teacher and assistant school superintendent, refers to himself as an instructional developer. "The question of my job's name is provoking," he says. "So few people do this kind of work that it's not an organized profession with its own name." Some educators would call Thier a curriculum developer, but he rejects the tag. "To me, the curriculum is something that happens between students and an instructional leader. We provide the materials that bring that about. We structure learning experiences."[1]

The experiences, grouped in self-contained modules, don't fall into conventional subject categories. Instead of creating lessons around conventional topics such as heat, electricity, or chemical bonding, SEPUP's staff of six takes the ideas for module subjects from students themselves through a process that a commercial organization would recognize as market research. "We know from talking to students that middle school is a period in which children become very interested in public policy issues," Thier explains. "Pollution and the environment are good examples. Our goal has been to identify public policy issues that interest students, to develop modules of materials that would teach the basic science underlying them, and to do so in a way that allows teachers to accomplish the existing goals of their science programs in more effective ways—without making extra burdens for them."

As part of its work, SEPUP pays close attention to new findings in cognitive science, developmental psychology, and other basic research in education. "Those inputs are vital to us," Thier emphasizes. "We work closely with people from those areas as we develop our materials. I compare good instructional development to the best relationships between science and engineering." Still, he notes, "Our modules use the findings of research, but don't originate solely in an attempt to prove a particular academic point. Instead, each module starts with an idea that gets kids' attention as a way of accomplishing our academic objectives."

After defining a new module's subject according to students' interests, Thier and his colleagues begin their research. To develop the module on plastics and the environment, they collected articles from newspapers and magazines that detailed related social and scientific issues. They studied an instructional approach to the same subject used in Britain and asked for help from the plastics industry, which, Thier says, "supplied not just information, but also ideas for experiments and activities."

Thier and his coworkers—which, as usual, included classroom teachers on leave to work with SEPUP—then drew on their diverse skills to organize and structure the information. Among the group were a biologist, a chemist, and an earth scientist with a master's degree in science education. "We're small, but that's somewhat deliberate," according to Thier. "Adding more people doesn't always make things quicker and, in fact, can slow things down." Instead, the group consults as needed with experts in curriculum development, cognitive psychology, and conventional scientific disciplines. With expert guidance, the SEPUP staff organizes a module's material in hierarchies of detail and creates a small kit of materials that students can use at their desks to perform experiments.

Each module is a mix of prescription and suggestion that grants teachers the freedom to shape the material to their own needs and those of their students. "If the subject matter isn't familiar to a teacher and they want to follow our lesson structure step by step, we give them all the detail they need to do that," Thier says. "If they feel they know the subject well enough and want to substitute some of their own ideas, they're free to do that, too." Such flexibility is deliberate; teachers often resent programs that present them with rigid lesson plans that must be followed precisely. "We define the game and organize the playing field," he says, and likens teachers to coaches: they may be playing a game that SEPUP designed, but they organize their own strategies and tactics according to their students' individual strengths, weaknesses, and needs. "Many teachers tell us that they use our outlines religiously the first time they teach the module, then feel more free to improvise the details as they become more familiar with the material. We provide a lot of detail for teachers who need it in a way that we don't think is obnoxious."

Teachers are similarly free to choose from the "item bank" of perhaps two dozen or more questions that ends each module. About half of the queries test low-level knowledge by asking for short-answer or multiple-choice responses. The next few challenge students' higher-order thinking skills by requiring them to interpret data and reason their way through carefully structured problems. The final few questions give students the chance to write essays analyzing the science behind a public policy question or to apply principles they've learned to new situations. It's an approach that works: teachers have found the modules' framework so comfortable that many have begun to adapt it to other subjects, and SEPUP is now developing instructional materials for two full-year science courses built around public issues.

The students' materials are somewhat less flexible. Modules don't come with textbooks. Instead, small groups of students use pages of recipelike instructions that show them how to perform experiments with the small trays of equipment that come with the materials. As students master basic concepts, the recipes give way to less structured activities and problems. "Each student takes his own data and draws his own conclusions, then the group discusses what they've learned," Thier explains. "We're attempting to balance individual and cooperative learning while we're patterning the students' experiences." It's a matter of efficiency. "Most kids can proceed on their own, giving the teacher the chance to help those who need help and to challenge those who need challenge."

Other aspects of the modules' design reflect concern about the efficient use of educational resources. "We've designed equipment kits that will let kids do activities and experiments in any classroom, without special facilities or equipment. The trays of equipment use eyedroppers to dispense very little material at a time, so there's very little waste. They clean up quickly and much of the equipment is reusable." Thier puts the total cost of a month-long module, with materials and supplies to equip a teacher's typical load of five daily classes, at just over $200, placing SEPUP materials among the least costly science programs now on the market.

After SEPUP develops a module's preliminary structure, it tests a prototype. Pairs of teachers from the SEPUP staff work in San Francisco area schools to teach the module in actual classrooms. One instructs while the other makes detailed notes about students' reactions and parts of the module that work well or poorly, and jots ideas and points to raise back in the design group. After several weeks of trials, SEPUP's staff reconvenes, often with a consulting specialist in materials design, to reconfigure and improve the module for a broader audition. The second-stage trial usually involves between ten and fifteen teachers from around the city who teach the improved version of the module while SEPUP staffers observe. After another redesign, the module goes to SEPUP's sixteen "field centers" around the country—schools from small to large and rural to urban—where trials are supervised by teachers SEPUP has trained as field coordinators. This "market test" involves as many as eighty teachers who use the module in up to five classes a day. After the trials are completed, each coordinator gathers participating teachers to talk about their own and their students' reactions to it. The meetings are recorded and the tapes sent back to SEPUP for review, and the module is revised again.

"We do all our own material on a desktop computer in our office, so we can change things very easily and quickly," Thier reports. "I have colleagues in other programs who commit themselves to producing a hardback textbook as soon as their programs receive funding. That's ridiculous, anachronistic—but schools still think they have to have one." When Australian educators wanted to try some of SEPUP's materials in their elementary schools, they found that they needed to translate some terminology and forms of notation into Australia's unique idioms. "With a textbook, that process would have been tortuous," Thier says. "But I was able to hand my colleague twelve computer disks; he took the whole program home with him, the teachers decided what they wanted, and they printed it themselves." After SEPUP finalizes a module, the materials are turned over to publishers and kit producers who distribute the lessons nationally. Between 1988 and 1992, SEPUP completed twelve modules covering subjects from plastics to groundwater purity, from food additives to the problems of solid-waste disposal.

The modules are on their way to becoming best-sellers, which augurs well for the innovations that the redesign process will yield. "In all the programs I've been involved in over the past thirty years, I've never seen growth like this," Thier marvels. "Soon, more than a million children each year will be experiencing SEPUP materials."

If Thier's group were only one of a growing corps of instructional designers and developers, all using SEPUP's redesign approach, SRSs would have a ready assortment of promising designs to work with. "But, unfortunately, for several reasons things aren't moving in this direction," Thier told us. In recent years the national push for quick, measurable gains in student achievement has emphasized the use and importance of standardized tests as a quick way to measure progress. "Shrinking budgets and increasing demands for being first in the world by the turn of the century are pressuring people into more rigid structures, and I'm talking about an open structure. We hear more and more now about 'aligning' the curriculum to those tests. That means narrowing the focus of instruction even more to dwell on the kinds of knowledge sampled by tests—not expanding it in new directions that might not fit as well with the conventional mode of testing."

He also notes that the National Science Foundation has recently funded several statewide pilot projects in science education, many having secured a commitment of $10 million or more over several years. "Because of political considerations, those statewide programs are often controlled by state education bureaucracies," he points out. "As a result, I'm concerned that these programs will be more concerned with taking small steps instead of bold ones. I'm concerned that we won't have the funding or a climate that will nurture people on the edge who want to try new things." Those people themselves might be hard to come by. "Graduate students who want to do this ask me where they should study, where they should work," he says. "If they're interested specifically in developing expertise in developing new approaches and materials, I have no idea. If you speak to any department of science education at any major university, they'd tell you, 'Yes, that's what we do now.' I can simply tell you that they don't. In terms of a specific academic program teaching people to do this kind of work, I don't know of one that exists or is being planned."

EDUCATION'S "TEACHING HOSPITALS"

There has never been any lack of zeal among educators to attempt to redefine what schooling is. In 1896, the philosopher John Dewey opened an experimental school on the University of Chicago campus to test his theories about curriculum and educational structure. In the 1960s, "laboratory schools" sprouted in many U.S. university schools of education. Lab schools, whose students were mostly children of university faculty, offered future teachers ready access to student groups on whom they could practice pedagogical skills and test new ideas in teaching and learning. Like most spasms of enthusiasm in education, the lab school movement was promulgated by a small group of passionate and persuasive educators. When lab schools' results proved inconclusive, and as more promising new intellectual fashions appeared, interest faded in what became yet another program offering no clear rationale to those obliged to fund and manage it. Lab schools soon disappeared.

A visionary effort now afoot to reinvent public schooling is the concept of the Professional Development School, or PDS. Conceived in conversations among three university deans of education in the mid-1980s, the PDS idea has grown into a vision of intimate partnership between individual public schools and research universities. It is a vision that resembles the Systems Redesign School in a number of aspects. The movement now counts nearly one hundred university-based schools of education among its adherents, who tend to view the PDS as education's equivalent of the medical profession's teaching hospital—an alliance between novice and master, research and practice, server and client. According to a 1992 report by the Holmes Group, the PDS movement's coordinating team, which is headquartered at Michigan State University, "The Professional Development School needs to be seen as the major focus of the university's threefold mission of preparing teachers and administrators, serving as the research and development arm of the profession, and providing direct services to schools—just as teaching hospitals assist in the training of physicians, conduct medical research, and provide high-quality patient care."[2]

The vision also has attracted dozens of public schools ready to take on the challenge of structural and cultural transformation. Participating educators picture a PDS as a place where "we might see experienced teachers working together with university faculty to better understand the range of . . . styles of learning in their schools," the group suggests. "We might see teachers testing curriculum modified for their own school's diverse students and explaining the results of their inquiry to their colleagues. We might see school and university faculty collecting and interpreting the practical knowledge of teachers for the purpose of establishing a case literature. We might see successful teachers writing and speaking about how they create a good learning community in their diverse schools. We might see teachers asking parents questions about culture and language, and using the answers to design programs for students in school and nonschool settings. We might see staff development activities spanning several years."[3]

Because even the most advanced Professional Development Schools are still new to the role, all are groping for working definitions of what they're becoming. But perhaps the direction of every PDS is reflected in the experiences of Morgantown High School, a PDS with almost 1,400 students and the equivalent of seventy full-time teachers in Morgantown, West Virginia. "A PDS is constantly changing," says the school's principal, Thomas Hart. "In fact, the only constant so far *is* change."[4]

Those changes reach far beyond the dozen or so education students from the University of West Virginia now at work in the school's classrooms. Since it became a PDS in 1990, Morgantown High has inaugurated a two-year integrated course in algebra and geometry taught by four teachers working as a team. The school's chemistry courses now require a good deal of writing from students. Teachers from the high school's social studies, English, and art departments have worked together to develop an interdisciplinary approach to the study of U.S. history and culture during the 1930s. Instructors in journalism, art, and the business-internship courses known as distributive education collaborate to teach a course in visual communications. Hart has asked his mathematics teachers to construct new kinds of tests that better measure students' abilities to think and apply the concepts they're learning, and the faculty is exploring more flexible ways to segment Morgantown's traditional seven-period school day. Morgantown, like other PDSs, is demonstrating that teachers are able and ready to exchange education's antiquated paradigms for more useful and dynamic ones.

Hart credits the school's university affiliation with having fostered such innovations. "I—and I think many other educators—had thought of an educated person as being someone with a lot of facts in his head," Hart admits. "Now we're coming to believe that analysis, problem solving, and critical thinking are more important." In the summer of 1992, the university invited the high school's teachers to a day-long seminar to discuss ways of incorporating higher-order skills into their courses. Fifty of the school's teachers showed up. "That turnout surprised me," Hart says. "They didn't have much notice, and they weren't paid for attending. In fact, we'd have had more come but a lot of them already had made their vacation plans."

Many of the school's teachers showed far less interest when Morgantown became a PDS. "At first, only a small number of teachers were eager to participate," Hart says. "That number has increased as more and more of our teachers have seen what others are doing and what the program can mean." The effort wins converts through consensus, not evangelism. "We're not forcing anyone to be involved," Hart points out. "We're letting this grow naturally. As a result, we're moving more slowly than we otherwise would, but we're building a stronger foundation."

Strong as it may be, the foundation Morgantown is building still isn't as large as the scope of the changes it hopes to make. Like the proposed Systems Redesign Schools, Morgantown has broken traditional cultural barriers between teachers. It fosters collaboration among them and with innovators outside the school. It emphasizes process rather than product. It invites, rather than coerces, its teachers to join in the continuing experiment. But the resemblance ends there. By nature—or, more correctly, by design—every Professional Development School carries within it three flaws that will hamper its impact at best and could defeat it entirely.

First, a PDS doesn't ease teachers' usual classroom crush but adds additional burdens to it. "What worries me most is the feeling that a lot of PDS teachers and principals are heading for burnout," says Ann Williams, the Holmes Group's executive assistant for management and operations. "They do their usual things very intensely all day long in class. On their lunch breaks, they're meeting with university faculty. After school, they're in more meetings or they go to classes. Some of the classes are at their partner universities, and some of them are education classes that these same overburdened teachers help to teach."[5] Computerized communications between universities and PDSs reduce mileage but do little to reduce the psychic toll a PDS exacts from its teachers. And for many schools the convenience of such sophisticated communications equipment is far beyond the reach of their budgets.

Second, becoming a PDS can carry a high price. Theoretically, a school's participation in the program needn't add to its expenses. But most PDSs find that theory and practice part company. Many of the schools have had to rely on special stipends, often channeled to them through their partner universities, to fund the time that staff members must take from their normal duties and give to needed study or preparation for their new roles. A Kentucky school pulled in a two-year federal grant to free its teachers and administrators from some of their routine chores so they could collaborate to define the school's new identity. Morgantown used a private foundation grant to pay for several planning and training sessions for teachers. "It's unreasonable to expect a school to take on several new activities and do them well within the regular school budget," Williams says.

Unfortunately, district offices may not couple their moral support for a PDS project with anything more tangible. Morgantown's school board designated the high school's role as a PDS as an official priority, but more than a year later it still hadn't allotted the funds the school needed to implement that role fully. "It's difficult [for a PDS to realize its potential] unless a central office decides to put in the funds that are necessary to make the needed changes—things like funding release time to let teachers out of their classrooms to take classes and attend conferences," Hart says. "If you're going to make changes, it takes money because you're going to have to do some retraining." Unfortunately, PDSs offer administrators too few reasons to make such a clearly major investment: improving the skills and effectiveness of teachers in a single PDS doesn't raise the quality of education in any of the district's other schools. The PDS teachers' additional training can make teaching and learning more efficient in one school, but it can never offer the scale of widespread efficiencies that would allow administrators to justify a sizeable investment in the first place. In addition, singling out one group of teachers or administrators for favorable treatment is a decision that stirs resentment among those not chosen.

The third flaw goes squarely to PDS's defining concept. While it may resemble a Systems Redesign School superficially, a PDS doesn't seek to combine innovations in integrated systems, nor does it seek to aid other schools. Those tasks might be implied in a PDS's role as a learning laboratory, but they're not specifically articulated or pursued. For all its boldness, the PDS concept confronts too few of the lingering, deeply rooted structural problems in U.S. education—problems that can be overcome through the approach of the Systems Redesign School.

THE PRICE OF PROGRESS

Fortunately, U.S. education can begin to fashion a redesign process without adding to the fiscal burden of taxpayers, legions of whom already are in revolt. Like any new venture, it will need seed money and support to establish itself. But there is ample reason to expect that school-based redesign eventually can become financially self-sustaining.

Exact start-up costs can't be forecast, but it's possible to calculate reasonable estimates. Each of the thirty potential SRSs should be expected to have a typical complement of teachers—to estimate generously, about twenty in an elementary school, thirty-five in a middle school, and fifty in a high school. Ten SRSs at each level, doubling their faculties, would thus recruit an additional 1,050 teachers from client school districts. According to National Education Association figures, during the 1991–92 school year the average salary for U.S. teachers was about $34,400. An informal survey of several random school districts around the country shows that the value of teachers' employee benefits averages about one third of their salaries—for our computations, about $11,450. The typical teacher's total annual compensation, then, can be estimated to be roughly $45,850. Therefore, doubling the teaching staffs at all thirty schools chosen as SRS sites for a year would cost about $50 million.

These additional teachers will need chairs, desks, and office supplies. To accomplish their mission, they'll need to travel and to make long-distance phone calls. They'll have to buy books, subscribe to journals, and pay tuition to attend university courses and professional conferences. The expense will vary from school to school and teacher to teacher as each takes on different tasks with different demands. How-ever, some reasonable estimates are possible for each teacher: $750 for equipment, $250 for books and subscriptions to professional journals, $1,000 for travel, another $1,000 for tuition, $500 in long-distance charges to communicate with colleagues and specialists, and perhaps another $500 budgeted for contingencies. During the program's first year, those expenses could be expected to average $4,000 for each member of an SRS's doubled teaching staff—a total of 2,100 teachers, or about $8.4 million in expenses.

As systems integrators, SRSs also will be the channels through which necessary investments in professional, curricular, and evaluatory devel-opment will flow to the independent suppliers creating the innovations that SRSs will test. Professional and curricular development cannot be separated, however; among the things that working teachers will study will be the proper use of new materials and approaches as they evolve. Indeed, reform's largest single investment must be made more or less simultaneously in the creation of new curricula—which include the approaches, techniques, materials, and technologies that will decisively move teaching and learning out of the old paradigm of schooling and into the new—and the expertise teachers will need to use them well. To begin to accomplish the huge task of redesigning every subject in all twelve grades and kindergarten, and continuously to improve teachers' own professional education programs, will demand an annual budget of at least $100 million, phased in over several years.

That $100 million figure, which grants $3.3 million to each SRS to allot among its suppliers, could be conservative. Consider a single exam-ple: Currently, materials for science classes are the most expensive, since they include equipment and chemicals as well as texts. Publishers' prices for conventional science curriculum materials currently range from $200 to $750 to supply a class of thirty students with study materials for one unit or module taking up anywhere from a quarter to half of the academic year. Because other subject courses will require no chemicals and less equipment, costs for other new curricular programs will be less. Let's assume that each SRS has a typical population of thirty students in each class, or total populations of six hundred in each of ten elementary schools, about one thousand in each of ten middle schools, and roughly fifteen hundred in each of ten high schools. Let's also assume that each student in each SRS studies six subjects a day, all of which will require revised material. Estimating an average cost of $600 to supply one class of thirty students with new materials in one subject, and estimating an average of three such packages to be used in each subject through the course of a school year, materials for a completely revised curriculum across all thirty SRSs would require an investment of $11.1 million. However, that figure represents the cost of buying existing programs "off the shelf." To invent and test new programs, as we recommend, is far more costly—more than enough, we believe, to justify our estimate of $100 million.

It's more difficult to estimate the amount that each SRS would need to spend on the services of consultants—seminar leaders for classes in teaching techniques, school management and curriculum specialists, and other experts. We can assume the typical consultant will charge $500 a day, including expenses—not an uncommon fee. An SRS's need for such advisers will be greatest early, as it struggles to shape its new structures and concepts; therefore, we suggest budgeting one hundred days of consulting costs for each SRS during its first year, at a total cost of $50,000 per school or $1.5 million programwide.

At each SRS, the processes of evaluation would necessitate a distinctly separate investment. Designing, building, and refining an evaluation system to monitor all subjects in all grades will be people-intensive: evaluators' skills and tools must develop apace with new curricula and approaches to teaching so that educators can discern with increasing subtlety the most effective experiments. That demands enough specialists to give each evaluation experiment detailed design, management, and oversight. We suggest an appropriation of $1 million in each SRS to begin to create and refine the necessary measurement methods.

Administering each SRS will demand the same degree of financial support. Running an SRS will go far beyond the usual tasks of school management. The constant exchange of information—among teachers, between SRSs and consultants, among SRSs themselves, between an SRS and its client schools, and between a school and program officials—will demand not only time but also more sophisticated communications and information-management technologies than most schools now possess. In addition, administrators and staff must be paid, and office, travel, and other expenses covered; the program will publish a journal and occasional papers, host meetings and conferences, and perhaps commission independent evaluations or studies. To cover the range of administrative expense, we estimate a $1 million outlay for each SRS during the program's first year, although nonprofit organizations often contribute to the overhead costs of innovative programs. The total administrative budget: $30 million for the entire program.

To test a year-long prototype of U.S. education's first system of progressive innovation, then, would require $230 million, including materials costs—about a tenth of one percent (.001) of our annual national $200 billion in education expenditures. The gains in educational effectiveness and efficiency already demonstrated by Reading Recovery, the Accelerated Schools Program, and other successful reforms using pieces of the redesign process only hint at the gains in effectiveness and efficiency that the Systems Redesign School program could offer.

Unfortunately, we need to seed school-based redesign at a time when the United States also is beginning to confront the consequences and remedies of its runaway national debt. The traditional source of investment in school programs—federal education spending—is likely to increase in the years ahead, probably enough to cover the costs of the pilot SRS program we propose. However, the costs of educational redesign can be met not only through additions to the national budget, but through redirecting existing portions of it. Some aspects of the process almost certainly can qualify for funding under the $6 billion Chapter One initiative to help failing children in poor areas, for example, while some existing work in the Department of Education's OERI (Office of Educational Research and Improvement) regional education laboratories should easily match the needs and projects at many SRSs. The balance can be funded by money dedicated to the redesign process from the budgets of all other existing U.S. Department of Education programs.

However, support means more than money. To create a constituency as broad as the SRS pilot program itself among those who will oversee it, responsibility for its successful implementation should be shared by the National Science Foundation as well as the U.S. Department of Education (and, perhaps, other agencies as well). There are precedents: federal interagency initiatives in materials science and global warming were organized because those issues were recognized as too important to be left to any single office. Education reform is no less urgent.

By helping to fund and manage the project, other agencies and education programs would have incentives not to sabotage or compete with it. Indeed, the more quickly SRSs multiply their efficiencies through client schools and districts, the sooner most of those agencies will accomplish their own goals.

And SRSs' client schools will see similar gains. After their year at an SRS, clients' teachers will return to their districts. There, they'll begin to help their schools implement the new professional-development schedules and other innovations developed at the SRS. As schools begin to implement those new ideas, they'll begin to educate students more efficiently and effectively. The same number of teachers will provide better instruction, and gradually the number of failing students will decline. Fewer kids will be assigned to remedial programs; fewer will receive "social promotions" unearned by academic achievement. Consistent evidence from a range of studies predicts that fewer will then quit school.

These changes aren't just heartening; they also save money. If the experience of most restructuring programs repeats itself, problems of vandalism and discipline will dwindle. If fewer children are doing physical damage to their schools, maintenance budgets should level off and might actually shrink. If more children are learning more quickly and effectively, educators will need to spend fewer resources to "rework" children through remedial programs. If more students remain in school long enough to earn a diploma, there will be fewer unproductive people needing public aid and more contributing taxes to the public treasury. As those savings begin to appear in school district budgets, some portion of them—perhaps all at first—can be reinvested in the redesign process to maintain its pace. As those efficiencies multiply, schools and districts will be able to shoulder a growing share of SRS funding out of the savings it brings them.

When SRS pilot schools have proved that a closely monitored process of continuous innovation can succeed in education, demand for more SRSs will spread nationwide. Such an expansion will require more school buildings, more teachers, more specialists, and more equipment—all of which will require additional investment. It won't be a tiny sum. Meeting the costs of a national infrastructure of Systems Redesign Schools might prove difficult at first, just as paying a child's college tuition can strain the budget of a middle-income family. But the strain is more than offset by an expectation of future rewards rich enough and real enough to justify short-term hardships. As redesign's efficiencies grow and multiply, federal programs will begin to reap savings greater than the amounts they've invested. Within a decade of its inception, Systems Redesign Schools could be virtually self-supporting through the budgetary efficiencies they create for all schools.

A SCHOOL FOR A NEW CENTURY

The year is 2014. For teachers and students at Second Avenue Middle School the day begins with meetings. Mrs. Atkinson, a science and mathematics teacher, begins this day with a routine one. For eleven-year-old Jeff, his first meeting is especially significant.

The teacher's meeting brings her together with the other instructors in her "house"—a group of sixty-four students who share four teachers (each training an apprentice) and an interdisciplinary, multiyear curriculum. Every morning, the teachers gather to discuss the day's lessons and address any issues or problems that have come up. The first order of business today is to review the plan for the next six weeks' coursework in electricity. Mrs. Atkinson, with her apprentice and an assistant teacher, will introduce the subject in the morning's main academic meeting by leading the students through a basic experiment and helping them to grasp its meaning. In Mr. Hardy's social science meeting the next day, the same students will begin to trace the history of electrical research and theory, which they'll summarize later in multimedia presentations. That research will continue in Mrs. Putnam's foreign-language seminars, where students will read, translate, and discuss related material in Spanish or French. Mr. Lund, the humanities teacher, is taking a wide-ranging approach. In studio sessions, he'll coach students using different expressive forms to explore the emotional and cultural connotations of electricity, while in reading seminars they'll consider how writers and philosophers have understood it. Later, in trips to a gallery, a sculptor's studio, and the city's art museum, students will confront and react to kinetic and illuminated art that relies on electricity for its meaning. This morning, Mr. Hardy and Mrs. Atkinson confer briefly to make sure that students won't encounter key technical concepts in their historical research until they've experienced them in the lab. Then the four teachers discuss the individual learning styles of eleven students who they fear might face particular difficulties. They determine which of the students are likely to have an easier time learning electricity's concepts through lab work and which through reading. They agree to monitor carefully each special child's learning and to supplement their regular coursework with special material from the Systems Redesign School's curriculum catalog if they need to.

Like Second Avenue's teachers and administrators, each of its students also is part of a management team. As usual, Jeff's first meeting this Tuesday is with the other members of the school's information resources committee. The information technologies supervisor and media coordinator get together with the committee's six teachers and six students to talk over problems, needs, additions, and possible changes to the school's mix of books, videotapes, sound recordings, and electronic databases. Jeff's fascination with computers led the committee to invite him to join last year. But this is his last morning with the group. His term with the panel is up and he has been accepted as a member of the academic committee, a panel of fifteen students that works on curricular issues with teachers, instructional designers, and school administrators. It's a coveted assignment, and Jeff worked especially hard on his application essay to win the seat. This morning, he first meets with the girl replacing him on the resources committee. He explains to her how the committee makes decisions, briefs her on its current issues, and gives her some judicious warnings and advice about some of the personalities she'll be working with. They then join the meeting in progress. Jeff introduces his replacement, makes a brief statement summarizing his views and concerns about issues and projects the committee is considering, and is thanked by the committee's student and teacher coleaders for his work.

The day's first two academic meetings—what used to be called "classes"—fill the balance of the morning. The meetings are carefully structured to integrate disciplines and to nurture in all students the steady growth of knowledge as well as the intellectual skills to use it creatively. This morning, Mrs. Atkinson explains to her students how they'll approach the study of electricity. Then the apprentice and assistant teachers give each four-person learning group a penlight battery, a wire, and a flashlight bulb. The assignment: to use the wire and battery to make the bulb light. One group presses the bulb's base against the battery's positive terminal. Another uses the wire to link the terminal and bulb base. A third asks if they can cut the wire into two pieces. The groups carefully diagram each arrangement they try and note the results. As each group works, it swaps ideas through a computer network with a partner-group in a Mexico City middle school tackling the same lesson at the same time. The Mexican children communicate their ideas and results in English, the students in Jeff's class in Spanish. (A Hispanic parent volunteer has stopped by to help the students with their Spanish if they need it.) As the experiment progresses, an older Second Avenue student serving as an assistant teacher moves from group to group, answering questions and prodding the students with queries of her own. The apprentice teacher, Helen Stewart, supervises the group and stands ready to field complex questions or issues that leave the assistant unsure.

After each group has found a way to make its bulb light, its members compare their successes and failures—first with their Mexican colleagues, then with the others in the room—to draw conclusions about why the bulb lit some times and not others. From those comparisons, students begin to formulate hypotheses about how and why their successful circuits worked, and what broad principles about electricity they can generalize from their results. In Jeff's second meeting today, an aesthetics workshop, he decides to write a poem to convey his emerging concept of what electricity is.

At noon, the tenor of the meetings changes. Instead of working on projects that develop skills and understandings needed by all future workers and citizens, the children now give the balance of their day to work that emphasizes their individual talents and interests. These are the projects that students themselves choose—efforts that help each of them to develop a unique constellation of specialized skills and knowledge that eventually will make him or her a uniquely valued member of the adult workforce and community.

Five children with a particular interest in fine art use the after-lunch meeting three days a week to sketch. Another group has asked Mr. Hardy, the social studies specialist among the four teachers who supervise this group of sixty-four students, for advice in organizing the next stage of their year-long research into the history, culture, and present plight of sub-Saharan Africa. The teacher recalls a recently published learning program that guides students through an interdisciplinary study of the region. He checks his electronic catalog and finds the program, then helps the students select a group of interrelated projects suitable for their level of analytical skills and levels of understanding. The students initially disagree about how effectively the program would help them reach the learning goals they've formulated for their research project. Mr. Hardy asks the four students to give him their written evaluation and decision by the start of the next day's meeting. He moves on to another group.

In another part of the room, Mrs. Atkinson sits in with Jeff's five-student group. The students have decided to take their study of electricity's practical possibilities farther than their regular morning meeting will: they're attempting to design a self-propelled robot whose lightbulb eyes will flash when it moves. As the science and mathematics specialist among the teaching group, Mrs. Atkinson has helped Jeff and his partners structure their project and will monitor its progress. But she also took a direct part in assembling the group itself. Left on their own, students tend to work with the same group of friends or partners they've worked with before. Children also gravitate toward others of their own social circle, ethnic group, or ability level. But in the world beyond school, groups form, change, and disband according to the demands of the work they undertake. To accustom students to that reality, teachers seek to mix students of diverse backgrounds and strengths. It's not enough for Mrs. Atkinson to ensure that a social studies project shows sound statistical reasoning and clear analytical language, or that the results of a mathematical investigation are presented in prose as clear and cogent as the equations. She also must see that the groups reflect the diversity of backgrounds and learning levels represented among the school's students and that each group makes effective use of that diversity. Toward that goal, she regularly coaches each group in communications skills, emphasizing that people from differing backgrounds may express and interpret the same ideas differently. In each group's organizational meeting, she also has stressed that when students who grasp a new idea quickly take time to explain the concept to a partner who understands it less readily, both are actively learning. It's often difficult to convince parents of that, and Mrs. Atkinson is prepared for their objections. When Jeff's mother expressed concern on this point, the teacher sent the results of several studies on the subject to her home computer by electronic mail.

This morning, Jeff and his partners are debating how to let the robot's eyes know the robot is moving and, therefore, to flash. Dan wants to design a special circuit to attach to one of the wheels. The circuit would sense that the wheel is turning and communicate that information to a control box that will then flash the robot's eyes. Carol argues that the arrangement is too complicated. Instead, she suggests a simple vibration sensor she's found in an electronics catalog. When the robot moves, it will vibrate; the sensor will detect the motion and can flash the eyes itself, without the aid of a separate control box. Jeff asks whether the vibration detector is so sensitive that a breeze might start the eyes flashing even if the robot isn't moving. Carol isn't sure, and Dan points out again that his device avoids the problem. Unwilling to give up so easily, Carol offers to research the vibration detector's specifications so the group can compare the two approaches in detail. Mrs. Atkinson rises to move to another group. "Remember," she says, "you'll have to make your decision about that by the end of this week so you can get on the next part of the project."

For the balance of the meeting, Mrs. Atkinson and the instructors working under her move among the groups, prodding them with questions, offering suggestions, mediating disagreements. As the groups adjourn, Jeff and his partners continue debating as they go on to their daily reading seminar. This week, they're analyzing a provocative novel for young adults about race relations and reflecting on the book's challenges to their own values.

Mrs. Atkinson, whose classroom teaching is over for the day, now resumes her own schedule of meetings. The afternoon's first brings her together with the six students working with her this semester as assistant teachers. Five of them are older Second Avenue students; the sixth is a sophomore from the local high school. The arrangement isn't unusual. All students in each of the city's schools spend part of their school year as assistant teachers in subjects they've already studied. The internships not only help students extend their mastery over the subjects they teach, but also help free teachers' time for professional study and improvement. Older students who express an interest in teaching as a career also may be assigned to coach students much younger than themselves—both to integrate their levels of knowledge about different subjects and to confront some of the deeper issues of teaching. This group works under Mrs. Atkinson's supervision, leading discussions in younger learning groups where they ask students to explain the results of actual experiments or to reason their way through problems that instructional designers have crafted to stretch students' understanding of the material.

The afternoon's colloquium is a coaching session to prepare for tomorrow's morning meeting. Mrs. Atkinson begins by showing a videotape of one of the assistants in a teaching session earlier in the day. After selecting several brief scenes, she asks, "Lee, why did you feel the need in each of those cases to provide those students with answers to your questions instead of letting them struggle a little longer to come up with their own?" After some discussion, Lee admits that he felt uncomfortable with the students' uncertainty as they groped for a response; he also worried that the pace of the class would slow and other students' attention would wander during the silence. "Can you think of any ways to keep their attention?" she asks. "If you were a student in that class, what would engage *you*?" Lee says that he likes to think about open-ended questions that lead him to speculate about a wide range of possible answers. Sarah, another assistant teacher, recounts an incident recently in which she used leading questions to keep the class discussion moving while one student spent twenty minutes devising a solution to the question posed to him. Lee is intrigued, and says he'll experiment with the method in tomorrow's session. "Remember," Mrs. Atkinson says, "if you get stuck, Mrs. Stewart or I will be in the room to help. If I'm tied up, you can use the group's computer to contact a subject specialist at the regional learning center and get on-line help. Now—any problems?"

Linda says, "I'm still not clear about the right-hand rule of current flow and that's probably going to come up in class tomorrow or the next day. I'm not sure how to talk about it."

"That's a good question—how *will* you say that?" Mrs. Atkinson asks. "We were going to get into that next, so you can start us off. We're your group; show us how you'd pose that subject." As Mrs. Atkinson helps the group frame the next day's discussion subjects and questions, she challenges both their academic knowledge and their resourcefulness as instructors.

Finally, she asks the group about Peggy Bailey. It's a crucial time for the student: Peggy's been slow to master the concepts of weather that the house has been studying. Now that the curriculum has moved on to projects in electricity, Peggy risks falling behind. Tom, an assistant teacher who has been tutoring Peggy privately after school, says that she's making some progress but that she's still tentative in her understanding of some key ideas. Mrs. Atkinson asks Lee and Mrs. Stewart how Peggy did in the electricity lab that morning. They tell her that she seemed engaged, confident, and showed no difficulty in mastering the concepts.

"If we can keep up the tutoring sessions for another week, I think she'll have mastered the weather material," Tom says. "Meanwhile, it sounds like she'll be able to keep up with the work in electricity just through the regular meetings."

Lee nods. "Since the material on electricity seems to interest her, maybe it would help her to relate the two. Maybe she could use some of her basic understanding of electricity to research the causes of lightning or something. That might not be the most useful example, but the approach might work."

Tom nods thoughtfully. "I'll look for opportunities to use that. It could give her some good intellectual leverage." Mrs. Atkinson does a quick database search through the room's desktop computer and finds two learning programs that relate weather and electricity. She gives Tom the programs' names and suggests that he scan them to determine their suitability to Peggy's need before the tutoring session that afternoon. "If one or both will be useful, you can explain to us tomorrow how you'll use them—and if they're not, you can tell us why," she says. As she gathers her papers to leave, Mrs. Atkinson tells Tom that she'll stop by the school office and reserve a tutoring room for him for another week.

Next, Mrs. Atkinson joins the rest of the school's seventy-two teachers in the auditorium. The assembly is an introductory session to a two-day workshop next week that will launch a three-month series of planning sessions. The occasion is a new curriculum and approach to teaching it, developed and tested at the nearby Systems Redesign School and now ready to be adopted by the SRS's clients. Today, the teachers watch a series of videotapes showing academic meetings being conducted under the new plan. The videos are introduced by a master teacher from the SRS, who also draws general contrasts between the new program and the current one and fields the teachers' initial questions. One difference is clear right away: when the school adopts the new plan at the beginning of the next academic year, the building will house four grades instead of the current three. As a result, the size of each house will increase from sixty-four to eighty students. In next week's sessions, the teachers will begin to analyze the new curriculum and practice the new techniques that will let them manage larger classes without compromising the quality of learning. They'll also begin to discuss how the school building can be remodeled and reorganized most effectively to accommodate larger classes and more students.

Mrs. Atkinson's last meeting this afternoon is more intimate. She's reviewing and critiquing the professional portfolio of her apprentice teacher, Helen Stewart. Mrs. Stewart began her portfolio to document her growing abilities as an instructor when she decided in junior high school that she wanted to become a teacher. Now she's completing the twenty-year apprenticeship of successful study and supervised instruction time that the National Board of Professional Teaching Standards requires in order to grant certification as a teacher. She asks Mrs. Atkinson's opinion on the best example she can present of her work with a troubled student. In one case, she helped a girl to find the right assignments to school-management committees that needed her gift for analyzing the reasons for conflict between people and suggesting workable compromises. After the girl spent several weeks as part of the group, her self-confidence rose, and so did her academic results. In another case, Stewart had worked with a boy's family to identify personal difficulties that distracted him from learning. She arranged counseling for the family and worked individually with the boy; after several months he'd been able to qualify for a special seminar for gifted science students. Mrs. Atkinson poses questions to her apprentice to test her ability to defend her approach in each case and to look at her own results critically. After a half hour, the apprentice realizes that she'd like to use the latter example, but needs to analyze it more carefully to understand exactly why it worked so effectively.

Because it's Tuesday, Mrs. Atkinson will be back in the same meeting room tonight. This semester, she's supervising a group of high-school seniors coaching an adult-education course in statistical analysis. The adults aren't the only ones who will be learning, though. By encouraging and fielding the adults' practical questions, Mrs. Atkinson and her students will gather a more accurate and detailed understanding of the kinds of skills the workplace is demanding. The teacher will carry that insight back to the school district's instructional-design committee, which will use her findings to help teachers and designers structure students' learning experiences more closely to the current needs and demands of the world beyond the classroom.

Welcome to one version of the twenty-first-century school. There will be many others. Each, however, will be a product of rigorous, effective research, development, mentoring, and redesign. Each will be a place in which teachers serve as coaches and facilitators rather than as information delivery services, and where technology multiplies and extends the number of effective exchanges between student and instructor.

We know that Mrs. Atkinson and her students won't be attending their school for at least another decade. As we've emphasized, cultural change can't be hurried. At least at first, the redesign process will probably spark as much anxiety and uncertainty among educators as it does exhilaration and hope. Some won't be able to surmount the challenges of redesign's uncertainties and new responsibilities. There will be calls to abandon unfamiliar new processes and to return to the old patterns—not because they're more effective or more efficient, but because they offer the certainty that comes with stability. Even if the old structures don't work, at least people know how to work within them. Educators, parents, and all of us must be prepared to confront that opposition to change, to expose it, and to keep pressing the case for innovation that builds on itself instead of always starting over.

In many ways, the tumultuous process of institutionalizing a system of redesign in education is reflected in the current struggle to create free-market economies in the newly liberated nations of Asia and Eastern Europe. Remote, centralized bureaucracies are being stripped of power. Individuals' voices and choices are gaining authority. Free and competitive markets, in goods and in ideas, are blossoming. Rigid, outdated institutions are crumbling as new, flexible, and unfamiliar ones are being built. But the similarities between school reform and those chaotic struggles need not continue past that point. In some of those nations, crowds have taken to the streets to protest the pace, and even the fact, of change. Fearing to step from the familiar into the unknown, they're unwilling to cope with the turmoil wrought by massive uncertainties. However, they can be forgiven: they've never glimpsed the society in which they're being asked to invest their futures. But U.S. educators *have* glimpsed our schools' future. They've seen research-based programs such as Reading Recovery and Physics By Inquiry make measurable differences in students' achievements and enthusiasm. They've seen the Accelerated Schools Program, Success For All, and other restructuring projects bring dying schools back to life by freeing teachers' expertise and creative power. They're watching as SEPUP demonstrates the synergy that results from combining the power of research, development, mentoring, and redesign.

American educators know that a more meaningful, challenging, and satisfying future waits on the far side of change. Until now, they have lacked a path that can lead them from today's antiquated education paradigm to the more effective and efficient ones that a new economy and century demand. The redesign process embodied in the Systems Redesign School can be that path—a route that leads unerringly toward excellence, even as our definitions of excellence change with our evolving conceptions about what it means to be educated. A future that holds change as the only constant leaves us no choice but to begin that journey.

Notes

1. Reforming School Reform

1. National Commission on Excellence in Education, *A Nation At Risk: The Imperative for Educational Reform* (Washington, D.C.: U.S. Government Printing Office, 1983), p. 5.
2. Ibid., p. 23.
3. National Center for Education Statistics, *The State of Mathematics Education* (Washington, D.C.: U.S. Department of Education, 1990), pp. 7–9.
4. National Education Goals Panel, *The National Education Goals Report*, executive summary (Washington, D.C.: U.S. Department of Education, 1991), p. 14.
5. John I. Goodlad, *A Place Called School* (New York: McGraw-Hill, 1984), pp. 207, 209.
6. National Education Goals Panel, *The National Education Goals Report*, p. xii.
7. David A. Hamburg, *Today's Children: Creating a Future for a Generation in Crisis.* (New York: Times Books, 1992).
8. William B. Johnston and Arnold H. Packer, *Workforce 2000: Work and Workers for the 21st Century* (Indianapolis: Hudson Institute, 1987), pp. 98, 99.
9. National Center for Research on Evaluation, Standards, and Student Testing, Program Two, Project 2.3, *Measurement of Workforce Readiness Competencies*, CFDA catalog no. 84.117G, (Washington, D.C.: U.S. Department of Education, 1992), pp. 2, 14, 15.

10. National Association of Manufacturers, public statement and press release accompanying *The NAM/Towers Perrin Skills Gap Survey* (Washington, D.C., 1991).
11. Thomas Kuhn, *The Structure of Scientific Revolutions*, 2d ed. (Chicago: University of Chicago Press, 1970) p. 5.
12. Ibid., p. 144.
13. Ibid., p. 109.
14. Ibid., p. 92.
15. Richard J. Sauer and Carl E. Pray, "Mobilizing Support for Agricultural Research at the Minnesota Agricultural Experiment Station" in Vernon W. Ruttan and Carl E. Pray, eds., *Policy for Agricultural Research* (Boulder, Colo.: Westview Press, 1987), p. 218.
16. Ibid.

2. The Pursuit of Excellence

1. Jeremy Main, "Betting on the 21st-Century Jet," *Fortune*, April 20, 1992, 117.
2. Historical figures provided by United Air Lines, September 21, 1992.
3. James Gleick, *Chaos: Making a New Science* (New York: Viking, 1987), p. 3.
4. Ibid., p. 38.
5. Ibid., p. 39.
6. Personal interview, August 26, 1992.

3. Reading Recovery

1. Personal interview, March 23, 1992.
2. Gay Su Pinnell et al., *Studying the Effectiveness of Early Intervention Approaches for First-Grade Children Having Difficulty in Reading* (Columbus, Ohio: Ohio State University, 1991).
3. Pinnell, personal interview, March 23, 1993.
4. Ibid.
5. Marie Clay, *Becoming Literate: The Construction of Inner Control* (Portsmouth, N.H.: Heinemann Educational Books, 1991), p. 19.
6. Ibid., pp. 61, 342.
7. Ibid., p. 323.
8. Ibid., p. 16.
9. Ibid., p. 20.
10. Ibid., p. 62.
11. Ibid., p. 18.
12. Ibid., p. 323.
13. Ibid., p. 62.
14. Ibid., p. 27.
15. Personal interview, March 23, 1992.
16. Richard L. Allington, "If They Don't Read Much, How They Ever Gonna Get Good?" *Journal of Reading* (October 1977): 58.

17. Philip C. Dyer, "Reading Recovery: A Cost Benefit Analysis," draft copy, 1990, pp. 3, 5–7.
18. Reading Recovery in California at California State University, San Bernardino, *Annual Report 1993*, p. 17.

4. Missing Links

1. Roland Barth, *Improving Schools from Within* (San Francisco: Jossey-Bass Publishers, 1990), pp. 49–50.
2. Dan Lortie, *Schoolteacher: A Sociological Study* (Chicago: University of Chicago Press, 1975).
3. Ibid., p. 160.
4. Michael Fullan and Susan Stiegelbauer, *The New Meaning of Educational Change* (New York: Teachers College Press, 1991), p. 119.
5. Lortie, *Schoolteacher*, pp. 61, 64.
6. John I. Goodlad, *Teachers for Our Nation's Schools* (San Francisco: Jossey-Bass Publishers, 1990), p. 173.
7. Lortie, *Schoolteacher*, p. 210.
8. Seymour B. Sarason, *The Culture of the School and the Problem of Change* (Boston: Allyn & Bacon, Inc., 1971), p. 115.
9. Lortie, *Schoolteacher*, p. 70.
10. Ibid., pp. 240, 77.
11. Fullan and Stiegelbauer, *The New Meaning*, p. 33.
12. Lortie, *Schoolteacher*, pp. 233–34.
13. Fullan and Stiegelbauer, *The New Meaning*, pp. 316, 317.
14. Ibid., pp. 53, 55.
15. Barth, *Improving Schools*, p. 18.
16. Lortie, *Schoolteacher*, pp. 242, 69–70.
17. Susan A. Walters, "Professional Teacher Development Through Research" in *Teachers and Research in Action*, ed. Carol Livingston and Shari Castle (Washington, D.C.: National Education Association of the United States, 1989), p. 41.
18. Jimmy E. Nations, "Using Research to Solve Student Grouping Problems" in *Teachers and Research in Action*, p. 29.
19. Lortie, *Schoolteacher*, pp. 69, 241.
20. Richard C. Atkinson and Gregg B. Jackson, eds., *Research and Education Reform: Roles for the Office of Educational Research and Improvement* (Washington, D.C.: National Academy Press, 1992), p. 17.
21. Harold W. Stevenson and James W. Stigler, *The Learning Gap: Why Our Schools Are Failing and What We Can Learn from Japanese and Chinese Education* (New York: Summit Books, 1992), p. 164.
22. Ibid., p. 160.
23. Ibid., pp. 161, 157, 159.

5. The Culture of the School

1. Josh Barnabel, "Legacy of a School Chancellor: Fernandez's Changes May Not Live On After His Departure," *New York Times*, June 30, 1993, B1.

2. Personal interview, October 26, 1992.

3. Michael Fullan and Susan Stiegelbauer, *The New Meaning of Educational Change* (New York: Teachers College Press, 1991), pp. xiv, 36, 47.

4. Seymour B. Sarason, *The Predictable Failure of Educational Reform* (San Francisco: Jossey-Bass, 1991), p. 99.

5. Seymour B. Sarason, *The Culture of the School and the Problem of Change* (Boston: Allyn & Bacon, Inc., 1972), p. 2.

6. Ibid., p. 42.

7. Ibid., p. 44.

8. Sarason, *The Predictable Failure*, p. 64.

9. Ernest R. House, *The Politics of Educational Innovation* (Berkeley, Calif.: McCutchan Publishing Corp., 1974), p. 73.

10. Fullan and Stiegelbauer, *The New Meaning*, pp. 345–46.

11. Ibid., p. xiii.

12. Harold W. Stevenson and James W. Stigler, *The Learning Gap: Why Our Schools Are Failing and What We Can Learn from Japanese and Chinese Education* (New York: Summit Books, 1992), p. 105.

13. Ibid., p. 106.

14. Ibid., p. 109.

15. Ibid., p. 111.

16. Jeannie Oakes and Martin Lipton, *Making the Best of Schools: A Handbook for Parents, Teachers, and Policymakers* (New Haven: Yale University Press, 1990), p. 168.

17. Ibid.

18. Stevenson and Stigler, *The Learning Gap*, p. 109.

19. Sarason, *Culture of the School*, p. 78.

20. Fullan and Stiegelbauer, *The New Meaning*, p. 119.

6. Measuring Up

1. Thomas Toch, *In the Name of Excellence: The Struggle to Reform the Nation's Schools, Why It's Failing, and What Should Be Done* (New York: Oxford University Press, 1991), p. 206.

2. George F. Madaus et al., *The Influence of Testing on Teaching Math and Science in Grades 4–12* (Boston: Center for the Study of Testing, Evaluation, and Educational Policy, Boston College, 1992), "Report," p. 7 and Executive Summary, p. 18.

3. Ibid.

4. Ibid., p. 9.

5. Ibid., p. 12.

6. Ibid., p. 15.

7. Personal interview, December 21, 1992.
8. Joseph McDonald, "Steps in Planning Backwards: Early Lessons from the Schools" (Providence, R.I.: Coalition of Essential Schools, Brown University, 1992), p. 1.
9. Ibid.
10. Joseph McDonald, "Exhibitions: Facing Outward, Pointing Inward" (Providence, R.I.: Coalition of Essential Schools, Brown University, 1991), p. 7.
11. Jody Podl et al., "The Process of Planning Backwards: Stories from Three Schools" (Providence, R.I.: Coalition of Essential Schools, Brown University, 1992), p. 4.
12. Joseph McDonald et al., "How to Redesign a School: Planning Backwards from Exhibitions" (Providence, R.I.: Coalition of Essential Schools, Brown University, 1992), p. 50.
13. Podl et al., "The Process," p. 12.
14. Personal interview, January 11, 1993.
15. Podl et al., "The Process," p. 12.
16. Personal interview, December 23, 1992.
17. Personal interview, December 29, 1992.
18. Lillian C. McDermott and Peter S. Shaffer, "Research as a Guide for Curriculum Development: An Example from Introductory Electricity, Part 1" *American Journal of Physics* 60 (November 11, 1992): 995, 1002.

7. Enacting the New Paradigm

1. Margarent Byrnes, personal interview, September 14, 1992, with information later confirmed by Candace Allen.
2. Ibid.
3. Personal interview, October 23, 1992.
4. Margaret A. Byrnes, Robert A. Cornesky, and Lawrence W. Byrnes, *The Quality Teacher: Implementing Total Quality in the Classroom* (Bunnell, Fla.: Cornesky & Associates Press, 1992), p. 84.
5. Byrnes, personal interview, September 14, 1992.
6. Susan Rosenholtz, *Teachers' Workplace: The Social Organization of School* (New York: Longman, 1989), quoted in Michael Fullan and Susan Stiegelbauer, *The New Meaning of Educational Change* (New York: Teachers College Press, 1991), p. 134.
7. Fullan and Stiegelbauer, *The New Meaning*, pp. 131–32.
8. Personal interview, September 6, 1992.
9. Gary Watts and Shari Castle, "Electronic Networking and the Construction of Professional Knowledge," *Phi Delta Kappan*, May 1992, 686, 685.
10. Personal interview, September 9, 1992.
11. Watts and Castle, "Electronic Networking," p. 689.
12. Personal interview, September 7, 1992.
13. Personal interview, September 21, 1992.
14. Personal interview, August 13, 1992.

15. Personal interview, January 15, 1990.
16. Howard Gardner, *The Unschooled Mind: How Children Think and How Schools Should Teach* (New York: Basic Books, 1991), p. 49.
17. Ibid., p. 91.
18. Ibid., p. 154.
19. Ibid., pp. 3, 154.
20. Arnold Arons, *A Guide to Introductory Physics Teaching* (New York: John Wiley & Sons, 1990), pp. 15–16.
21. Ibid., pp. 289, 314.
22. Personal interview, March 23, 1992.
23. E. H. van Zee and Lillian McDermott, "Investigation of Student Difficulties with Graphical Representation in Physics" in *Proceedings of Second International Seminar: Misconceptions and Educational Strategies in Science and Mathematics III* (Ithaca, N.Y.: Cornell University Press, 1987), pp. 531–39; also Arons, *A Guide*, pp. 35–37.
24. Arons, *A Guide*, pp. 2, 3.
25. David Johnson and Roger Johnson, "The Internal Dynamics of Cooperative Learning Groups," quoted in *Learning to Cooperate, Cooperating to Learn*, ed. Robert Slavin (New York: Plenum Press, 1985) p. 105.
26. Ibid., p. 114.
27. Personal interview, June 4, 1992.
28. Ibid.
29. Personal interview, December 17, 1991.
30. Personal interview, August 28, 1992.
31. Bert K. Waits and Franklin Demana, "The Calculator and Computer Precalculus Project (C²PC): What Have We Learned in Ten Years?" (preprint; Columbus, Ohio: Ohio State University, 1990), p. 22.
32. Ibid., pp. 21–22.
33. Tom King, quoted in "St. Paul Sketches 'School of the Future,'" *Wichita Eagle*, October 31, 1989, 2.
34. Personal interview, August 5, 1992.
35. Edward B. Fiske, *Smart Schools, Smart Kids: Why Do Some Schools Work?* (New York: Touchstone, 1992), pp. 247–48.

8. The Key to Reform

1. Personal interview, December 18, 1992.
2. The Holmes Group, *Tomorrow's Schools: Principles for the Design of Professional Development Schools* (East Lansing, Mich.: The Holmes Group, 1990), p. 81.
3. Ibid., p. 39.
4. Personal interview, January 6, 1993.
5. Personal interview, January 8, 1993.

Bibliography

Adler, Mortimer J., and Charles Van Doren. *How to Read a Book: The Classic Guide to Intelligent Reading.* New York: Simon & Schuster, 1973. A classic that demonstrates how a typically passive activity can be transformed into a higher-order skill.

Arons, Arnold. *A Guide to Introductory Physics Teaching.* New York: John Wiley & Sons, 1990. A detailed example of how physics—and, by implication, other courses—can be redesigned according to the insights of cognitive science.

Barth, Roland. *Improving Schools from Within.* San Francisco: Jossey-Bass Publishers, 1990. An essay on the potential value of a technical culture within education.

Bennis, Warren, and Burt Nanus. *Leaders: The Strategies for Taking Charge.* New York: HarperCollins, 1985. Techniques and visions of leadership from those who know.

Byrnes, Margaret A., Robert A. Cornesky, and Lawrence W. Byrnes. *The Quality Teacher: Implementing Total Quality in the Classroom.* Bunnell, Fla.: Cornesky & Associates Press, 1992. An introduction to the principles of Total Quality Learning.

Clay, Marie. *Becoming Literate: The Construction of Inner Control.* Portsmouth, N.H.: Heinemann Educational Books, 1992. The research framework underlying Reading Recovery, a paradigm-shattering reform program.

Comenius, John Amos. *The Great Didactic,* 2d ed. trans. M. Keating. London: A & C Black, 1910. Among the earliest examples of educational design, laying out a plan for systematic schooling.

Covey, Stephen. *The Seven Habits of Highly Effective People: Restoring the Character Ethic.* New York: Simon and Schuster, 1989. Essential traits for success in family life and in a global economy based on personal services.

————. *Principle-Centered Leadership.* New York: Simon and Schuster, 1991. Skills demanded by an increasingly group-oriented workplace.

Csikszentmihalyi, Mihaly. *The Evolving Self: A Psychology for the Third Millennium.* New York: HarperCollins, 1993. A guide to personal happiness and wisdom in a changing world.

Deming, W. Edwards. *Out of the Crisis.* Cambridge, Mass.: Massachusetts Institute of Technology, 1986. The principles of Total Quality, by the engineer who inspired Japan's quality revolution.

Drucker, Peter. *Innovation and Entrepreneurship: Practice and Principles.* New York: Harper and Row, 1985. Survival skills for tomorrow's economy.

————. *Post-Capitalist Society.* New York: HarperCollins, 1993. Trends and problems arising from the emergence of a knowledge-based economy.

Eisenstein, Elizabeth L. *The Printing Revolution in Early Modern Europe: A Parable for Today's Communication Revolution.* Cambridge: Cambridge University Press, 1983. The impact of printing on the Renaissance and its implications for today.

Fiske, Edward B. *Smart Schools, Smart Kids: Why Do Some Schools Work?* New York: Touchstone, 1992. A survey of promising education reforms.

Fuhrman, Susan, ed. *Designing Coherent Education Policy.* San Francisco: Jossey-Bass, 1993. Research perspectives on efforts to achieve the U.S. national education goals.

Fullan, Michael, with Susan Stiegelbauer. *The New Meaning of Educational Change*. New York: Teachers College Press, 1991. A research review of organizational barriers to education reform.

Gardner, Howard. *The Unschooled Mind: How Children Think and How Schools Should Teach*. New York: Basic Books, 1991. Cognitive science's new insights into teaching and learning.

Glasser, W. *The Quality School: Managing Students Without Coercion*. New York: Harper and Row, 1990. Using the principles of Total Quality to motivate learning.

Goodlad, John I. *A Place Called School*. New York: McGraw-Hill, 1984. Problems of current educational structures, extensively documented.

_____. *Teachers for Our Nation's Schools*. San Francisco: Jossey-Bass Publishers, 1990. Problems and challenges in teacher education.

Hamburg, David A. *Today's Children: Creating a Future for a Generation in Crisis*. New York: Times Books, 1992. A research perspective on the worsening problems of U.S. children.

Hirsch, E. D., Jr. *Cultural Literacy: What Every American Needs to Know*. New York: Random House, 1987. Literacy as a basis for cultural unity and stability among Americans.

The Holmes Group. *Tomorrow's Schools: Principles for the Design of Professional Development Schools*. East Lansing, Mich.: The Holmes Group, 1990. A noble and valuable attempt to reconceive school structure.

Hughes, Thomas P. *American Genesis*. New York: Penguin, 1990. History and analysis of early technological systems and early stages of the redesign process.

_____. *Networks of Power: Electrification in Western Society, 1880–1930*. Baltimore: Johns Hopkins University Press, 1983. The first fifty years of a redesign process, including its social and political aspects.

Johnson, D. W., R. Johnson, and K. Smith. *Cooperative Learning in the College Classroom*. Edina, Minn.: Interaction Book Co., 1989. A reform proposal based on twenty years of research.

Johnston, William B., and Arnold H. Packer. *Workforce 2000: Work and Workers for the 21st Century*. Indianapolis: Hudson Institute, 1987.

Krugman, Paul. *Peddling Prosperity.* New York: Norton, 1994. The effects of economic nostrums on U.S. policy and performance since 1970.

Kuhn, Thomas. *The Copernican Revolution: Planetary Astronomy in the Development of Western Thought.* Cambridge, Mass.: Harvard University Press, 1957. A useful historical analogy for the challenges of education reform today.

———. *The Structure of Scientific Revolutions*, 2d ed. Chicago: University of Chicago Press, 1970. The definitive analysis of paradigm shifts, the process through which organizational cultures are transformed.

Livingston, Carol, and Shari Castle, eds. *Teachers and Research in Action.* Washington, D.C.: National Education Association of the United States, 1989.

Lortie, Dan. *Schoolteacher: A Sociological Study.* Chicago: University of Chicago Press, 1975. Landmark study of the teaching profession and its differences from other fields.

Lyons, Carol A., Gay Su Pinnell, and Diane E. DeFord. *Partners in Learning: Teachers and Children in Reading Recovery.* New York: Teachers College Press, 1993. The latest summary of the Reading Recovery program, including results of recent research.

McDermott, Lillian C. "A Perspective in Teacher Preparation in Physics and Other Sciences: The Need for Special Science Courses for Teachers." *American Journal of Physics* 58 (1990). On physics education, from the director of a breakthrough physics instruction project.

Marshall, Ray, and Marc Tucker. *Thinking for a Living: Education and the Wealth of Nations.* New York: Basic Books, 1992. The relation of education reform to current economic change.

Naisbitt, John. *Megatrends: Ten New Directions Transforming Our Lives.* New York: Warner Books, 1986.

Naisbitt, John, and Patricia Aburdene. *Megatrends 2000: Ten New Directions for the 1990s.* New York: Avon Books, 1990. (Both *Megatrends* books emphasize trends that leave the uneducated behind.)

National Council of Teachers of Mathematics. *Curriculum and Evaluation Standards for School Mathematics.* Reston, Va.: National Council of Teachers of Mathematics, 1989. A catalyst for the current standard-setting movement in education.

National Research Council. *Fulfilling the Promise: Biology Education in the Nation's Schools.* Washington, D.C.: National Academy Press, 1990. Seventy-three critical problems plaguing biology education and recommendations for solving them, any one of which would be daunting to implement.

Oakes, Jeannie, and Martin Lipton. *Making the Best of Schools: A Handbook for Parents, Teachers, and Policymakers.* New Haven, Conn.: Yale University Press, 1990. A collection of good advice on basic issues.

Quality Education for Minorities. *Education That Works: An Action Plan for the Education of Minorities.* Washington, D.C.: Quality Education for Minorities, 1990. A minority perspective on educational improvement.

Rogers, Everett M. *Diffusion of Innovations*, 3rd ed. New York: Free Press, 1983. How innovations permeate a culture and the barriers they must overcome.

Sarason, Seymour B. *The Culture of the School and the Problem of Change.* Boston: Allyn & Bacon, Inc., 1972. A classic study of the reasons why most past education reforms have failed.

_____. *The Challenge of Art to Psychology.* New Haven, Conn.: Yale University Press, 1990. The absence of meaningful artistic experiences in public schools.

_____. *The Predictable Failure of Education Reform: Can We Change Course Before It's Too Late?* San Francisco: Jossey-Bass, 1991. Wise advice directed toward achieving a positive answer.

_____. *Letters to a Serious Education President.* Newbury Park, Calif.: Corwin Press, 1993. A delightful summary of Sarason's ideas on education reform and its implementation.

Schor, Juliet. *The Overworked American: The Unexpected Decline of Leisure.* New York: HarperCollins, 1991. Insight into a major U.S. social and cultural dilemma.

Schultze, Charles L. *Memos to the President: A Guide Through Macroeconomics for the Busy Policymaker.* Washington, D.C.: The Brookings Institution, 1992. Sound advice from a wise veteran.

Secretary's Commission on Achieving Necessary Skills. *What Work Requires of Schools.* Washington, D.C.: U.S. Department of Labor, 1991. Skills needed in the emerging workplace.

Silberman, C. E. *Crisis in the Classroom: The Remaking of American Education*. New York: Random House, 1970. An examination of deeply rooted problems in our schools.

Sizer, Theodore R. *Horace's School: Redesigning the American High School*. Boston: Houghton Mifflin, 1992. Concepts from the Coalition of Essential Schools, presented by an experienced reformer.

Slavin, Robert E. et al. *Success for All: A Relentless Approach to Prevention and Early Intervention in Elementary School*. Arlington, Va.: Education Research Services, 1992. A solidly researched and field-tested program to revitalize inner-city schools.

Smith, Page. *Killing the Spirit*. New York: Penguin, 1990. The breakdown of long-standing paradigms within the humanities and social sciences.

Stevenson, Harold W., and James W. Stigler. *The Learning Gap: Why Our Schools Are Failing and What We Can Learn from Japanese and Chinese Education*. New York: Summit Books, 1992. An excellent example of comparative observation in classrooms. The book also highlights the vital role cultural differences play in structuring and conducting education in different countries.

Tyack, David, and Elizabeth Hansot. *Managers of Virtue: Public School Leadership in America 1820–1980*. New York: HarperCollins, 1982. A history of U.S. public education, more reliable than childhood memories.

Index

Ability models, 119–23
  effort downplayed in, 119–21
  "shopping-mall high school" and, 121
  tracking and, 121–23
Academic achievement, as matter of in-born ability vs. effort, 119–23
Accelerated Schools Program (ASP), 167–71, 174, 197, 200, 218, 229
Administrative bureaucracies, flattening of, 42–46, 108–9
Agriculture, 93
  support for change and improvement in, 17–19, 78–80
Agriculture Department, U.S., 17–18
Airplane industry, 81, 98, 199–200
  cockpit instruments and, 137–38
  redesign process and, 24, 31–32, 33–34, 35–38

repairs and, 79–80
  vision and, 26, 27–28
Air Transport Association, 37
Allen, Candace, 158–60, 161, 163, 164, 166
Allington, Richard, 65–66
American Marketing Association, 97
Apple Computer, 32–33, 34, 35, 41–42
Arithmetic and Mathematics Educational Practice Lectures, 87
Arizona, portfolio programs in, 146
Arons, Arnold, 179–80, 181
Asia, 139
  assumptions about education in, 119–21, 123
  class size in, 130
  question asking in, 102–3, 124–25

Asia (*cont'd*)
  teaching profession in, 100–103, 104, 105
  See also Japan
Assembly line, creation of, 33
Assembly-line workers
  in industrial age, 9–10
  in postindustrial age, 11–12
Assessment, 138–44
  in education redesign, 138–39, 150–51, 154–55
  new forms of, 144–48
  research program on, 151–52
  in TQL, 161, 163–66
  See also Tests
Automobile industry
  redesign process and, 30, 33–35
  vision and, 28

Baker, Eva, 149, 150
Baltimore, Success For All in, 8
Barth, Roland, 84, 91–92
Barton, Eileen, 146
Becoming Literate (Clay), 59
Behaviorism, 175
Benton Harbor, Mich., school system, 174
Binckney, Ron, 74–75
Blacks, dropout rate among, 6
Board of Examiners (New York City), 107
Boeing, 31–32, 34, 35–37, 137, 199–200
Boston College, 140–41
Broady, George, 31
Brockway, Penny, 169, 170
Brown, Bob, 188–90
Bruner, Jerome, 81
"Building tenure," 106–7
Burnett Academy (San Jose), 174
Bush, George, 7, 9, 27
Byrnes, Lawrence, 164
Byrnes, Margaret, 159, 160, 162, 164–66

"Calculator and Computer Precalculus Project" (C²PC), 191–92
Calculators, in mathematics instruction, 110–12, 190–92
Calculus, preparing students for, 191–92
California
  adult-student ratios in, 130
  curricular mandates in, 125
  educational reform in, 8
  testing innovations in, 143
Canada, curricular mandates in, 126
Care Bears, 182
Carnegie Corporation, 93
Carter, Jimmy, 94
Castle, Shari, 172
Centennial High School (Pueblo, Colo.), 158–60
Central Park East Secondary School (New York City), 146–47, 148
Change
  as familiar part of industry, 113
  human dimensions of, 38–42
  orderly processes of, 16, 17–19, 20, 25, 110–11, 112, 113
  political dimensions of, 109
  resistance to, 39–42
  schools' cultural resistance to, 112–13, 116–18
  See also Educational reform; Innovation; Redesign process
Chaos (Gleick), 39
Chaos theory, 39–40
Chapter One, 64, 73, 218
  conventional remedial reading classes funded by, 65–67, 74
  program costs in, 70–71
Charlottesville, Va., education summit (1989), 7–8
Chemical Education for Public Understanding Program (CEPUP), 205
Chemistry, SEPUP and, 205–10

Chicago, flattening of administrative bureaucracy in, 43, 108–9
Chicago School Reform Act (1988), 109
China. *See* Taiwan
Christian theology, 108
Class size, 100, 130–31
  electronic learning technologies and, 189
Clay, Marie, 59–64, 65, 204
Coaching toward mastery
  subject skills needed for, 83
  teacher training and, 84
  teaching by information transfer vs., 82–83
Coalition of Essential Schools, 144–46, 148
Cognitively Guided Instruction, 8–9
Cognitive science, 157, 175–82, 186, 194, 196, 206
  and unconscious misconceptions about world, 177–81
  whole learning and, 176–77
Coldrick, William, 33, 41–42
Comer, James, 167, 173, 174
Competition, cooperative learning and, 183, 184, 185
Computer industry
  redesign process and, 32–33, 34, 35
  resistance to change encountered by, 41–42
  vision and, 26–27, 28
Computers
  electronic learning technologies and, 26, 187–95
  e-mail and, 188–90, 202
  at Saturn School, 192–94
Condit, Phil, 31
Condom distribution, 106, 108
Congress, U.S., 5, 7, 94
Connecticut, testing innovations in, 143
Constructivism, 176
  See also Cognitive science

Cooperative Extension Service, 17–19
Cooperative learning, 27, 47, 157–58, 182–87, 194, 196
  combining children of different ability levels in, 183–84, 185
  fears abated in, 183
  group learning and, 182–86
  peer tutoring and, 186–87
  as preparation for adult life, 185–86
  in SRSs, 201–2
  studies on, 184–85
Copernicus, Nicolaus, 12, 13, 14–15
Cornesky, Robert, 164
Corporal punishment, 174
"Creation science," 108
Creemer, Joyce, 169
Culture of schools, 106–36
  absorbed by all of us during our schooling, 127–28
  educational politics and, 107–8
  and fallacies of reform, 127–34
  larger national culture and, 118–23
  resistance to change in, 112–13, 116–18
  SRSs and, 200
  time issues and, 123–25
Culture of the School and the Problem of Change, The (Sarason), 113
Curriculum, 25, 26
  educational politics and, 125–27
  exhibitions and, 145–46
  measurement in development of, 151
  new math and, 113–16
  shaped by tests, 126, 142–43
  state mandates and, 125–26
  textbook selection and, 126, 127
  See also specific programs

Darling-Hammond, Linda, 148
Demana, Frank, 191–92
Deming, W. Edwards, 160

De Revolutionibus (On the Revolution of Celestial Spheres) (Copernicus), 15
Dewey, John, 210–11
Douglas, Donald, 24
Dropouts, 6
   retention linked to, 64
Dyer, Philip, 70, 71

Economy
   in industrial age, 9–10
   See also Postindustrial economy
Educate America Act (1994), 7
Education
   Americans' assumptions about, 119–23
   behaviorists' view of, 175
Educational politics, 106–18
   in Chicago school system, 108–9
   conflicting sovereignties and, 134–35
   cultural and social aspects of, 107–8
   curriculum and, 125–27
   and introduction of calculators into math classes, 110–12
   new math and, 113–16
   in New York City school system, 106–7
   and schools' cultural resistance to change, 112–13, 116–18
   state mandates and, 125–26
   test scores and, 142
Educational reform
   class size and, 130–31
   coordinated and supportive research and extension system lacked in, 19–20
   determinants of success in, 167
   expense of, 131–32
   failed, teachers scapegoated for, 116, 117
   goals for, 7
   immediate results sought in, 129–30
   imposed from above, 110–12, 135, 199
   individual initiatives in, 8–9, 25–26, 27, 47, 197–98; *see also* Cognitive science; Cooperative learning; Electronic learning technologies; Reading Recovery; Science Education for Public Understanding Program; Teacher power; Total Quality Learning
   integration of successes in, 195–96
   measuring cost efficiencies of, 151–52
   measuring improvement in, 138–39, 150–51, 154–55
   mentoring in, 198–99
   need for, 1–3, 5–7, 9–12, 20
   new math and, 113–16
   new paradigm needed in, 12–13, 15–16, 20, 27
   orderly processes of change and, 16, 17–19, 20, 110–11, 112, 113
   political dimensions of, 106–18, 125–27, 134–35
   proposed in *A Nation At Risk*, 3–4, 7, 8, 9, 14, 126
   redesign process in, 46–47, 132, 135–36, 195, 198–99
   resistance to change encountered in, 40–41, 112–13, 116–18
   six fallacies of, 127–34
   systems redesign schools (SRSs) as laboratories of, 199–205
   teachers as key to, 104–5
   teacher training as barrier to, 86–87
   test scores as gauge of, 133–34
   understanding of reform process needed in, 128–29
   and version of twenty-first-century school, 220–29
   vision required for, 26–29, 46
Educational research, 80, 92–98, 135, 136
   controversies in, 94

federal government and, 92–93, 94

flaws in, 93, 95, 99

funding of, 92, 93, 96–97

inadequate links among designers in, 97–98

lab school movement and, 211

lack of coordinated system of, 19–20

marketing deficiencies and, 96–97

on measurement, 151–54

not utilized by teachers, 94–96

PDS and, 211–15

private sources of money for, 93

Educational Testing Service (ETS), 4–5

Education Department, U.S., 4, 5, 6, 64, 72, 93, 94, 97, 117, 218–19

Effort, academic achievement as result of innate ability vs., 119–23

Electronic learning technologies, 27, 158, 187–95, 196

class size and, 189

e-mail and, 188–90, 202

in mathematics instruction, 110–12, 190–92

overestimation of, 188

at Saturn School, 192–94

Electronic mail (e-mail), 188–90, 202

Elementary-school teachers, education of, 83–84

Emerging literacy, 60

"Empty vessel" approach, 175–76

English courses, 129

Estrada, Kristine, 174

Evaluation, 148–50

in education redesign, 138–39, 151, 154–55

infrequency of, 149–50

research programs on, 152–54

SRS costs and, 217

typical methods of, 148–49

Exhibitions (mastery demonstrations), 144–46, 147–48

"Exhibitions: Facing Outward, Pointing Inward" (McDonald), 145

Faculty lounges, 91

Faculty meetings, 91

Fairbanks Elementary School (Springfield, Mo.), 169, 174

Fears

abated in cooperative learning, 183

vanquished by TQL, 161, 165–66

Fernandez, Joseph, 106–7

Fiske, Edward, 195

Flunking (retention), 64–65, 71

Ford, Henry, 33

Ford, Joseph, 40

Ford, Roy, 169–70, 174

Ford Foundation, 93

French, Mark, 193–94

Fried, Mary, 56, 57, 64, 67, 68, 69, 72, 73, 74–75

Fullan, Michael, 85, 90–91, 104, 112–13, 117, 125, 126, 128, 130, 170

Gainsburg, Julie, 147

Gardner, Howard, 177–79

Gender gap, 94

Gleick, James, 39

Godbold, John, 109

Goodlad, John, 86

Grading and evaluation, 126

cooperative learning and, 184, 186

new assessment techniques and, 146–47

TQL and, 159–60, 161, 164–66

Group learning, 182–86

See also Cooperative learning

Guide to Introductory Physics, A (Arons), 179–80

Hamburg, David, 7

Handicapped students, cooperative learning and, 185

Hart, Thomas, 212–13, 214
Hechinger, Fred, 176
Higher-order thinking skills
  needed in postindustrial age, 3, 10–12
  standardized tests and, 141
  teacher training and, 82–83
High school, 9
  course offerings in, 121
  dropping out of, 6
  graduation from, 2, 5, 6
Hispanics, dropout rate among, 6
Hodgson Vocational-Technical High School (Newark, Del.), 145
Holland, Robin, 54, 56, 66
Hollibrook Elementary School (Houston, Tex.), 169–70, 174
Holmes Group, 211
Hopkins, Joe, 37
House, Ernest, 117
Hudson Institute, 11

IBM, 32–33
Improving Schools from Within (Barth), 84
Industrial age, educational needs in, 9–10
Influence of Testing on Teaching Math and Science in Grades 4–12, The, 140–41
Innovation, 95
  educational politics and, 126, 127
  inadequate marketing of, 96–97
  institutionalized structures of, 79
  measuring cost efficiencies of, 151–52
  organizational hierarchies and, 42–43
  teacher training and, 88–89
  thwarted by structure of teaching profession, 78, 90–92
  See also Change; Educational reform

Integration of improvements, 25, 30–31, 195–96
Interdisciplinary classes and projects, 145, 146
  in twenty-first-century school, 220–21, 223
Interruptions, 125

Japan, 123
  assumptions about education in, 119, 120–21
  teaching profession in, 100–103, 105
  technical culture of teaching in, 87–88
  TQM in, 160
Jasinowski, Jerry, 12
Johns Hopkins University, 25, 167
  Center for Research in Effective Schooling for Disadvantaged Students, 96–97
Johnson, David, 184–85
Johnson, Roger, 184–85

Kammerer, Douglas, 67, 75
Kentucky, educational reform in, 8
King, Tom, 193
Knapp, Seaman, 17–19
Kuhn, Thomas, 13–15

Laboratory schools, 211
Labor Department, U.S., 11–12
Langford, David, 160, 161–62, 163–64, 165
Lea, Suzanne, 180
Learning Gap, The (Stevenson and Stigler), 100–103, 119–21, 122, 123, 124, 139
Learning groups, 182–86
  See also Cooperative learning
Levin, Henry, 167, 168, 171, 173
Lipton, Martin, 122–23

Literacy, 5
  as personal evolution, 60
Local school councils, 43
Lortie, Dan, 84–86, 87, 88, 90, 94, 95, 99

MacArthur Foundation, John D. and
  Catherine T., 51, 54
McClure, Robert, 172
McDermott, Lillian, 151, 180–81
McDonald, Joseph, 144, 145, 148
McDonell Douglas, 199–200
McIlquham, Leslie, 169
Macintosh, 32–33, 41–42
Magic Bullet Syndrome, 130
Making the Best of Schools (Oakes and
  Lipton), 122–23
Manufacturing
  in industrial age, 9–10
  in postindustrial age, 11–12
Mastery In Learning, 94, 171–72
Mathematics, 139, 165
  Asian vs. U.S. students' skills in, 102
  assumptions about ability vs. effort
    and, 120
  calculator-based approaches to, 110–
    12, 190–92
  chaos theory and, 39–40
  Cognitively Guided Instruction and,
    8–9
  gender gap in, 94
  intuitive misunderstanding of, 177–
    78, 179–81
  new math and, 113–16
  reports on achievement in, 4–5, 6
  tests on, 141, 143
  workforce skills in, 12
Measurement, 137–55
  in education redesign, 138–39, 150–
    51, 154–55
  exhibitions and portfolios in, 144–
    48
  research program on, 151–54

in TQL, 161, 163–66
  See also Tests
*Measurement of Workforce Readiness
  Competencies,* 11
Medicine, technical skills in, 80, 81
Mentoring, 198–99
Michigan State University, 211
Microprocessor industry, 26–27
Minority students
  dropout rate among, 6
  standardized testing and, 142–43
"Mobilizing Support for Agricultural Re-
  search at the Minnesota Agri-
  cultural Experiment Station"
  (Sauer and Pray), 19
Morgantown High School (Morgan-
  town, W.Va.), 212–13, 214
Mount Edgecumbe High School (near
  Sitka, Alaska), 161–62, 163–64

National Academy of Education, 93
National Academy of Science, 92, 99
National Alliance of Business, 6
National Assessment of Educational
  Progress, 4–5
National Association of Manufacturers,
  11–12
National Commission on Educational
  Excellence, 3–4
National Council of States for In-Service
  Education, 89
National Diffusion Network (NDN), 97–
  98, 99
National Education Association, 94,
  171–72, 215
National Education Goals, 27
  panel on, 5, 6
National Institute of Education, 93, 94
National Institutes of Health, 92
National Research Council, 95
National Science Foundation, 92, 140,
  205, 210, 218

Nation At Risk, A, 3–4, 7, 8, 9, 14, 126
Nations, Jimmy, 95
New math, 113–16
New Meaning of Educational Change,
  The (Fullan), 85, 104, 112–13
New York City school system, 106–7
New Zealand, Reading Recovery in, 63

Oakes, Jeannie, 122–23
Office of Educational Research and Im-
  provement (OERI), 94, 96, 99, 218
Ohio State University's College of Edu-
  cation, 63–64, 74–75
Oral language acquisition, 60, 176–77

Paradigms
  defined, 156
  new, foundations for, 156–58, 194–96;
    see also Cognitive science; Cooper-
    ative learning; Electronic learning
    technologies; Teacher power; Total
    Quality Learning
  new, needed in educational reform,
    12–13, 15–16, 20, 27
  scientific, 13–15
  shifts in, 14–15
  teacher training and, 81–82
Peer tutoring, 186–87
Phi Delta Kappan, 172
Physics
  chaos theory and, 39–40
  electronic learning technologies
    and, 188–90
  intuitive misunderstanding of, 177–
    78, 179–81
Physics By Inquiry, 179–81, 195, 197,
  198, 204, 229
Piaget, Jean, 176
Pinnell, Gay Su, 51, 52, 53, 54, 55, 66, 68,
  70, 71, 73, 75
Planning backwards, 144, 147–48
Podl, Jody Brown, 146, 147

Politics of Educational Innovation, The,
  117
Portfolios, as assessment technique,
  146–47, 148
Postindustrial economy
  educational needs in, 2, 3, 9–12, 20
  skills needed by workers in, 11–12
  teacher training and, 81–82
Pray, Carl, 19
*Predictable Failure of Educational Re-
  form, The* (Sarason), 113, 116–17
Principals, "building tenure" of, 106–7
Prison, 72
Professional Development School
  (PDS), 211–15
  flaws in, 213–15
Program evaluations, 138–39, 148–50

Quality control, 99
Quality Teacher, The (L. Byrnes, M.
  Byrnes, and Cornesky), 164
Question asking
  by e-mail, 190
  simple vs. complex questions and,
    102–3, 124–25
  by students vs. teachers, 124

Reading
  Asian vs. U.S. students' skills in, 102
  conventional remedial programs in,
    65–67
  typical instruction in, 53–54
  whole-language approach to, 176–77
Reading readiness, 59–60, 61–62
Reading Recovery, 25–26, 27, 47, 48–77,
    152, 197, 198, 204, 205, 218, 229
  budget limitations and, 72–73
  candidates for, 55, 72–73
  confidence built in, 58
  conventional remedial programs vs.,
    65–67
  cost-benefit analysis of, 69–72

delays in implementation of, 72–73
description of, 48–49, 54–58
development of, 59–64
features of redesign process incorporated in, 50–51, 76–77
high-level champions needed for, 73
no good alternatives for, 64–67
program administrators threatened by, 74–75
retention in first grade vs., 64–65, 71
spread in use of, 75
statistics on use of, 50
studies on effectiveness of, 51–53, 54–55, 74–75
teacher training in, 51, 67–69
typical reading instruction vs., 53–54
Reagan, Ronald, 4, 94
Redesign process, 22–47, 105
absent from educational reform, 22–23, 24, 26, 38
candidates for, 30
continual change in, 25
continuous collaboration in, 23–24, 31–33
defined, 22
economies made possible by, 36–37
in educational reform, 46–47, 132, 135–36, 195, 198–99
expensive to support, 34–36
goals of, 30
growing pains in, 37–38
human resistance to change overcome by, 41–42
increasingly complex products in, 33–34
in industry, 23–24, 30–38
integration of improvements in, 25, 30–31, 195–96
orderly pattern of change in, 16, 17–19, 20, 110–11
power structures and, 42–46
processes improved by, 33

Reading Recovery and, 50–51, 76–77
role of vision in, 26–29
specialized professions, businesses, and industries arising from, 24, 25, 34
Rekrut, Martha, 186–87
Remedial programs, 219
costs of, 69–72
typical, in reading, 65–67
See also Reading Recovery
Research
in industry, 96
See also Educational research; Redesign process
"Research as a Guide for Curriculum Development" (McDermott), 151
Retention (flunking), 64–65, 71
Rosenholtz, Susan, 170

Sanders, Theodore, 108, 109
Santamaria, Willie, 167, 168
Sarason, Seymour, 86–87, 113, 114–15, 116–17, 118, 124, 125, 127–28, 130
Saturn School (St. Paul, Minn.), 192–94
Sauer, Richard, 19
Savo, Cynthia, 174
Scholastic Aptitude Test (SAT), 133, 143, 192
School Development Program (SDP), 167, 173–74
School Renewal Network, 171–72
Schoolteacher (Lortie), 84–86
Schwarz, Paul, 147
Science, 129, 165
chaos theory and, 39–40
cost of curriculum materials for, 216
gender gap in, 94
intuitive misunderstanding of, 177–78, 179–81
tests on, 141

Science Education for Public Understanding Program (SEPUP), 205–10, 229
  choosing subjects for, 206
  preparation of modules in, 206–7
  students' materials in, 208
  teachers' flexibility in, 207–8
  testing of prototypes in, 208–9
Self-esteem, 122, 193
Sex education, 108
Sizer, Theodore, 144
Slavin, Robert, 96–97, 99, 144, 149, 150, 167, 171, 204
Smart Schools, Smart Kids (Fiske), 195
Smith, Wesley, 137
South Pointe Elementary School (Miami, Fla.), 8
Specialization, 24–25, 34, 204
Speech acquisition, 60, 176–77
Sports programs, 119
Standards-based systemic change, 8
Stanford University's Center for Educational Research with the School of Education, 167
State of Mathematics Education, The, 4–5
States, curricular mandates of, 125–26
State University of New York at Albany, 65–66
Statistical process control, 11–12
"Steps in Planning Backwards," 144, 147–48
Stevenson, Harold, 100–103, 104, 105, 119–21, 122, 123, 124, 139
Stigler, James, 100–103, 104, 105, 119–21, 122, 123, 124, 139
Structure of Scientific Revolutions, The (Kuhn), 13–15
Subject skills, teacher training and, 83–84
Success For All, 8, 25, 27, 47, 96–97, 167, 171, 172–73, 183, 197, 200, 229

Sullivan High School (Chicago), 146
Superintendents, 127
Systems redesign schools (SRSs), 199–205, 210
  applying for participation in, 201
  client districts of, 202, 219
  costs of, 215–20
  educating students during participation in, 201–2
  faculty size in, 202
  as integrators vs. lone reformers, 204
  as laboratories of educational change, 199–205
  new approaches, techniques, and materials tested in, 203–5
  new scheduling patterns designed in, 202–3
  number of participants in, 201
  PDS compared with, 211, 213, 214–15
  qualities needed by, 200–201
  specialization and, 204
  and version of twenty-first-century school, 220–29
  volunteering for, 200

Taiwan, 123
  assumptions about education in, 119–20
  question asking in, 124–25
  teaching profession in, 100–103
Teacher power, 157, 167–74, 186, 194, 195
  Accelerated Schools Program and, 167–71, 174, 197, 200, 218, 229
  framework for change offered in, 173–74
  and pooling of expertise in areas outside classroom teaching, 172–73
  uniting teachers separated by distance in, 171–72
Teachers, teaching profession, 78–105
  in Asia, 100–103, 104, 105

assessed by students' test scores, 140, 141, 142

classroom workloads of, 90, 100, 103, 123, 202–3, 213–14

educational research and, 80, 92–98

empowered to work collaboratively, 157, 167–74; *see also* Teacher power

individualism and subjectivity in, 87, 88, 91, 98–99

innovation thwarted by structure of, 78, 90–92

as key to reform, 104–5

limited opportunities for interaction in, 91–92, 98–99, 100–101

scapegoated for failed reform, 116, 117

specialization of, 204

subject skills lacking in, 83–84

technical culture lacked by, 79, 80–81, 87–88, 104, 105

Teachers and Research in Action, 94–95

Teachers for Our Nation's Schools (Goodlad), 86

Teacher-student ratios, 100

Teachers' Workplace (Rosenholtz), 170

Teacher training

absence of time and psychic resources for, 90

in Asia, 101

as barrier to reform, 86–87

as career-long process, 84–92

coaching skills and, 82–83, 84

collision of old and new paradigms and, 81–82

expense of, 132–33

flaws in, 81–84

freeing faculty time for, 202–3

innovation and, 88–89

lack of funding for, 89–90

new math and, 114–15

in Reading Recovery program, 51, 67–69

subject skills and, 83–84

teacher's colleges vs. experience in, 84–85

teacher's own schooling and, 85–87

Technical culture, 79–81, 92

lacked by teaching profession, 79, 80–81, 87–88, 104, 105

Tests, 121, 139–44

alternatives to, 144–48

curriculum shaped by, 126, 142–43

in education redesign, 139

as gauge of effective reform, 133–34

innovations in, 143–44

standardized, 139–43, 210

TQL and, 165

Texas

comprehensive school reform in (1980s), 119

curricular mandates in, 125

Textbooks, 126, 127

new editions of, 24

Thayer Junior-Senior High School (Winchester, N.H.), 145–46, 147

Thier, Herbert, 206–7, 208, 209–10

Time demands

constant interruptions and, 125

question asking and, 124–25

teachers' classroom duties and, 90, 100, 103, 123, 202–3, 213–14

Total Quality Learning (TQL), 157, 158–66, 194, 195, 196

concentration on process in, 161, 163

concepts and techniques of, 160–61

data collection in, 163–64

development of, 158–60

fear driven out of learning by, 161, 165–66

Total Quality Learning (TQL) (*cont'd*)
  grading in, 159–60, 161, 164–66
  power sharing between students and
    adults in, 161–62
  standards set by students in, 162–63,
    164–65
Total Quality Management (TQM), 160
Tracking, 121–23
  standardized tests and, 140, 141
Trans Continental, 24
Tutoring
  by e-mail, 189–90
  by peers, 186–87

Union meetings, 91
Union Pacific Railroad (UP), 43–46
United Airlines, 31, 32, 36–37
United Parcel Service, 43–44
University of Chicago, 210–11
University of Minnesota's Cooperative
    Learning Center, 184
University of Washington at Seattle,
    179
University of West Virginia, 212–13
Unschooled Mind, The (Gardner), 177–
    79

Vaughn, Stephanie, 170
Vermont, portfolio programs in, 146

Vision, 26–29, 41, 46
  demonstrations of workability and,
    28–29

Waits, Bert, 191–92
Walsh, Mike, 44, 45
Walters, Susan, 94–95
Warwick, R.I., school system, 186–87
Watkinson School (Hartford), 147
Watts, Gary, 172
Webster, Daniel Elementary School
    (San Francisco), 167–68
Western Air Line, 24
Whole learning, 176–77
Williams, Ann, 213, 214
Wilson, Kenneth, 95
Wisconsin
  Cognitively Guided Instruction in, 8–9
  curricular mandates in, 125
Workforce 2000, 11
Wozniak, Steven, 35
Wright brothers, 27–28, 34
Writing skills, 5

Yale University's Child Development
    Study Center, 167
Yanscik, Jan, 48–49, 55, 56–57, 58, 66–
    67
Yoshida, Makoto, 88